The Last Lynching

The Last Lynching

How a Gruesome Mass Murder
Rocked a Small Georgia Town

Anthony S. Pitch

Skyhorse Publishing

Skyhorse Publishing books may be purchased in bulk at special discounts for sales promotion, corporate gifts, fund-raising, or educational purposes. Special editions can also be created to specifications. For details, contact the Special Sales Department, Skyhorse Publishing, 307 West 36th Street, 11th Floor, New York, NY 10018 or info@skyhorsepublishing.com.

Skyhorse® and Skyhorse Publishing® are registered trademarks of Skyhorse Publishing, Inc.®, a Delaware corporation.

Visit our website at www.skyhorsepublishing.com.

10 9 8 7 6 5 4 3 2 1

Library of Congress Cataloging-in-Publication Data is available on file.

Cover design by Rain Saukas
Cover photo by iStock

Print ISBN: 978-1-5107-0175-5
Ebook ISBN: 978-1-5107-0176-2

Printed in the United States of America

For two very brave men: Robert "Bobby" Howard, civil rights activist and my guide, who endured a firebombing, jail, and other horrors; and Richard "Rich" Rusk, Secretary of the Moore's Ford Memorial Committee and my guide, who stuck his neck out where others feared to go.

And for Joseph "Joe" J. Bell of the firm of Bell, Shivas & Fasolo, P.C. in Rockaway, New Jersey, for volunteering an enormous amount of work, time, and finances, and admission to the Georgia Bar solely to petition for release of the sealed testimony in the grand jury hearing.

And for my grandchildren, Kayla, Maya, and Eli, who I hope will be inspired by the above.

Note to the Reader: Throughout this book, Roger and Dorothy have a surname spelled "Malcolm." This spelling is in defiance of a marker over Roger's grave, which spells his name "Malcom," as well as his first marriage certificate, which has not been located but is said to read "Malcom." Such mistakes are possible. On page 31 of this book, I describe how Roger was mistakenly charged with stealing a dog instead of intent to murder. It was human error. That is what I think happened on the marriage certificate. The FBI, attorney general, lawyers, court officials, journalists, and many others spelled the name "Malcolm," and I have chosen to follow the spelling used in the vast majority of official documents.

Lynch: To murder by mob action and without lawful trial
—Webster's New World Dictionary of the
American Language, second college edition

Irish lore claims origin of the word.

The case of James Lynch Fitzstephen, Mayor in 1493 of the town of Galway, on the west coast of Ireland, will always stand out as the supreme of implacable parental justice. It is recorded that he hanged his son for some infraction of the law from the window of his own house, which stands today as Lynch's castle, and from which incident he came down to us as "lynch law."
—Letter to the Editor from Jacob Lempit, NY,
in the *New York Times*, January 7, 1934

CONTENTS

PREFACE

Our nation cries out for arrests and justice for the heinous crime of July 25, 1946, when two African American couples were ambushed and lynched in rural Georgia. One of the victims was even a decorated veteran who had served in North Africa and the Pacific during World War II. No one, of whatever color, creed, or gender, deserves to die at the hands of a bloodthirsty mob. The foursome who lost their lives had no one to help them resist. They died as if they were wildlife. They were slain without any dignity, but their memory is enshrined by the living.

Our Declaration of Independence proclaims that all men are created equal, that they are endowed by their Creator with certain unalienable Rights, and that among these are Life, Liberty, and the pursuit of Happiness. We are a country of laws. The Bill of Rights is firm that no person should be deprived of life, liberty, or property without due process of law.

And yet four of our citizens had their lives violently ended by vigilantes. They died without the benefit of lawyers or courts, stripped of all constitutional rights, and without a shred of mercy. Laws were flouted, human beings degraded, and murder committed out of the way of witnesses. The four were left to rot and stiffen by the lazy Apalachee River while festive hunters took away ropes and shell casings as trophies.

The N-word is horrific, offensive, ugly, and degrading and has no place in our modern lexicon. However, I use it extensively throughout this text to show what was normal and in daily use in rural Georgia in 1946. To have censored or sanitized the language would have glossed over the indignities and slurs suffered by so many, and falsely portrayed the times as they were. Nothing so evokes the essence of yesteryear as the language in common use. Today the word is scorned in public utterance and is unacceptable. It is hoped that frequent use of this word will faithfully record what it was like then, not the past as heard through the ears of our present.

"Lynch," incidentally, is used throughout, since the dictionary defines it as "murder by mob action," and the FBI, National Association for the Advancement of Colored People (NAACP), and others referred to these murders as lynchings.

Many might ask why this story is not left alone as it might exacerbate tensions between the races. My response is simple. It is a slice of American history that deserves to be commemorated in the long narrative of who we are, what we did, and what we believe in today. The people and events described herein are authentic and real. Not a single person or episode has been tailored to make the account either more dramatic or more palatable to modern sensitivities. This is how it was, and no amount of tinkering can alter that. The facts are brought to light through about 10,000 documents from the FBI and National Archives, many obtained through the Freedom of Information Act, or declassified at my request. They form the basis and backbone of this book.

A child of this generation was surprised that time would be spent on offering up such a "dated" story. Why bother with the past, she asked in all seriousness, when the world is filled with so much violence today? It may seem irrelevant to someone brought up with the new phenomenon of irrational and random terrorism, where life is cheapened and vile deeds are committed in the name of religion. But this story is a part of history, which cannot be denied, and therefore deserves to be told and remembered.

Fear and terror continue to stalk the land near where the four bodies were found close to Moore's Ford Bridge. When I went down to Georgia to witness the annual reenactment of the lynchings, I asked a white congregant whether he would accompany me and show the way to the scene of the crime. The man agreed, but when he found out the purpose of the visit he warned, "You had better leave this place immediately. Don't answer any questions from whites. They'll make history out of you within thirty seconds."

While I was driven by the homes of surviving children and grandchildren of the major suspects, an African American civil rights activist and passenger, who acted as guide, said we would slow down but not stop beside the residences because "that would be too dangerous."

Nothing untoward happened when, accompanied by a white secretary of the Moore's Ford Memorial Committee, I joined Sunday worshippers, among whose grandparents some of the suspects had knelt and prayed. But strangely, on exiting one church after a brief period inside, we found that the hood of the car belonging to the Georgian host was raised, though nothing had been tampered with.

Next, I carefully walked to the closely-dug graves of the suspects, now well-tended and silent. They are all dead and buried. If they knew anything of the lynchings, or even if they took part in mass murder by the Apalachee River, none had spoken out before they died.

The suspects were never identified.

Did the killers get away with murder?

I have always been captivated by stories that are epic, true, and horrific. That is why I wrote three previous books that were poles apart but fit the criteria and challenged me as a writer and researcher: vile bestialities of the Holocaust, on a scale too colossal to comprehend, in *Our Crime Was Being Jewish;* the saddest story in American history, in *"They Have Killed Papa Dead!"—The Road to Ford's Theatre, Abraham Lincoln's Murder, and the Rage for Vengeance;* and the wanton destruction of the White House and the nation's capital, in *The Burning of Washington: The British Invasion of 1814.* Like this book, they took years to complete, and each time they were finished I felt a lingering sense of sorrow. I had to part with a subject that was as familiar as taking a walk.

For decades I had yearned to chronicle a lynching because it matched the prerequisites mentioned above, but it was hard to find sufficient documentary evidence to substantiate my story. Finally, I sensed that what took place near Moore's Ford Bridge, Georgia, in 1946 stood out above all the others. Not only was there a massive bonanza of written evidence to research, but one of the tethered men murdered by fanatics was a veteran of World War II, only recently returned from victory over barbarians. How could it be that the very depravity Americans fought against had taken root in our soil?

The crime had to be exposed from contemporary top-secret correspondence and confidential reports of the FBI. I did not intend to accomplish what others could not by solving the crime, but I would try to uncover details of the hunt for the killers, and see why even courts were looked upon with suspicion. I also hoped to unmask the methods then sanctioned by the state of Georgia to enforce segregation and the subservience of people of color. This would show what the victims were up against and put the era in historical perspective.

Now we can see for the first time how the atrocity was handled and why the investigation failed to meet expectations. Extracts of documents that were circulated at the highest levels of the FBI, the Justice Department, and investigators on the spot are now there for all to read. They even include the personal comments scratched on the correspondence by the attorney general and J. Edgar Hoover, the lonely and secretive director of the FBI.

After conducting my research, I now think that the Georgia Bureau of Investigation may have been at fault. The murders should have been treated as a state crime, before and certainly after the FBI was compelled to admit that it may have lacked jurisdiction. No federal statute had been infringed and no conspiracy proven of a state official colluding with others, without which the FBI had no jurisdiction or power to search for weapons. But we also know that the GBI did not have the manpower, the skills, or the resources to match those of the FBI, and besides, they had gradually distanced themselves from the case, due perhaps to lack of interest.

Readers will have to decide for themselves whether the FBI did all within its circumscribed authority to find the murderers, which would have strengthened its case before the grand jury. But even then, with the FBI saying most people lied before the grand jury, what chance was there for the truth to emerge?

The last hope lies with those killers who might still be alive to come forward and confess their role. Perhaps the imminence of death will encourage them to admit to the lynching. Otherwise we may never know who committed this unspeakable crime.

BACKGROUND

Nobody knew whether the four victims would have been spared near Moore's Ford Bridge if anti-lynching laws had been in place in 1946. Their absence was not for want of trying. Ever since the aftermath of the Civil War, Congress had tried unsuccessfully to pass anti-lynching laws, with some 200 such bills introduced during the first half of the twentieth century.[1] Three bills passed the House of Representatives but were stymied by filibustering, or the threat of it, by Southern senators.[2]

Those who wanted the federal government to step in and stamp out lynching had only to look at the statistics to see how it had flourished over the years. The respected Tuskegee Institute of Alabama published figures showing that from 1882 through 1937 there were 4,680 people lynched, 3,387 of whom were black and 1,293 white. In the last three years for which figures are available, thirty-five black and two white people were lynched.[3]

As recently as 2015, the Equal Justice Initiative in Montgomery, Alabama, documented 3,959 racial terror lynchings in twelve Southern states between the end of Reconstruction in 1877 and 1950, which, it wrote, is at least 700 more than previously reported.[4]

One of the most sickening lynchings took place in 1934 in Florida. The body of a white woman, Lola Cannidy, twenty, had been discovered close to the farm where she lived with her parents. Her head was smashed in and she had been strangled so violently that her eyes protruded from their sockets. Both arms were broken and the fully clothed corpse was partially covered with brushwood and pine logs. A black man, Claude Neal, twenty-three, admitted acting alone and was arrested. Later it was discovered that Neal, who lived with his mother across the road from the Cannidys, had played with the deceased when they were children, then worked on her family farm.

A Southern white professor, investigating on behalf of the National Association for the Advancement of Colored People, submitted his findings on this case. He learned that the two had an intimate romantic relationship going back months or maybe years. He said blacks knew about it and told Neal he was skirting danger. At their fateful meeting Lola had apparently wanted to end it. Neal reportedly said, "When she didn't want me to speak to her and then told me that she'd tell the white men on me, I just got mad and killed her."

After the local sheriff sensed a mounting spirit of revenge he arranged for Neal to be whisked to safety twenty miles away. The prisoner stayed on the run to escape vigilantes, fleeing to Panama City, then Pensacola, and finally across the Florida line to the jail at Brewton, Alabama.

A few hours after midnight on October 26, 1934, about 100 armed men drove up and threatened to dynamite the jail and burn through blockades with acetylene torches. "We'll tear your jail up and let all the prisoners out if you don't turn him over to us," someone shouted. Obediently, the jailor unlocked the cell and the mob hauled out the prisoner, who was screaming and crying. Neal was shoved in the front of some thirty cars with Florida license plates and driven almost 200 miles across the state line to the woods near the dead girl's farm.

There he was savagely tortured for hours. The NAACP investigator wrote that the bloodthirsty mob cut off his penis and testicles. They sliced his sides and stomach with knives, chopped off a finger and toe, and burned him with steaming irons. The lawless lynchers tied a rope around his neck and hoisted him up a tree, only to lower him as he was about to choke to death and repeat the torture all over again. Daylight had come when they were finally sated and decided to kill him.

Neal's emasculated remains were attached by rope to a car and dragged along the road to the farm of the dead girl's parents. The mob had now swollen to thousands when a woman came out of the Cannidy home and plunged a butcher's knife through the black man's heart. The vengeful mob moved in to kick the carcass and some even drove their cars over the dead man.

They took what remained of Neal to Marianna, Florida, the seat of Jackson County, where they hung the nude body from a tree on the courthouse square. Hundreds of photographs of the brutal sight sold for fifty cents each. Three fingers from one hand and two from the other were prized souvenirs. One man offered to divide a finger with a friend as "a special favor." Another preserved his trophy in alcohol. Onlookers stayed to view the body as it hung motionless in the square. Eventually someone came forward and shielded it with a burlap sack. Only then was it cut down. A full day and a night had passed since he was taken screaming from his cell.

The professor's report to the NAACP summed up this murder with chilling finality. "They seemed to believe that lynch law was really the only way they could 'keep the nigger in his place.' The chain-gang, prison, and the electric chair are not enough. To have a negro suddenly disappear, never to return to his people, seemed to them to be the best method of 'handlin' the niggers.'"[5]

A horrified lady in New York City felt compelled to write a plea to President Franklin Roosevelt, urging enactment of an anti-lynching law. "It is as safe for a white man to torture and kill a black man as it would be for him to play a game of quoits with his neighbor by the barn," she cried out. "Local courts do not, and I believe, cannot punish the lynchers."[6]

Two years later, in 1937, the House of Representatives approved anti-lynching legislation by a vote of 277 against 120[7] and it went to the Senate. The debates that followed spilled over into 1938 amid competing sides, who strained to utter the courtesies normally extended to fellow senators.

The bill would have imposed a collective fine on those living within the boundaries of the crime in an effort to tame and even do away with lynching. But senators from the South rose one after the other in a pre-arranged ploy to stifle debate and hold the floor while savaging the content of the bill. The senior senator from Georgia, Walter George (D-GA), and his junior, Richard Russell (D-GA), played major roles in tearing apart the proposed legislation and marshaling their forces against it.

"Oh, these great guardians of law and order, these jealous defenders of their law-enforcement officers, are attempting to legislate against a crime that showed . . . one out of sixteen million was lynched in the year 1937, when we know that murder in all its forms was rampant everywhere," Russell thundered[8] in an effort to show the duplicity of Northerners, who did not have special laws to stamp out murder and racketeering, which the FBI said were on the rise.[9] Russell addressed the dignified body, declaring: "Last year there were only eight murders by lynching, the only crime with which this bill even purports to deal, as compared with 12,000 murders in other forms."[10] He argued that lynching had all but been eliminated over the past few years. As a reward, he noted sarcastically, the world would be told that Southerners "are incapable of enforcing the law. You are a clan of barbarians. You cannot handle your own affairs unless we apply to you the lash and spur of federal power."[11]

Russell, a former governor of Georgia, then launched into a long diatribe against the Communist Party of America, accusing it of sharing the goals of those backing the bill. The proposed statutes would be the forerunner of legislation to strike down laws prohibiting the intermarriage of whites and blacks.[12] Legislation to follow would, Russell contended, "enforce social equality between the races, which includes wiping out all segregation of the races in schools and colleges and churches and hospitals and in homes and in every public place." Supporters of the bill, Russell insisted, "are contributing to a horrible and sickening situation and are encouraging this nefarious movement of the Communist Party in the South."[13]

Russell claimed the pending bill was number one on the program of the Communist Party. It would be followed by laws to take over the electoral machinery of the states, to prescribe the qualifications for suffrage, and to provide that "some little federal agent from Washington" should sit at every ballot box throughout the United States and control the elections of the people within the states. "The Communist Party hoped to elect to the House and Senate members of the Negro race, and that at least one state would have immediately a Negro Governor, due to the fact that there was a majority of colored people in that state, and that was to be the beginning of the establishment of a Soviet form of government in the South, to be known as the Negro Soviet Republic," he insisted.[14]

Senator Russell, who became president pro-tem of the upper chamber and had a major senate office building named after him, said if the bill was passed "it would work an awful hardship on the good Negroes of the South." They would be taxed just as would whites living in a community judged to be liable for a lynching. "Perhaps living at the far side of the county, on the forks of the creek, is a good old Negro who has a little farm which he has acquired after years of arduous toil. Perhaps he has worked and stinted and slaved to acquire a little piece of land, forty or fifty acres. He sees the tax collector and the sheriff coming down upon him. They say, 'John, you heard about this nigger that the sheriff had in his custody getting killed, didn't you?' 'Yes, I heard about it, but I didn't know him. I didn't have nothing to do with it, boss. I didn't even know that nigger.' 'Well, judgment has been secured against the county for $10,000 and your share of that judgment is $22.50. That is the tax on your farm.'"[15]

Senator George was no less outraged. He told a packed debating chamber of eighty-six senators, "I think the country will look with more or less derision upon the Senate of the United States if it continues to waste its time in an effort to bring up for consideration the anti-lynching bill."[16] He argued the folly of the federal government, which could declare it to be a federal offense for three people in any American state to do a certain act. It could tell three men from North Dakota, "You are guilty of a federal offense because the Congress has said you are a mob; you are an unlawful assembly. If the federal government can do that in the case of a lynching, it can do it in the case of cattle stealing; it can do it in the case of ordinary theft."[17]

George was not content with ridiculing the bill. He needed to evoke sympathy and even gratitude for putting his life in the hands of others. "We love the Negro," he announced. "We try to protect him. As a simple judge upon the bench I have gone through the dead of the night to the place where a mob had been formed, once to protect a white man, more than once to protect the life of a poor colored man charged with and convicted of the most serious offenses. I have gone down alone or with but one single court official—possibly a reporter—by my side, without an arm, without a weapon. I have gone down for the purpose of giving these poor, humble, unfortunate people every bit of protection that I could give them. Through all the years the judges and the officers of the law in the South have striven and have done their best. They could not always succeed. They will not succeed any better if this bill is enacted into law."[18]

A Democrat from South Carolina, James Byrnes, was succinct and eventually clear even to the most partisan of senators. "Lynching is murder," he began misleadingly. "The fact that murder is committed by a mob does not lessen the offense, it only aggravates it. Murder in punishable by the laws of every State in the Union. The only justification therefore, for this bill must be that the States of the Union have not enforced to the satisfaction of the authors of the bill, the law against persons guilty of murder." Then the Southern senator launched his personal attack. "The purpose of this bill . . . is to punish the crime of lynching. Its title should be, 'A bill to arouse ill-feeling between sections, inspire race hatred in the South, and destroy the Democratic Party.'"[19]

Senator Robert Wagner (D-NY) would not be intimidated. Earlier he had argued that "the crime of lynching is all too frequently accompanied by planned and prolonged orgies of mob brutality that would have shocked the soldiers of the Inquisition."[20]

But he was snuffed out by the preponderance of Southerners holding the floor in a united front against what they termed "an assault on State's rights."[21] Senator Charles Andrews (D-FL) said it would even be wrong to call the bill an anti-lynching bill because it failed to provide a remedy. "If we could pass an anti-rape bill and thereby prevent rape there would not be any cause for the introduction of this present bill," he concluded.[22]

Racial differences marred an otherwise sober look at the bill. Senator Allen Ellender (D-LA) digressed to scorn the beliefs of blacks and portray them as a threat. It was immaterial to him what they prayed to. "They may pray to an ox. They may pray to this desk formerly occupied by Webster," he scoffed. "The point I desire to make is that I do not want that kind of people to rule this country. That is what I mean. I do not want that kind of 'barbaric lunacy' to prevail in this country and head our government. That is what I am fighting to prevent. And the moment you give to them rights leading to social equality, they are going to come here the next time and demand legislation bringing them nearer and nearer to it."[23]

Occasionally the debate sank to the level of a street gang at odds with others. Senator Thomas Connally (D-TX), who held the floor for long spells, was blunt. "Do not fool yourselves. Everyone in the country understands why this bill is here," he declared. "You are not fooling the people. Theoretically speaking, you can go out in the desert and stick your head down in the sand and imagine you are an ostrich. No one else thinks you are an ostrich. The people know why you are seeking to pass this bill. You are cheapening the Senate of the United States. Everyone knows the bill is unconstitutional."[24]

Crossing party lines to echo similar thoughts, Senator William Borah (R-ID) insisted that the bill would foster racial tensions, arguing, "It is not in the interest of national unity to stir old embers, to arouse old fears, to lacerate old wounds, to again, after all these years, brand the Southern people as incapable or unwilling to deal with the question of human life. This bill is not in the interests of that good feeling between the two races so essential to the welfare of the colored people."[25]

An outspoken white supremacist, Senator Theodore Bilbo (D-MS), wanted to solve the problem by exiling all African Americans to Liberia. "The African colony is the home of the negro," he pronounced. "He is there in his wild state. He is there uncivilized. He has no religion except that of cannibalism and fetishism. He knows nothing of the Christian religion." Bilbo, who died while under senate investigation for improper racist behavior during his re-election campaign a decade later,[26] wanted the African *émigrés* to "rejuvenate and revolutionize the black man of the African jungle" and convert him to Christianity.[27]

One of the few who argued the other way, Senator Sherman Minton (D-IN), welcomed the involvement of federal authorities. "We have had some horrible bandits in Indiana," he said. "When we found out we could not handle them, thank God the federal government stepped in and helped us catch them. I never objected."[28]

But the bill's foes prevailed on a motion to shut down debate. On February 16, 1938, with eighty-nine senators answering their names for a quorum, a vote on cloture was defeated in a 46 to 42 vote. Those who objected so vigorously to the proposed legislation had finally won and succeeded in filibustering it to death.

Realizing there were other matters to attend to, senators abandoned the divisive issue.[29]

Then, in 2005, the Senate made an about-turn, wondering whether to apologize for refusing to pass anti-lynching laws that might have stifled the atrocities. Documented incidents showed that lynching had occurred in all but four states, and that the number of victims, predominantly African Americans, had risen to at least 4,742 from 1882 to 1968.[30] In language that could never bring back the dead, the Senate debated its contrition. If passed, the resolution would apologize to the victims of lynching for the failure of the Senate to enact anti-lynching legislation. It would also express sympathy and solemn regrets "to the descendants of victims of lynching, the ancestors of whom were deprived of life, human dignity, and the constitutional protections accorded all citizens of the United States." The text also promised to remember the history of lynching, so that the tragedies would neither be forgotten nor repeated.[31]

Senators who gave voice to their outrage were hypercritical of long-dead predecessors for failing to quell the curse of lynching. Before the debate began in earnest, majority leader Senator William "Bill" Frist (R-TN), described the issue before them as "one of the worst failings of this institution in our history." The heart and lung transplant surgeon flayed the horror as "nothing less than a form of racial terrorism." Lynching was a way to humiliate, to repress, and to dehumanize, whose "deep scars will always remain." He acknowledged that nearly 250 victims were from his home state of Tennessee.[32]

In one of the most memorable moments of orations in favor of passage, Senator Mary Landrieu (D-LA), chief sponsor of the resolution, said "justice was mostly deaf, but never color blind." Forthright but soft-spoken, she pointed to a blown-up photograph of an African American hanging from a tree, as people, including children, took part in the jamboree. "Some businesses closed down so that the whole town could attend these lynchings," she said. "In many instances it was a form of public entertainment." She was particularly scathing toward fellow senators who had once sat at the same desks, asserting, "There may be no other injustice in American history for which the Senate so uniquely bears responsibility."[33] And in what amounted to self-flagellation she continued, "Federal authorities were impotent to stop this murder. State authorities seemed to condone it, and the Senate of the United States refused to act."[34]

The Southern senator made a poignant reference to jazz legend Billie Holiday, who had performed the classic song "Strange Fruit" in 1939, and whose life had been threatened because she continued to sing it. She read the haunting words that had touched the hearts of Americans of all colors, who had responded with speeches and marches: "Southern trees bear a strange fruit / Blood on the leaves and blood at the root / Black body swinging in the Southern breeze/ Strange fruit hanging from the poplar trees."

"But the Senate of the United States," she rued, "one of the most noble experiments in democracy, continued to pretend, to act like this was not happening in America, and continued to fail to act."[35] Senator Barbara Mikulski (D-MD) also paid homage to Billie Holiday and decried retribution against the singer whose record label refused to record the song and some of whose concerts were canceled. "Yet her perseverance turned 'Strange Fruit' into one of the most influential protest songs ever written."[36]

In language diluted for senatorial ears but just as condemnatory, Mikulski recounted how previous senators had tried several times to end "this monstrous practice by outlawing it. This is a horrific failure that cost American lives," said the lady who would serve in Congress longer than anyone else of her gender. "This failure will always be a scar on the record of the United States Senate."[37]

Senator John Kerry (D-MA), who would become secretary of state, confessed that like most Americans, he always thought that a lynching xxii *The Last Lynching*

was just slinging a rope over a branch of a tree. But, he said, the story was so much more gruesome, dark, and horrendous. Lynchings were "organized torture. People were literally tortured for sport . . . and crowds would cheer. Children were brought to be spectators," he recalled with solemnity.[38]

A Southerner, and lead Republican co-sponsor, Senator George Allen (R-VA), bemoaned how "Senators ended up looking the other way. They turned their eyes, they turned their heads when something positive could have been done to disapprove, deplore, and obviously pass a law making lynching a federal crime."[39] Time and again senators pointed out that the House of Representatives had passed anti-lynching legislation, only to have the Senate say no. The Senate had even defied calls from seven presidents, from William Henry Harrison to Harry Truman, to follow the lead of the House of Representatives.[40]

In the end the non-binding resolution passed by unanimous consent rather than through a roll-call vote.[41] In this way those opposed to the resolution would not have their names recorded, but their identities would be known by their absence from the list of co-sponsors. Ten senators, all Republicans, took advantage of this option by refusing to back their colleagues. They included Senators Trent Lott and Thad Cochran, both from Mississippi, where more recorded lynchings took place than in any other state.[42]

"It's a statement in itself that there aren't a hundred co-sponsors," Senator Kerry pointed out at a press conference after approval.[43]

Murder

The store owner's wife looked up in alarm.

"Mrs. Aycock, call the sheriff for me, quick!" Loy Harrison burst out. "They took all of my negroes from me and I suppose they shot them."

"All of them?"

"I suppose so," the agitated Georgia farmer replied.

"How?"

"They blocked the bridge and made me put my hands up. They got Roger out and then pulled George and said, 'We want you too, Charlie,' and pulled him out. I told them this was George and not Charlie, and they said 'Keep your damn mouth out of this! This is our party!'" Then, he said, a group of twenty to twenty-five men had taken the two black men and their wives from him.[1]

Deputy Sheriff, Lewis Howard was eating supper at his home in the Walton County jail, in nearby Monroe, when his wife handed him the phone.

"Somebody took my niggers away from me at the Moore's Ford Bridge and shot them! What must I do?" Harrison exclaimed. According to the deputy sheriff, Harrison said he wanted to go home before his wife heard about the killings, which would upset her.

"You go on home," the deputy sheriff urged, but told Harrison to meet him afterwards at Aycock's store on the Athens highway.[2]

Walton County Sheriff Emory Gordon had just finished listening to the news broadcast at 6:15 p.m. when his deputy called about a band of men seizing a carload of blacks. He continued his meal until he was finished, then set out with two deputies, Howard and Charles "Doc" Sorrells.[3]

It was still light and no one was present when they parked ten miles east of Monroe,[4] near the isolated Moore's Ford wooden bridge over the sluggish Apalachee River, which cut through brush, undergrowth, and thick clumps of grass overlooked by jack pines.[5] Gordon found tire tracks of vehicles that had turned around sharply and sped off. Howard walked down a side path before he came upon the mutilated, blood-stained bodies—two black men and two black women. All had been shot multiple times and had cracked skulls, shattered limbs, gaping wounds, and shredded flesh. The three lawmen did not stay long. They were so overcome by the grotesque array of bodies that one of them would later say they forgot to protect the scene or collect physical evidence before racing back to Monroe to assemble a coroner's jury.[6] As dusk fell over the quiet riverside, the bloodied corpses lay stiffening and unattended.

Bailiff Ray Flanigan was idling at the intersection of Highway 78 and Broad Street in Monroe, the usual meeting place for members of the sheriff's office at this hour, when the three rattled lawmen drove up. Howard told Flanigan to get together a coroner's jury of half a dozen men, then meet him at the crime scene.[7] Flanigan's first call was to brief the one-armed county coroner, sloppily dressed in rumpled clothes and unshaven for days, who would have to oversee formal proceedings beside the corpses.[8]

One man drafted to serve on the coroner's jury was sitting on a bench in Monroe's business district talking with the chief of the city's police, Ben Dickinson, when Deputy Sheriff Howard approached and said, "Uncle Ben, we've played hell. We let the negro go on bond and we have four of them dead at the river."[9]

Meanwhile Deputy Sheriff Sorrells had recruited a mortician with the white-owned E.L. Almand funeral home to serve on the coroner's jury and organize removal of the bodies to the mortuary in Monroe.

Howard made no attempt to inform his wife, so when she became alarmed at his absence, she telephoned Sheriff Gordon's wife, from whom she learned that four blacks had been abducted and shot dead, including Roger Malcolm, whom she had seen leaving the jail on bail less than an hour earlier.[10]

Within half an hour the coroner's jury had been appointed. At about 8:00 p.m. the first carload with Flanigan, Sorrells, the coroner, and two other jurors arrived at the secluded site of the massacre. By now it was darkening and they had to leave the auto headlights on and use flashlights to survey the terrain.[11] Flanigan was swiveling his flashlight near the bridge, trying to locate the bodies, when Howard drove up with the remaining jurors and Loy Harrison. The jury foreman arrived with a physician, followed by funeral home staff in an ambulance, its headlights throwing more light through the quickening darkness.[12]

Word of the slayings had already reached beyond the Walton County seat of Monroe, and scores of people stopped by Aycock's store to ask directions to Moore's Ford Bridge.[13] They continued to come for days after. One carload of visitors unfamiliar with the area explained that they were "just riding around and wanted to see where those niggers got killed."[14]

By the time the coroner had sworn in jurors and the physician, an estimated thirty-five to forty men, women, and children had swarmed in to gawk at the carnage.[15] The sheriffs who had seen the lifeless quartet an hour earlier led jurors down a wagon path to the macabre tableau about fifty yards from where the dirt road reached the bridge.[16] Loy Harrison, who had been driving the victims home until, he said, he was blocked on the bridge, identified each by name.

With the aid of flashlights and beams from autos they saw all four corpses lying close together, about thirty to forty yards south of the river.[17] They were somewhat parallel to one another. The coroner and jurors agreed that none of the victims appeared to have tried to run from their captors. They were either facing their executioners or in a profile position when murdered. It also appeared that some shots had been fired into the bodies after they had already fallen. Many of the wounds came from weapons fired at point-blank range into the victims' faces and arms.[18] Laboratory evidence would later find that between six and twelve weapons, including shotguns and pistols, had been fired during the slaughter.[19]

The two males were furthest from the river. The inquest began with George Dorsey, the five feet seven, 131-pound,[20] darker-skinned of the two males. He lay with his face and stomach almost flat with the ground. The bullet and shotgun wounds on his head, back, and arm[21] showed he had had no chance of surviving. George Dorsey, thirty, had come back from World War II only to be gunned down in the boondocks by a band of fanatics.

Roger Malcolm's shattered figure indicated, according to one juror, that he had been singled out for "the worst punishment" of the four. He had apparently looked directly at the firing squad and taken a shotgun blast to the face.[22] Roger, twenty-five, five feet ten, may have fallen backwards, thrown off balance by the velocity of gunfire. He lay on his back with the remnants of his face pointed skywards, and had a ten-foot-long four-ply rope pulled tightly around his neck. One of his assailants had fashioned a halter hitch loop and closed it with two overhand knots, a method commonly used to tie up horses.[23] The hands of both men were bound by a single rope. Gunshots had left reddened paths through Roger's forehead, breast, and hip. In a departure from reports on the other three bodies, the coroner now inserted Harrison's comments to the jurors that he had been blocked at the bridge by twenty or more men, in three Fords and a single Chevrolet car.[24]

Dorothy Malcolm, twenty-four, the smaller of the women, had sustained ghastly wounds when gunned down near Roger, her reputed husband. She had fallen on her left side, with her disfigured face pointed toward her husband. Gashes to her head, chest, and an arm proved the ferocity of the gunmen.[25]

George's wife, Mae, twenty-four, had fallen closest to the river and settled in a somewhat crouched position, touching Dorothy's body.[26] She lay on the edge of the rutted road with her face turned toward the river.[27] A large-caliber bullet, shot downward through her head, illustrated how the killers had moved in to silence their fallen victims at close range. Other gunshots had smashed both of her shoulders.[28] Mae had attended high school, and, according to the FBI, "was apparently from a higher class of negro families than the other victims."[29]

Laconically, the coroner listed the cause of death of three victims as "gunshot wounds at the hands of persons unknown." Only in the case of

Mae Dorsey did he write "death by *violence* [author's italics] of gunshot wounds at the hands of persons unknown."[30]

During the inquest, jurors and law enforcement officers snipped off pieces of the plow line rope to take away as keepsakes. Deputy Sheriff Sorrells cut the noose around Roger Malcolm's neck, but it had been pulled so tightly that when it was sliced loose the rope's impression remained firmly outlined on the skin.[31] One juror cut off a two-foot-long piece from the same rope to take home. "I borrowed a knife from one of the other men who was present and cut off a piece of this rope which was still tied around the dead man's neck," said the juror.[32] Another snipped the rope off Roger Malcolm's hands.[33] A twelve-inch segment of rope, and a separate section eight inches long, both of which Sorrells had cut from George Dorsey's hands, were given to Bailiff Flanigan, who was also given a bullet taken from George's abdomen.[34]

Two of the bodies were loaded into an ambulance even as inquests continued on the remaining pair.[35] An hour passed before they were finished;[36] then the coroner and every juror signed off on reports written up by the physician.[37]

All four coroner's reports recommended payment per victim for services rendered, at the rate of ten dollars to the attending physician, five dollars to the sheriff, and one dollar for each of the six jurors.[38]

The unusual passage of an ambulance, hearse, and other vehicles descending on Moore's Ford had prompted one inquisitive local farmer, Ridden Farmer, and his young son, Emerson, to walk the quarter mile from their house to the crime scene. However, the inquest had not yet begun on the remains of the fourth body when the farmer was overcome by revulsion, threw up, and immediately returned home with his son.[39]

As they left, souvenir hunters came forward, with more arriving later that night and in days to come, leaving their headlights on to illuminate the crime scene and make it easier to scavenge for mementoes.[40] They pried loose bullets embedded in tree trunks behind where the victims had fallen, and carried off pieces of rope and even an empty Luger pistol cartridge case.[41] One scrounger picked up and pocketed a decayed tooth thought to have broken loose from one of the victims during the gunfire.[42]

Back in Monroe, Lewis Howard, a big man with a voice like a frog,[43] returned to the jail. While locking up the inmates he announced, "I done something I sure am sorry about. You know that negro that got bonded out? They have overtaken them and got them."[44]

Sometime after 9:00 p.m., a radio operator in the Atlanta headquarters of the Georgia State Patrol received a call from Sheriff Gordon, asking to speak with anyone from the Georgia Bureau of Investigation. Told that none were present, the sheriff said he wanted to report a lynching. The operator asked who had been lynched and by whom.

"Four negroes were killed in Walton County," Gordon replied. The radio operator, who quit his job shortly afterwards to operate a grocery store, did not take notes and could not recall whether the sheriff said that they were killed by white men.

"Well, would you like for us to send some GBI men down there?" asked the operator.

"I don't think it is necessary. I have already investigated it," the sheriff answered.

"Well, if you do not request them to come down they probably won't come down as they have all been mighty busy lately," said the operator.

The sheriff hesitated, then said, "Well, you can tell them and they can come on down if they want to."[45]

When the radio operator called the director of the GBI to report the killings, he emphasized that the sheriff had not given any other information or even requested assistance. The chief knew that it was GBI policy never to assist with investigations unless specifically requested by the sheriff or local police. Nevertheless, it had always been the policy of the sheriff's office in Monroe to report even minor offenses to the State Patrol Barracks at Madison, Georgia, a district that covered Monroe. This unprecedented quadruple slaying, however, had gone unreported to Madison, which would have been equipped, according to the GBI head, to send troopers to Monroe at a moment's notice.[46]

Not long after the lynchings, Loy Harrison drove up to the home of Moena Williams, the mother of two of the victims, Dorothy Malcolm and George Dorsey. Moena, forty-four, had been only fifteen years old when she had given birth to George. For the past four years she had lived with her family on a patch of farmland owned by Harrison.

"Come over here, Moena, I've got something to tell you which I know you don't want to hear," he said.

As the portly farmer spoke with her, his brother-in-law waiting in the vehicle heard Moena shouting and crying.[47] They sat on the porch with her slightly deaf husband, Jim Williams.[48] Harrison told her he had been waylaid at gunpoint and that all four passengers had been forcibly hauled off.[49] "I don't know what happened to them."[50] He told her to accompany him back to his house and wait there until he could get news of their fate from the sheriff's office.

After he had driven back, two of his farming friends arrived at Harrison's roadside home. They said Harrison told them, "I had one of the worst experiences I have ever had, a while ago. I was coming from Monroe and when at the Moore's Ford Bridge a bunch of men came out of the bushes and put a gun to my head, walked up to the car and said, 'Get out of there, Charlie!'"

Harrison said he replied, "This ain't Charlie. This is George. What you all up to? You want my money?"

"No, we just want your coons."

Harrison continued, "The group threw a rope around the wrists of both of the negro men and took them about fifty yards down the road." Harrison then heard shooting but he did not know if they were dead. After the shots were fired, the abductors came back to the bridge, appearing to be perfectly calm. Harrison did not appear to be nervous either while relating what had happened because, said one of his visitors, "He ain't that type."[51] Harrison invited his visitors to go down to the river with him "to see about them," but they backed off, one of them explaining he had ten cows to milk. When one of the visitors asked if Harrison had a pistol with him, he replied that he didn't even have a pocket knife.

Moena interjected, "Mr. Loy, you going down there?"

"I ain't scared," Harrison answered. "That crowd done gone."[52]

Williams said he and Moena waited at Harrison's home until he came back between 9:00 and 10:00 p.m.

"All four of them are dead and are now at the undertaker's parlor," he said.

When she heard that one of her sons and only daughter had been killed, Moena slumped down in a faint.[53]

After she came to, Harrison told her he had made arrangements for the bodies to be prepared for burial.[54] That night Moena and Jim stayed in Harrison's basement at his house. At daybreak he told her to be brave, since they were dead, and nothing could be done about it.[55]

Meanwhile, the nighttime embalming had begun on the bodies of George Dorsey and the two females, but it came to an abrupt halt at the mortuary when it was decided it would be more prudent to let them be handled by a black-owned funeral home. The white mortician felt the move would "facilitate the visits of colored friends and relatives and create a more harmonious handling of the situation."[56] Shortly after midnight, the corpses were delivered to the Dan Young funeral home in downtown Monroe,[57] the owner of which speculated that the transfer was made to save the white undertaker from "the trouble that was coming."[58] As Dan Young received the dead, an observer recoiled, for Roger looked as if he "had as many holes in him as a sifter."[59] Another eyewitness shuddered when he saw "one side of Roger's face shot off."[60]

Abruptly, a few FBI agents who had arrived in Monroe the night after the lynchings were ordered to collect spent ammunition that might still be embedded in the bodies. The crime scene remained unprotected until 8:30 that morning, July 27, when the first FBI agents arrived at the location.[61] A full day and two nights had passed without anyone closing off the bloodstained site to the public.

The order for an additional autopsy was issued by a Walton county superior court judge on the second day after the shootings,[62] when the mortician once again brought the dead out of refrigeration. The autopsy would have to be finished in time for the burial the following morning.

Young had gone to Atlanta earlier that day to get the coffins and other funeral supplies. While there, he had spoken confidentially with Eugene Martin, a board member of the NAACP Legal Defense and Educational Fund, and brother-in-law of Walter White, the formidable executive secretary of the NAACP.[63] Young passed on all manner of information about the unfolding events in Monroe, including unsubstantiated talk among Monroe's blacks of what they had heard and believed. He even spoke of the E.L. Almand funeral home, saying that the son was mayor of Monroe while the father, defeated in the recent primary election for representative to the state legislature, was reportedly a member of the Ku Klux Klan.[64] He talked openly with Martin and an attorney but refused to be quoted. Young was so fearful for his life that he said he might be killed if such information leaked out.[65] The prospect of retribution so alarmed him that he even wondered whether he ought to flee Monroe. "Under no circumstances does he want his name mentioned in any shape, form or fashion as he had been sought after, and talked to so much, that he is beginning to fear that he might in some way be considered a dangerous man by the guilty parties," Martin wrote to White.[66]

Significantly, a member of one of the families of the victims was earnestly willing for the stomachs of the slain to be examined. A finding might answer Harrison's assertion that they had been drinking before the abductions. Young was confident that his experience in embalming would establish the truth.[67]

Only a few days had passed since Young had conducted a funeral service attended by Roger Malcolm's grandmother. The elderly lady had once taken him aside for a confidential plea. Conditioned by a lifetime of hardscrabble subservience on white-owned farms, she feared for Roger's life after he had stabbed a farmer. She told Dan Young that if anything happened to her grandson, she wanted the undertaker to take care of the body.[68] Now that same grandson lay dead and stretched out before him, awaiting the respect that Young had promised the frail old lady.

Just three bullets had been taken from Roger's corpse because the coroner had given instructions to remove only those that were visible.[69] Young began the macabre task of searching for the bullets inside the victim. As representatives of the FBI and GBI took notes, he found nothing more inside the butchered remains of Roger Malcolm. The day before, the three slugs had been delicately picked from his bloodied head, arm, and hip. Other shots had burst through Roger's body and left gory signs of execution.

Ignoring the painful sight of Dorothy Malcolm's ravaged body, Young searched for but did not find any more slugs. He made simultaneous notes of her pellet-riddled corpse. Shotgun blasts had wreaked havoc with the bones and tissues of an ear, cheek, chin, and neck, while splintering her left wrist.

Young, a graduate of the Atlanta School of Mortuary Science,[70] and rated by the NAACP as "an important character" in Monroe,[71] retrieved a single slug and three pellets from the innards of George Dorsey. A bullet had crashed through his defenseless frame and slowed to a stop just below the skin of the right armpit. Holes from exiting shots left tattered flesh in both ears and an arm.

The mortician delicately removed thirteen shotgun pellets from Mae Dorsey. A .38-caliber slug that tore through the top of her head was extracted from her spinal column. The murderers left her with a torn breast, mangled shoulder, and perforated lungs.[72]

Slugs removed from the corpses, bloodied earth, and pieces of pierced trees were sent to the FBI laboratory in Washington, but the results were inconclusive. Five bullets possibly were fired from the same gun, though there was "some indication two weapons may have been used."[73]

When the autopsy was over, Young stated definitively that they had not been drinking, an assertion he later repeated to his confidant in Atlanta, where no mention was made of any defilement of the body of Dorothy Malcolm to remove a fetus from her remains.[74] Neither he, nor representatives present from the FBI and GBI, made any verbal reference at all to accusations that the cadavers had been tampered with after death. Notes scribbled at each of the autopsies, and initialed and dated by Young and the onlookers, were retained as exhibits in the case file.[75] Much later, their unknown whereabouts would spawn wild theories of ghastly depravity on the body of Dorothy Malcolm. Critics of official investigations said the killers had cut open her torso and yanked out a seven-month-old fetus, a charge repeatedly made decades later by the Georgia Association of Black Elected Officials, sponsors of the annual reenactments.[76]

At daylight on Sunday, mourners gathered on the hard, uneven ground beside the isolated Mount Perry Baptist Church, a small white-washed clapboard structure topped with a low steeple and barely visible off the quiet country road beyond the tiny settlement of Bishop. Young and old were dressed in their Sunday best, some of the women in simple prints and many of the men in ties and jackets, holding their porkpie hats. This day they came to bury the siblings, George and Dorothy, alongside each other. Their mother, Moena, stayed home, no one knowing whether her sorrow was too heavy for ceremony or if fear had kept her indoors. A woman who said she was Roger's estranged wife told the media decades later that she had refused to allow Dorothy and Roger to be buried side by side.[77] Silently, the grieving lined up and filed slowly and solemnly past the coffins for a last look at the faces of the dead. An American flag draped the closed portion of the veteran's casket. When the prayers and the preacher were done, they crossed the virgin land and stood beside the spades and fresh mounds of rocky earth as the coffins disappeared below.

Mae Dorsey was buried quietly at the Tabernacle Baptist Church, just off Monroe's main street. The day after, Roger was laid to rest at Chestnut Grove, eleven miles southeast of Monroe. More than two decades had passed since Buster Malcolm had given the infant Roger his surname when he moved into the birthmother's home after her husband abandoned the family. Now Buster looked on as the earth closed over the child he had raised as his own.[78]

Monroe

A visitor could drive from one end of Broad Street to the other and pass through the built-up area of Monroe in not much longer than it took to fill the car's tank with gas. Named in honor of President James Monroe and established as the county seat in 1821, the town lay forty-five miles east of Atlanta and twenty-four miles southwest of Athens.

There was a sense of languid ease to this urban base for the surrounding farming community. The red-brick county courthouse overlooked Broad Street with aging authority, as if mindful of its role as keeper of a settled way of life. From its expansive front grounds rose a sculpture of a Confederate soldier in memory of those who fought in defense of the South during what many locals still regarded as the War of Northern Aggression.

Fifty years earlier the city's boundaries had been measured from the same courthouse to include all the land within a radius of three quarters of a mile.[1] It was sufficient to contain half a dozen bars whose rowdy patrons frequently shattered the peace of weekends and public holidays with brawls, riots, and gunfire. Outraged residents retaliated in 1894 with a vote that banned the sale of whiskey as far as the distant limits of the county. Triumphantly, a local resident boasted in the local newspaper that "It may be safely claimed that few towns or cities anywhere have a healthier moral and religious atmosphere."[2]

Demolition crews removed all traces of the ramshackle wooden barrooms to make way for sturdy brick buildings in which pioneer families opened businesses that flourished under the same bloodlines over generations. Continuity of family ownership gave a feeling of stability buttressed by the opening of the Walton Cotton Mills and plants by Coca Cola and the Ford Motor Company. Prominent retail outlets became more than landmarks and compass points. They were the anchors of the fledgling community, comforting reminders of its solid base.

The venerable Hotel Monroe, open since 1921 at the corner of Broad and Court Streets, loomed over the heart of the commercial area like a beloved matriarch, offering abundant servings of family-style plain cooking in a dining room grand enough to host wedding receptions, banquets, and regular meetings of the Rotarians and Kiwanis.[3] One of its tenants, P. N. Briscoe, founded in 1892, was a lustrous presence as the state's preeminent cotton merchant that bought twice as much cotton as any of its statewide rivals.[4]

The black part of Monroe was "around the corner" from the paved sidewalks of the main uptown shopping district.[5] It was markedly different, with squalor rife in the roads, huts, and the rear of a movie theater, topped by a red neon sign above the doorway proclaiming to all that it was the "Colored Entrance." A squalid-looking clapboard room, adjacent to Young's funeral home, sold soda pop, pork chops, and fish sandwiches. There was also a beauty parlor and another eatery. An air of listlessness prevailed, and the locals loitered beside the buildings, some watching idly as others played checkers all day.[6]

Monroe had been plagued by periodic outbursts of racial tensions and violence, but that had hardly stained its reputation in a state where segregation was the norm. In 1939 a black male was arrested and charged with raping a white woman. He was secretly taken out of the county, but days later grim men surrounded the jail in Monroe demanding officials hand him over. After a fruitless search their leader waved off enraged followers as one hundred townspeople stood by. Subsequently, tear gas had to be used to disperse the mob when the man was electrocuted after a Walton County superior court found him guilty and sentenced him to death.[7]

More recently, about 1941, a black male recollected seeing klansmen riding the streets of Monroe garbed in white sheets and masks. Their presence was not new. Almost a quarter century back, the old-timer remembered talk that the KKK "had beaten up some colored folk in the Blasingame district," close by.[8]

As far back as thirty-five years earlier, a black man living just south of Monroe was thought to have attempted to rape a white widow. The man's aunt, who fiercely denied his guilt, never forgot his grisly end. He was protected by Georgia National Guardsmen until his trial in Monroe was rescheduled and he was temporarily guarded only by the sheriff. When the train neared Monroe an armed mob blocked it, dragged the man out, shot him, and hung his body from a telephone pole.[9]

While the racial tensions and violence persisted, other aspects of the town were changing. By the end of World War II, Walton County had the distinction of being the state's second largest producer of cotton,[10] with an acreage yield higher than anywhere else in Georgia.[11] But peace and prosperity magnified local problems, one of which was Monroe's pressing need for more telephones and relief from congestion on long-distance calls. The utility company urged patience, with assurances that fifty additional lines had been ordered.[12]

And yet the chief of Monroe police was forced to take out a front page advertisement in the local newspaper in 1946, warning that several people had almost been hit by stray bullets, and that this danger had to be stopped. "It is illegal to discharge firearms of any sort in the city of Monroe, except in defense of life and property," the lawman threatened. "This applies to .22 rifles and other dangerous firearms."[13]

By war's end, Monroe's population had held steady at only a few thousand people, but it was already identified by the businesses that carried the names of its prominent families. They were in such familiar locations that print advertisements did not bother to include addresses. Farmers flocked to Aycock's to buy everything from horse wagons, combines, and cotton-picking sacks to leather kneepads, feeds, and seeds.[14]

From about the Fourth of July to the end of August, farmers lay down agricultural implements and silenced the tractors to relax during "lay-by time," a period spanning the end of cultivation to the start of harvesting. Many would drive into Monroe during the broiling heat to hang out on the shaded grounds of the courthouse or in the cooler interiors of Hearn's Hardware Store (which also sold firearms), Vernon Wright's radio shop, Harry Arnold's fertilizer plant, Robinson's ten-cent store, Prather's service station, Allen's five-and-ten-cents store, or the Mendel family's furniture and grocery stores. Others might slip into Daws Flour and Feed Company to pick up a special treat of chocolate pudding for ten cents a box or cherry pies at thirty-nine cents a can.[15] Some would while away the hours at Jack Ford's pool room or Wright's pool hall, leisurely downing beers away from the scorching sun. A few would meet up to play cards or checkers at Levy Adock's general store at the intersection of a dirt road leading to Hestertown, or at other venues along rural stretches. The brief hiatus from farm work gave way to neighborhood fish fries and barbecues, visits to friends and relatives, and above all attendance at nightly church revival services. "Picture shows" were another option, with Troy offering continuous movies from mid-afternoon and Cherokee bringing back popular oldies. Adults paid twenty-five cents for admission.[16] The American Legion Fairgrounds at Church Street were always a draw for the summer appearance of the Bailey Brothers circus, which featured lions and tigers, Arabian stallions, clowns, and acrobats.[17] Sanders furniture company touted a collection of 5,000 albums, from two dollars and seventy-five cents to four fifty, for those wanting to use "all-electric" or "hand-wind portable phonographs" and listen to Tex Ritter, Tommy Dorsey, Glenn Miller, or semi-classical favorites by Fritz Chrysler. The 1946 summer sale slashed record prices to a mere twenty-five cents each.[18]

The farming community in the Blasingame district of southern Walton County, just minutes from where Roger Malcolm stabbed Barnett Hester, was located seven miles southeast of Monroe.[19] Fronting a network of country roads, with even rougher stretches of by-roads, were the homes of so many Hesters, or people related to or descended from them, that the area was better known as Hestertown. Marriage between those closely related to one another was not uncommon.[20] Other families had also multiplied and remained in Hestertown so that the surnames Hester, Malcolm, Peters, Adcock, Hawk, and others were plentiful.

Hestertown had evolved into clannish turf, a bastion, within which the residents shared a common culture, economic interests, and a rigidly uniform outlook. But that did not preclude family feuds, some of which were unforgiving and lasting. For a quarter century the longtime bailiff of the Blasingame district had not visited the home of his first cousin, the wife of Barnett Hester, because of a falling out of relatives over the administration of a grandfather's estate.[21]

Most families farmed cotton, though many had dairy cows they milked in the morning and evening. The fields sprouted corn, wheat, tomatoes, cucumbers, butterbeans, peas, and watermelons. Rainfall was a mixed blessing because it multiplied the numbers of boll weevils feeding on plant lice. Every year the farmers fought back with a poisonous mix of rotenone and calcium arsenate, adding a killer dose of nicotine sulphate if the lice infestation was severe.[22]

Nearly all the farmers in the vicinity of Hestertown owned a shotgun or small-caliber rifle[23] as hunting was one of the most popular year-round outdoor diversions. They shouldered weapons in the search for doves, hawks, squirrels, hogs, chickens, polecats, snakes, foxes, turtles, and rabbits. Little heed was paid to game laws.[24] Children, too, enjoyed the thrill of shooting and relished swimming, or fishing in the creeks, rivers, and ponds for minnows, and graveling turtles, which involved lifting snapping turtles from beneath the water and brought them up by shoving sticks under their upper shells. The Apalachee River near Moore's Ford Bridge was a popular destination for swimmers and adventurers looking for turtles.[25] Others would claim the hours to can peaches and vegetables or to sort watermelons. By Labor Day many of the farmhands were out in the fields, picking cotton and baling and loading hay.[26] In late fall they sharpened the knives to kill and dress hogs in a seasonal ritual extending well into winter.

But there was a darker side to Hestertown, which some outside observers deplored. They were notorious for treating their black farmhands "like horses and mules,"[27] and for being "nigger haters, determined to keep them under their thumbs."[28] Within days of taking command of the case in the field, FBI special agent Charles Weeks informed Washington about whom they were up against. "Their reputation as to the handling of negro tenants on their farms in the past has been to take the discipline into their own hands without calling upon the law for assistance."[29]

The community felt no conflict between its firm conviction in racial superiority and its fervent attachment to churches that preached a creed of goodwill to all. It was an attitude shared by the larger community. Hestertown's week-long revival meetings at the Ebenezer Baptist and Union Chapel United Methodist churches were always filled to capacity with the devout and those who felt obliged to be present. But at their conclusion, which in 1946 coincided with the quadruple lynchings, a participant ironically reflected in the local newspaper: "If everyone could or would always have the brotherly love and devotion, and feel the nearness of Christ as during the summer revivals, what a glorious world this would be."[30]

Primary Election

3

Roger Malcolm's incarceration came in the closing days of an election campaign dominated by race-baiting provocations. After the US Supreme Court lifted the ban against blacks voting in Georgia's 1946 primary elections, white supremacist gubernatorial candidate Eugene Talmadge stiffened his resistance and coarsened his rhetoric. The inflammatory campaign would come to a head with balloting on July 17, 1946, just three days after Roger Malcolm stabbed Barnett Hester.

Seeking a fourth non-consecutive gubernatorial term, Talmadge criss-crossed the state, thundering, "The nigger should come in the back door with his hat in his hand."[1] As though he were repeating a refrain, the plain-speaking rabble-rouser, wearing red galluses, told voters, "I believe in treating the negro right, but I want to deal with them with their hats in their hands, saying 'yes sir' and 'no sir.'"[2]

Talmadge and his unwavering followers were the faithful heirs of earlier generations who held sway when slavery went unchallenged. The candidate and his devotees were as rigidly white supremacist as their ancestors had been, even after their defeat in the Civil War. Abolition of slavery made no dent in their insistence that blacks should remain subservient. Six years after destruction of the Confederacy, Congressional hearings in Washington, DC exposed widespread lawlessness and intimidation meant to subjugate blacks by murder and whippings and to terrorize them into staying away from voting booths. Asked how whites generally treated blacks in Georgia, the native-born solicitor general for six of the state's counties told US Senators and Congressmen, "They expect obedience and submission generally. When they come in the house we expect them to pull off their hats. Any language that we would regard as not offensive at all from a white man would be impudence from a negro." Asked whether whites would punish blacks outside of the law, the witness replied affirmatively. "I have heard frequent remarks that would go to show that they would justify the whipping of a negro."[3] A former Georgia professor of classics testified that it was natural for former slaveholders "to domineer over the colored people."[4] The legacy of belief in racial superiority bound the generations as tightly as shrouds wrapped around ancient mummies.

There had been many lynchings in Georgia, even though Talmadge proudly claimed that there had been none during his three terms as governor. This claim was disputed by an institution promoting better race relations, which listed five lynchings during Talmadge's first term, eight in his second, and one in his third.[5]

Campaigning as though the outcome of the Civil War had not led to a broadening of voting rights for men of color, Talmadge ran advertisements promoting himself as "the white people's candidate" and urging voters, "Let's keep Georgia white."[6] He had threatened the inevitability of black dominance over white women in the workplace if blacks gained political power,[7] citing with outrage an alleged instance of "a feather-in-his-hat negro zoot-suiter" trying to sit down in a Baptist church alongside a white woman.[8]

Pledging to ban blacks from voting if reelected,[9] Talmadge echoed the past, warning, "Wise negroes will stay away from white folks' ballot boxes. We are the true friends of the negroes, always have been, and always will be, as long as they stay in the definite place we have provided for them."[10] The ultimatum was an unsettling reminder of the violent aftermath of the Civil War, when armed horsemen cloaked in sheets and headcovers with eye holes materialized out of the night to gun down unsuspecting victims or to lacerate their naked flesh. Then, as now, black communities panicked, with many succumbing to demands that they stay away from ballot boxes. Others fled their homes for the safety of the woods or towns.[11] It had been futile in the past to finger the assailants or plead for prosecution because, as one black man had testified to Congress seven decades earlier, "If a man knows two or three men in a crowd, or knows one man for certain, that man gets 40 or 50 men to swear that he was at some other place that night."[12]

The same malevolence plagued the countryside during the 1946 primary election, with Talmadge inciting boisterous overflow crowds to

the edge of reckless enthusiasm. During Reconstruction, white supremacists were said to have "Ku Kluxed" their black adversaries.[13] Now,
Talmadge's cohorts enforced the same limitations on blacks without the
need to murder or wear outlandish disguises as had been done by members of a gang notorious for its triple alliterative lettering.

Over 135,000 blacks had registered to vote for the first time in 1946,
but tens of thousands would be disqualified in a systematic campaign
that challenged their literacy and competency.[14] About 120,000 challenge forms were printed on instructions from the Talmadge For Governor Club and distributed to followers throughout the state. Investigators later found that a large proportion of whites could not have passed
the educational qualification tests given to blacks.[15] Talmadge's Atlanta
office sent a Lamar County official "suggestions" for questions to stump
and disqualify blacks, such as, "In whose charge are the navigable rivers
of the US?" and "Who has the right to coin and issue money in the
US?"[16]

Thousands of blacks were removed from voting lists based on challenges signed in many cases by persons not even acquainted with them,
and who knew nothing of their qualifications.[17] In Meriwether County,
about thirty to forty challenge forms arrived at the home of a septuagenarian for his signature below the names of blacks registered to vote.
However, because he was ill, he told his wife to fill in his name as the
challenger. "I only knew three or four of these negroes," he admitted. In
Warm Springs, a white man knowingly questioned the eligibility to vote
of a black schoolteacher, even though he knew the educator was qualified. "All I had to do was sign my name below in the space provided,"
he said.[18] After arranging for 1,500 challenge forms to be sent to the tax
collector in Liberty County, Eugene Talmadge wrote him, "After a few
have been challenged, they will quit registering. The next problem will
be to challenge all the negroes presently registered."[19]

In southern Worth County, over 200 white spectators jeered as prospective black voters had to answer whether they had been convicted of
crimes or committed adultery. If they could read, they were told to interpret a section of the Georgia Code. Periodically a spectator would loudly

demand of the registrar, "Aren't you going to disqualify him!" During an adjournment, some hundred men encircled two registrars considered too impartial. One of the mob cried out, "I've been appointed by this crowd to demand your resignations! It won't do for you to go back up there—is that right boys?" "Yes!" the crowd responded. One of the ruffians, armed with a knife, followed a registrar home, warning from an open window that he should not return to the courthouse. The registrars promptly resigned, but even though reinstated by a judge, one of them later confessed that he disqualified more blacks than he ordinarily would have to save himself from being killed.[20] The night before polling in Greenville, Meriwether County, a furniture store owner instructed half a dozen Talmadge enthusiasts to burn a cross in the negro section of town "to keep many of them from showing up to vote."[21] One of the participants made light of the escapade by referring to it as "a little fun."[22] Other white supremacists armed with rocks and sticks scared off fifty-two blacks from entering a polling station in Manchester.[23]

In southernmost Grady County, men firing rifles, shotguns, and revolvers pulled up in twenty-one trucks and cars outside the homes of blacks, then ordered them not to vote and to relay the directive to their friends.[24] When a white attorney in eastern Chatham County complained to electoral officials about the delay in opening ballot boxes and the deliberate slowing down of black voters waiting for hours in misleadingly unlabeled lines, a furious official turned on him, warning, "If you do not get the hell away from here immediately, I will break every bone in your body."[25]

Candace Phipps, daughter of a black farmer in southwestern Baker County, pleaded with a US district attorney for help. Though she could read and write, she had been struck from the roll by registrars after being told to interpret a page of text she had just read on the right of a citizen to appeal to a higher court if justice had been denied in a lower court. "It may be too late to help in this election but there will be others and I think all qualified citizens should have the privilege of citizens, regardless of color," Phipps wrote to the district attorney. "We have to be very careful of our lives. If there is anything you can do without me having to appear as witness [sic] I would appreciate it, but I am truly afraid to have to come out in the open as we colored people never have protection here, and if you can't do anything without me as a witness, you may drop the matter, and I'll continue to pray that some day deliverance will come to the worthy people of our race."[26] On that same day, about fifty other blacks waiting their turn to be challenged were told to return the following day because officials said they had run out of time.

The personal whim of a single woman blocked untold numbers of blacks from registering to vote in northwestern Fayette County. After her husband, the tax collector, suffered a disabling stroke, she said she "took over his duties as best I could," registering more than 100 white voters in her home. But when blacks came to her house to register she turned them away, explaining that her husband was too ill to register them at his office. "I refused to turn my living room over to negroes and I didn't feel it was necessary to register them outside or elsewhere," she explained.[27]

A certified public accountant in northern Polk County mimeographed a blank challenge form and entered the names of 499 blacks, reasoning that "it would be easier to disqualify 100 negroes than to persuade 100 whites to vote for Talmadge." He said he made up his expenses by betting on the outcome of the primary election. However, his efforts were foiled by registrars who ruled there was not enough time for hearings, or to draw up voter lists.[28]

Past military service by blacks was of no consequence. In Monroe County, about twenty-five black veterans were turned away from a polling station when told they were not on the voter list.[29] A white attorney who went to the Atlanta office of Talmadge's son, Herman, to suggest that he did not think it necessary to challenge the right of 221 blacks to vote in northwestern Haralson County was told "it made no difference to him, that all he expected was for us to carry the county for his father."[30]

Walton County, the location of the lynchings, provided one of the most conspicuous exceptions to the campaign to undercut the black vote. When Superior Court Judge Henry West heard there might be challenges in Walton County, which fell within his judicial circuit, he told the board of registrars, all avowed Talmadge men, that he would replace one of them with a supporter from another political faction to stymie monopolistic partisanship.[31] It proved unnecessary after the registrars met with fellow Talmadge backer Walton County Sheriff Emory Gordon in the lawman's Monroe office nine days before the election. All four men agreed that targeting black voters might antagonize the electorate into voting for someone other than Talmadge. The sheriff firmly believed that "the people of Walton County are an aristocratic type of Georgia people, who would not stand for such a purge," and who would very likely turn against the Talmadge crowd and vote for other candidates if blacks were erased from the rolls.[32]

Some electoral officials had quit their jobs in protest and a few editors had railed against the glaring discrimination against blacks. But the tally of those disqualified soared across the state.[33] Talmadge predicted that "very few negroes will vote if registrars do their duty."[34] He dismissed as "intimidation" the US district attorney's promise to investigate illegal purging[35] and warned, "I think it would be extremely wise for negroes to stay away from the white folks' ballot boxes on July 17, for neither the US attorneys nor Jimmy Carmichael [his principal opponent] will have a corporal guard to back them up."[36] To reinforce his stance, Talmadge shared the stage with a South Carolina state senator who praised Ku Klux Klanners from Georgia for having helped overthrow black rule in his state during Reconstruction.[37]

Confident of victory and stridently boastful, Talmadge predicted an avalanche of votes in his favor to restore the whites-only primary.[38] Carmichael decried Talmadge's scare tactics but was careful to reassure the edgy white electorate that if elected, he too would never desegregate schools and that "there would be no interracial marriages, and no mixing of the races in our institutions."[39] However, ten days before election day, polls predicted the former governor's defeat.[40] Registration of black and white voters had reached historic highs and in Walton County surpassed all previous tallies. In Monroe, almost one in four registered voters were black. This number was not representative, however. In Blasingame, the heart of the Hester family clan, all but twelve of the 256 voters were white.

Undaunted, Talmadge took comfort from the county unit system, peculiar to Georgia, in which gubernatorial candidates had to win a majority of the 410 county unit votes to win on a first ballot.[41] Each county was allotted either two, four, or six unit votes, according to population. The system gave smaller counties an overwhelming advantage because the superior numbers of voters in large counties would receive only two or four more votes than much smaller counties. Combined wins in many of the smaller, more conservative rural counties would trump predictable losses in the more liberal but far fewer large counties.

Two days before the election, Talmadge canvassed votes in Monroe and the surrounding farming community. The adjacent Blasingame area, where Barnett Hester had been stabbed, was fertile territory for Talmadge. It was thickly populated by generations of families sharing a mentality of "keeping the negro in his place."[42] Talmadge was reportedly seen "in close conversation" with Barnett Hester's brother, George, and was understood to have offered immunity to anyone "taking care of [the] negro."[43]

Toward midnight on the day of the election, just hours before polling booths opened, drivers passing by a wooded area a few miles south of Monroe saw as many as fifteen cars parked alongside the road, with groups of white men milling around, smoking and talking. Towler's Woods was well known as a rendezvous for buying and selling liquor, heavy drinking, card games, smooching, or just hanging out. Yet there was something disturbing about this late night cluster of upward of twenty men, especially with the outermost cars pointed in different directions, as if on the lookout for infiltrators.

A black bicyclist returning from a movie was so shaken by the sinister outlines of men and vehicles in the dead of night that he detoured out of sight through the woods.[44] A preacher who had delivered a sermon at the Methodist Church in Monroe had not yet heard about the stabbing of Barnett Hester, and thought the crowd at Towler's Woods might be conspiring to foil black voting rights.[45] One motorist felt a chill of fear when the fog lights of a car at the head of the line suddenly brightened.[46] Terror gripped two black men on their way home from a meeting in the Monroe Colored High School, where they had been coached on how to cast votes for the first time in their lives. They immediately suspected they had stumbled upon a lynch mob. "We thought these people might be planning to get Roger Malcom because he stabbed the Hester boy," said one.[47] A twenty-five-year-old discharged white veteran and his wife, who lived about 100 yards from where the gathering took place, said it broke up sometime after 1:00 a.m. "Both my wife and I were scared," the man admitted.[48]

Some days later, a few white men passing the time in a Monroe general store were overheard talking about nightriders who had met in the woods to plan the lynching.[49] Word of the clandestine plot to kill Roger Malcom spread throughout the community, even though it was hearsay. The mob aborted the lynching, according to rumor, only because no one took the lead and they had drunk too much.[50] "That nigger was lucky to live as long as he did because before the lynching they had a meeting out there and they were going to lynch him that night, but one man was fool enough to bring along his twelve-year-old boy, so they had to call it off," said one informant.[51] Another man said his wife had heard it talked about at work, but she gave no names. "You know how a crowd of women is," he said.[52]

Someone in another group outside the Monroe Bank remarked that "they were down at Towler's Woods splitting up the Talmadge whiskey last night."[53] Deputy Sheriff Howard made a cryptic remark to the same group that if they took Roger Malcom they would have to come to the jail after him, leaving it unclear whether he would resist or cooperate with a lynch mob.[54]

Violence erupted even before the sun rose on election day. A black man had woken up to the sound of white men shouting from his front yard, several miles north of Monroe. "Come out you son-of-a-bitch or we'll kill you and your family!" A month earlier he'd punched a white man in a store after a dispute over sugar he said he'd paid for. Now they had come to settle the score. One of the whites was armed with a shotgun and another with a pistol as they drove him through the countryside. They told him he was "a bad nigger. We're going to rule the niggers around here." Then the black man said the sedan pulled up and a man named James Verner, thirty-six, and a number of other attackers stripped him of his clothing and beat him with a hose, sticks, and the pistol.[55]

At dawn, intimidation broke out in earnest. Another black man and his wife were awakened by the dull bang of shotgun blasts. From his porch he looked across the road to the home of his neighbor, the afore-mentioned James Verner, a former firearms marksman with the Army Air Corps. Verner, and a number of his friends were firing shotguns pointed upward, but in the direction of the black man's home. The pellets fell like heavy hail onto the tin roof. Some hours later, when the black man told his employer he was going to vote, the boss man warned that people were "a little rough" about letting colored people vote in Gratis and suggested he vote instead about ten miles south in Monroe.[56]

Blacks who tried to vote in Gratis were chased off with threats and vulgarities. Two men who parked their car opposite a polling booth in a general store were confronted by James Verner and his brother-in-law, who commanded, "Don't put your damn foot on the other side of the road." The black men obeyed. "We never did try to vote after they told us not to cross the road," said one. They left the town, he admitted, "because we were afraid."[57]

With Verner and two other white men remaining inside the polling station most of election day, not a single black person came in to vote. "I don't know why the negroes in the community did not vote and I do not know of any who were run away or refused the right to vote," said the store owner.[58] Verner rebuffed critics, saying he "did not give a damn who voted, or who they voted for."[59]

When the polls closed and the ballots were counted, Talmadge emerged triumphant. He had lost the popular state-wide vote to Carmichael by some 16,000 votes out of almost 700,000 cast, but he still came out the winner. He had swept the county unit votes with a handsome majority, trouncing his opponent in Walton County despite losing to him in the most populous city of Monroe. In the Blasingame district, close to where the black sharecropper had impulsively stabbed his white employer, Talmadge chalked up 85 percent, winning over all but twenty-two of the votes.[60] It was a foregone conclusion that he would triumph in the general election.

That night, as Talmadge's supporters celebrated victory, Deputy Sheriff Lewis Howard spoke gravely to his new inmate, Roger Malcolm. "If that fellow dies that you stuck, you better be praying if you want to go to heaven because your time won't be long."[61]

Stabbing

Roger Malcolm started drinking shortly after Dorothy decided not to continue their morning walk to church that Sunday, July 14, 1946. "I'm going to leave you in the fall anyway!" he snapped at the woman he lived with.[1] Neither Roger's grandmother nor his sister knew for sure whether the black couple were husband and wife,[2] though his mother-in-law, Moena, said they had married seven months earlier.[3] However, almost forty-six years later, another woman, Mattie Louise Campbell, insisted she had then been Roger's estranged wife.[4]

The relationship was a tumultuous one. For some time Roger and others had suspected Dorothy was carrying on with Barnett Hester,[5] the white man on whose farm they had been living for the past half year.[6] Some of Roger's family and friends thought Dorothy, twenty,[7] was just the kind of woman to be flirting around. One of Roger's friends from childhood said it was "common talk" among the black community that Barnett Hester, twenty-nine, had been paying attention to and "fooling around" with her.[8] Roger's closest blood relatives had no doubt that Dorothy, nicknamed "jitterbug" by some,[9] was a "fast" woman.[10] A neighboring farm worker said she was "what we call a rough girl, and from seeing her at parties I know she would go off with any colored man who had a pint of liquor."[11] Above all, Roger had complained to the man who had raised him that he was having trouble with Dorothy because she was showing signs of too much "independence."[12]

Roger had already had too many drinks as the sun set slowly over Georgia farmland that summer, when he jumped off the side of an auto and chased Dorothy out of another car. She broke free and ran screaming to the front yard of the house where Barnett lived with his parents.[13]

About this time Barnett and his oldest brother, George, had returned from milking cows. Barnett said he first learned about the domestic fracas when his wife called out to him that Roger and Dorothy were "fussing." He told Roger he didn't want any trouble and ordered the black man off his property.[14] A different account came from a passing black eyewitness who said Roger was still on the road when Barnett struck him with a wagon standard, knocking his hat off. After a second blow, Roger lashed out and stabbed the white man.[15]

The black farmhand's move was so quick that Barnett did not notice right away that the knife had pierced his torso, perforating the diaphragm and lacerating the base of his stomach.[16]

"I've been cut!" Barnett cried out in shock as he grasped his left side and staggered indoors.[17]

White bystanders and relatives claimed the assailant then taunted, "From now on call me *Mister* Roger Malcolm!"[18] Black eyewitnesses, however, said Roger exclaimed, "I thought you were going with my wife; now I know it!"[19] Shrieks and screams broke the calm of dusk as Roger sprinted away from his employer's home to hide in the field of ripened corn.

Ida Hester, fearing her son would bleed to death, cried out to her husband, Bob, to rush Barnett to the hospital.[20] At that moment a stupefied George ran into the house for his car keys.

The hollering alerted some of the Hester clan living within earshot. Grady Malcolm, fifty-three, walking with his wife and grandson near a cucumber patch, spotted the black man running toward him just as the wounded man's father shouted at him to head after the attacker. Grady's brother, Wayman, fifty, stopped milking his cow and joined in the chase. Roger veered off into the cornfield but the brothers had closed in. They told Roger to throw away his knife, then surrender. Roger asked who they were, and after they identified themselves he hesitated. Then he realized they had him cornered, with no possibility of escape, so he hurled away his knife, and they dragged him back to Barnett's home.

Two black men walking to find out the cause of the commotion halted when a car pulled up and the white driver gloated, "No use in you all going down there. We done got him and we gonna make away with him! Roger will never walk this road no more!"[21]

At the Hester home the hard-of-hearing Claude Malcolm, fifty-five, saw two "damn restless" white adolescents guarding the fugitive, so the brick mason "tied a rope around the nigger's feet" and stayed put until the lawmen arrived.[22]

More relatives and neighbors gathered around, most of them women.[23] From a safe distance in a field, Dorothy looked on in terror as white men kicked her trussed-up mate.[24] She was so shaken that she slept at a friend's house that night. She would never return to her own home, directly in front of Barnett's dwelling, in a tenant's house on a field.[25] Meanwhile, Bob Hester was driving Barnett to the hospital. He made a stop in the middle of the road near a general store in order to tell the owner to pass on news of the stabbing to Weldon, the wounded man's brother.[26]

It was a dangerous turn. Weldon delighted in bullying, beating, whipping, and cursing Roger Malcolm, never letting up since they were children growing up on the same farm. Everything Roger had suffered in the past would pale beside the consequences of knifing Weldon's younger brother. He had put himself at risk of the ultimate revenge from a community that believed in "keeping the negro in his place."[27] A former Monroe area resident said if a black got into an altercation or physical encounter with a white man, "it was the same as a death sentence for him."[28] A local resident later said that lynching was a bad thing for the county because three of the victims were probably innocent, but "it was probably not too bad to kill Roger inasmuch as he had stabbed a white man."[29] Roger might as well have put his head through a noose and kicked away the supporting chair.

As soon as he learned of the stabbing, Weldon stormed onto Roger's front porch, brandishing a shotgun with such rage that he left no doubt he wanted to blast the occupants with its lead pellets. "Come on out of there, you sons-of-bitches! I'm gonna kill both of you!" he roared.[30] When he realized no one was home, he raced to the scene of the stabbing at his parents' house. Weeks later, still smoldering, Weldon spluttered, "If Papa had left me and George [his brother] alone we might have killed him that night."[31] Eyewitnesses had no doubt that Weldon would have slain Roger had he not been restrained by his mother, who demanded he go immediately to the hospital to check on his brother's condition.[32]

Grady and Wayman Malcolm had driven seven miles into the Walton County seat of Monroe and told the sheriff they had captured a black man who had stabbed Barnett Hester, but the sheriff replied that he had already sent lawmen to make the arrest.[33] The brothers then returned to their homes in "Hestertown."[34]

Half an hour later, when it was dark enough for car headlights to be turned on, deputy sheriffs Lewis Howard and Charles "Doc" Sorrells arrived at the Hester home to make the arrest.[35] Roger lay in the front yard, his legs still lashed together. Howard would insist Roger did not look as if he had been kicked, punched, or physically abused, and the deputy sheriff claimed the encroaching darkness made it impossible for him to recognize anyone in the thick group of men, women, and children, even though he was distantly related to the extended clan. As Howard began loosening the restraints on Roger's feet, a woman cried out, "Don't let him get away!"[36]

The lawmen returned to Monroe and locked Roger in a cell in the red brick Walton County jail, which doubled as Deputy Sheriff Howard's residence.[37] Though the sheriff's affidavit charged him with a misdemeanor assault and battery with intent to murder, a justice of the peace drawing up the warrant turned to the wrong page of the criminal docket and charged Roger with another person's offense of stealing a dog. The careless mistake would go unrecognized for weeks until detected by the FBI.[38]

A staffer at the Walton County Hospital instantly recognized Barnett and Weldon Hester, who had both been patients at the hospital before. They both arrived drunk on the Fourth of July. Barnett had his head split open and Weldon was "so obnoxious" that she called the police, but by the time they arrived the brothers had left.[39]

This time, medical staff held out scant hope for Barnett Hester's survival. He was wheeled into the operating room at 11:00 p.m. for more than three hours of surgery, then placed in an oxygen tent for a further six hours. His anxious family stood vigil at the hospital throughout the night, not knowing whether he would pull through or succumb to his injuries.

Many in the neighborhood learned about the stabbing immediately, as the news spread by word of mouth. Others learned the news from the local newspaper, the *Walton Tribune,* which reported that hundreds of friends and relatives were praying for the recovery of "a splendid citizen."[40]

The stabbing instantly became the talk of the little town studded with nineteenth-century churches and a conspicuous monument to Confederate dead on the grounds of the county courthouse. Some stated openly that "the nigger should have been taken care of" before being handed over to the deputy sheriffs.[41]

Jail

Rumors that a lynch mob would storm the jail to drag out Roger Malcolm gained additional credibility when Deputy Sheriff Howard appeared to make access easier for a break-in after dark. He told the black janitor, a trusty, that he would have to sleep upstairs because Howard expected a mob to burst in. Until then Major Jones, forty-nine, serving a fifteen- to twenty-year sentence for murder, had been sleeping on the main floor outside the cell block in the downstairs porch, known as "the runaround."[1] After the lynchings, Jones told the FBI he had been warned by the deputy sheriff's wife, Lorena, not to talk about his move upstairs "under any circumstances, as this would ruin them if the FBI should find out about it."[2]

Lorena confided her anxieties to a black female employee, telling her she had heard that "a mob crowd was coming to the jail to get the boy out," but her fears subsided after she learned Barnett Hester's condition had improved.[3] When the FBI agents eventually learned of the move upstairs and confronted the trusty, he was visibly in fear of physical abuse as retribution from the deputy sheriff, before whom he cowered. He did not like Howard, thinking him "mean and rough" toward blacks,[4] but his punishment was limited to withdrawal of privileges to run unaccompanied errands in the streets of Monroe.[5] Howard's word was doubtful because he had already compromised himself by buying a pistol from an inmate for five dollars while the prisoner was in a chain-gang for shooting a black man dead.[6]

There was talk swirling among the inmates that Roger would be abducted by vigilantes. Word was that they were going to seize him on election day.[7] A newspaper reporter said he had been told that an anonymous group had warned the deputy sheriff that if Barnett Hester died they would expect him to turn over the keys to the jail. Both deputy sheriffs denied it and insisted they had no hint of any plot to take reprisals or overpower the jailers.[8] But such assurances did not quell suspicion among the inmates of either race.

At first, Roger gave no clue to his feelings, playing cards with another prisoner most of the time and keeping quiet about the stabbing.[9] One inmate later said, however, that Roger told him he would never be a free man, and that if he did get released he would have to leave town or "they" would kill him.[10] Mattie Louise Campbell, who resolutely claimed to be his estranged wife, visited Roger, gave him four hamburgers and, at his request, handed him a cheap wristwatch with a black leather band in a steel-covered case, costing twelve dollars.[11] She would always remember how Malcolm hollered out a window of the jail, "I ain't gonna get out of this. They're gonna kill me."[12]

A week into his confinement Roger was visited by Buster Malcolm, the man who had raised him as his own son after the biological father abandoned the toddler. Buster brought him clean clothing and smoking tobacco, even though a white woman had told her servant "it won't do them any good to buy them. He won't be able to wear them. He won't be able to walk around anymore 'cause he stabbed that man for nothing. It will just be money wasted."[13] The two men talked through a grated window within earshot of other inmates as the stepfather kept his distance on the outside. When Roger asked if he could get bail, Buster suggested it would be wiser to stay put because the Hesters were "mad" at him, though he had not heard any talk about harming Roger. Then Roger mentioned what he had withheld from others, telling his surrogate father that he did not want to get out of jail because he was afraid of what a mob might do to him.[14]

Moena and her family had not let up in their desperate pleas for their employer to bail him out, however. Moena had been "in the field busting middles of cotton" when Dorothy told her Roger had "some trouble" with his boss man and wanted to know if "Mr. Loy" could get him out of jail.[15]

Harrison had replied, "How come Roger locked up?"

"Him and boss man had a little falling out."

"I don't know whether I can get him or not," the farmer had told her.

"I will go with you and see him," she answered.

"I'll let you know about it," he said.

But the heavy-set landowner kept stalling, repeatedly, telling them he was too busy. Once, Harrison said he could not do anything about bail because of Barnett Hester's condition and that "they were looking for the white man to die," the implication being that the black assailant would have no hope if this happened.[16] But later, Moena recounted, he had left open the possibility of bail by saying, "If I get any spare time when I catch up I will go and see if I can get him out." When she raised the issue for the last time, he replied that his car was "not running good" and he did not know if he could make it into Monroe.

Even though Moena never had an opportunity to go to school,[17] she was articulate and outspoken, or, in the words of the FBI, "a rather shrewd and sharp-tongued negro."[18] But as Harrison drove up to her house just before lunch on the day of the lynchings, she was timid and submissive. "Mr. Loy," she begged, "have you thought anymore about going up to Monroe and getting Roger out for us? Please, sir." She did not yet know that Barnett Hester was out of serious danger and that day would sit up on the side of his bed for the first time since the stabbing eleven days earlier.[19] Now Harrison hinted at good news. "I might go up there and get him since you have all been after me so much," he replied. "Now you all give him such a good recommendation, I don't want him to cause me no trouble. You know he is a stranger and I don't know him." Then, abruptly, he committed himself, telling her, "I am going to get him. Maybe my car will hold out. I'll come by and see you at 2:00 p.m. and we will go and see if we can get him out."

Reflecting on the situation, Harrison added, "Ain't no use in him sitting in jail and be punished. He wouldn't have done that if he hadn't been drunk. Them people is really hot about it and didn't like it at all."[20]

Moena's oldest son, George Dorsey, spoke up. "I'll be ready. I want to go, too. I'll slip on a shirt." Mae, his wife, announced she, too, would join them. Moena turned to her husband, Jim, sixty-four, whom the FBI described as "thoroughly dominated by his wife,"[21] and asked, "Reckon I ought to go, too, Biggun?" "No, ain't no use you going. Mr. Loy will already have a load if he gets Roger out."[22]

Harrison was confident he had left his farm at 2:15 p.m. on the day of the massacre because he had waited for his children to return from school at the regular hour of 2:00 p.m. in the same Pontiac sedan he then drove fifteen minutes later to Moena's house, a third of a mile away.[23] A little over three hours before gunfire erupted near Moore's Ford Bridge, Harrison pulled up in Moena's yard. None of her family had eaten the midday meal. They waited a few minutes for Mae to finish dressing, then she climbed into the run-down Pontiac to join George and his sister, Dorothy, Roger's wife. A mile and a half later, Harrison passed over Moore's Ford Bridge before taking the dirt road by the Mountain Lodge School and picking up speed on Highway 78 until he pulled up at the courthouse in Monroe, just over ten miles from the crime scene.

Harrison had a brief conversation outside the sheriff's office with Deputy Sheriff Howard, telling him he wanted to have a word with Roger in the county jail. Ostensibly, he wanted to start sawmill operations and, being short of hands, thought Roger might "trade with him" if bailed out.[24] The landowner and the lawman agreed to meet at the county jail a few blocks away.

As soon as Howard got to the county jail he instructed another inmate, a World War II navy veteran now imprisoned for violating parole after an auto accident, to wake up Roger Malcolm and let him out of his cell so he could talk to Harrison through the barred open window.

Within earshot of Harrison, his passengers, and several inmates, Howard was overheard saying, "Roger, if Mr. Harrison gets you out will you leave liquor alone?" Roger answered that he would never touch another drop.

Harrison cut in. "If I get you out will you go to work?"

"Yes, sir," Roger replied.

Howard then asked Harrison, "Are you going on his bond?"

Harrison indicated that he would and that he would return about 5:00 p.m. to get Roger. "That will be best," Howard declared, according to an eavesdropping inmate. "He might get into something else. Don't carry him uptown."

Harrison, who owned farmland in Oconee and Walton counties, replied that he was going to take Roger out of the county.[25]

Back at the courthouse George, Mae, and Dorothy waited under the shade of a tree near the fountain while Harrison went into the sheriff's office, asking how much the bond would amount to.[26] Sheriff Gordon set it at $600, a normal amount for Walton County. Asked when he wanted to get "the nigger," Harrison replied, "I'll be back in a couple of hours."

Howard said, "That will be about 5 o'clock and I will likely be home at the jail. You need not come by the courthouse. You just come on down to the jail."[27]

The FBI would later learn from an unidentified informant that in Walton county a black man was never bonded out of jail while a white man's life was in danger, and that prior approval would have to come from "interested" people.[28]

Outside, on the front lawn near the statue of a Confederate soldier, Harrison instructed his three passengers to do any shopping they needed to do and meet him back at the same location in two hours. After they parted, he made multiple stops to talk with at least ten friends and acquaintances in Monroe before returning to the county jail. By all their accounts, the conversations amounted to nothing more than small talk about farming, the need to repair his car, and concern for the health of mutual friends. Later, he would repeatedly claim that he had said nothing about the imminence of Roger's bail.[29] But the FBI's special agent in charge was skeptical, suggesting that there were only two likely ways the killers could have learned about the timing of Roger's release. "One, that Harrison was one of the plotters and had arranged to make this bail as part of the lynching, and that he had fixed the time of 5:00 p.m. to take Malcolm out of jail and arrive at a pre-arranged spot for the crime at approximately the time he did. The other possibility is that in view of the extremely informal manner in which the public offices of this county are administered, information flows quickly and freely from the sheriff's office, or any other office, to the nearby loungers on park benches, and it is not at all improbable that the mob could have been organized in the two-hour period after the bond was signed, and while

Harrison was transacting his business in town prior to departing for home and picking up Malcolm en route."[30] Harrison would later grudgingly agree with this logic even while stubbornly denying involvement.[31]

In a series of interviews with federal agents, Harrison outlined his movements that afternoon, claiming he stopped first at Gunter's garage to repair the Pontiac's gearshift but left when he saw all the mechanics busy and the owner absent. Then he drove to the Monroe ice plant where he woke up the operator, Will Perry, who was asleep in the office. FBI investigators focused intently on this stopover, which apparently lasted about an hour and a half, because Harrison insisted he spoke only with Perry and the night operator, Vivian Tillman, who arrived two hours before his regular 6:00 p.m. shift. Perry noted that it was Harrison's first visit in a month and that they talked only about farming, the sawmill, and a colt that had broken a leg.[32] Tillman told the FBI that Harrison was definitely not at the ice plant at the same time as James Verner that day. He regularly bought chicken feed from Harrison for his turkeys and said he could not recall what they spoke about, but that they did arrange to have supper together over the coming weekend. Then, about 5:00 p.m., Harrison left, saying, "I'll be seeing you."[33]

But their claims of trivial talk only between themselves were discredited by independent eyewitnesses who also saw and recognized Verner as he leaned on the Pontiac while talking with Tillman and Harrison in the ice plant yard. Verner's familiar green LaSalle Coupe was parked close by, and it was no secret that the former firearms marksman with the Army Air Corps had terrorized blacks with gunfire and ultimatums of physical violence if they tried to vote on the day of the primary election.

After filling up with gas and water at the White Star service station,[34] Harrison said he continued on to Hearn's Hardware Store on Broad Street, parked his car, and spoke outside for some minutes with Ernest Dillard, whose Walton County farm lay a quarter mile from the crime scene.[35] Dillard told investigators he could only recall joking that his crop was better than his friend's.[36]

As they were talking they were joined by Lamar Hearn, who co-owned the store that sold arms and ammunition and also served as the town's tax assessor. They returned his greeting, after which, according to Hearn, Harrison left almost immediately while the other two went into the store.[37] Harrison claimed to have spent the next twenty minutes in a fruitless search at three crowded grocery stores for meat and lard for his farmhands.

Meanwhile, a number of people acquainted with Mae, Dorothy, and George chatted with them on the sidewalks and inside a few retail businesses. Major Jones, the jail trusty, hailed them near a grocery store.

"Thought you was going to get that boy out of jail?" he asked.

Mae replied, "We are going to get him. Mr. Harrison said he had to go somewhere and would meet us at 5 o'clock up town."[38]

Later, a black preacher who also worked at a funeral parlor saw them in front of Robertson's Dime Store. He asked Mae about "her way of living."

Mae replied, "Can't I come home?"

"What you doing here?" he queried.

"I just come over here. Just come home."

"How did you come," he asked.

"With my boss man."

"Who is your boss man?"

"Mr. Loy Harrison."[39]

Mae and George stopped in at a store and bought twenty cents' worth of candy.[40] Then they purchased meat[41] before all three ate custard pie in a café catering to blacks.[42] All of the retailers reported that the victims did not drink any beer or wine.

About this time inmates at the jail heard a familiar clock strike the hour of five. One of them turned to Roger and remarked that "it looked like his man had forgotten him." Nobody thought Roger looked scared.[43] However, he confessed to another prisoner, "I'm hot."[44]

Harrison parked next to the deputy sheriff's residential quarters at the county jail and was led into the back yard, where he found Howard eating a watermelon.[45] They walked through to the prisoners' quarters, where the deputy sheriff unlocked Roger's cell door. Roger placed his mark on the bond then accompanied Harrison to the Pontiac. It was about 5:30 p.m. when he climbed into the back seat between his wife and Mae. George was up front, next to the driver. Harrison drove up Church Street and made a few turns before they picked up speed on the Athens Highway, headed for home.

Recounting that last stretch before nearing Moore's Ford Bridge, Harrison told the FBI that his passengers had evidently been drinking beer or wine and were talking louder and somewhat faster than usual. "Just negro talk," he told the agents, to which he paid no attention. They seemed, he declared, "happy and contented."[46]

Ambush

The drive should have taken no more than fourteen minutes from the courthouse to Moore's Ford Bridge, based upon the route and speeds Harrison gave to the FBI. He said he traveled at fifty miles an hour along the highway and twenty to thirty miles an hour on the narrow, winding dirt roads.[1] During that short span, his fleeting presence was registered by the steady eyes of inquisitive neighbors. As the Pontiac cut through the sparsely settled countryside, black and white residents took customary note. It was the habitual pastime of those who sat on porches fringing the roads to scrutinize passersby, as if seeking reassurance that nothing irregular was taking place. From these advantageous overlooks they could define patterns of activity, detect abnormalities in rural rhythms, and stay in touch with their circumscribed world. They were so close to the slow-moving vehicles that they often identified faces and made mental snapshots of clothing. Some remembered Harrison driving with his passengers toward Monroe three hours earlier. Now they watched even more intently as he returned with one extra passenger.[2]

"We always talk about the models of cars as they pass the house," a black woman told the FBI.[3] Another black onlooker, describing himself as a "jack-leg" auto mechanic, took endless pleasure in testing his skills by rattling off the makes and models of passing vehicles.[4]

Harrison turned off Highway 78 immediately below Aycock's store into Mountain Lodge Road, which was dry, dusty, and deserted. This was the longest way home and Harrison never explained why he took it[5] despite having to pass by the Dorseys' home. Had he stayed on the main highway, he would have shortened the distance back to his farmhouse.[6] Two miles later, as he approached a fork, with the right one leading to Good Hope and the other going down to Moore's Ford Bridge, he said he asked George Dorsey if he wanted to get out at his home set back from the road at the intersection. "No, I'll just go on down to Mama's house," Dorsey replied, according to Harrison.[7]

While Harrison offered an account of ferrying a carload of carefree, lightheaded, and chattering passengers to their homes, other onlookers in the vicinity had glimpsed unsettling movements along the gravel roads leading to the isolated wooden bridge. By late afternoon, carloads of white males were converging on the remote rendezvous point with synchronized precision and grim determination.

A black female in the front yard of a neighbor at the intersection of High Shoals, northeast of Good Hope, and the road leading to Moore's Ford Bridge, stared hard at two passing cars loaded with white men driving toward the bridge "sometime between 5 and 6 p.m." When it slowed down at the intersection, she got a clear look at the passengers, all of whom wore large hats and appeared "serious looking."[8]

Her neighbor's conflicting account described a procession of cars passing by her home toward Moore's Ford Bridge shortly before acquaintances arrived to exchange a billy goat for a nanny goat between 5:00 and 6:00 p.m. The first two cars, traveling close together, appeared along the road leading from Good Hope. A third shiny vehicle approaching from a road leading toward Monroe got in behind the other cars. Simultaneously she saw a fourth join the line as it edged closer from the High Shoals road. Accustomed to studying occupants of vehicles driving by her house, she told the FBI that all four cars were filled with white men with fixed looks, as if on "a serious mission."[9]

A black woman living close to George's home later related that she was sitting on her front porch when she made out Harrison's car coming from the direction of Aycock's store toward Moore's Ford Bridge. As it passed by her home she had no difficulty in recognizing the occupants, all of whom she knew well.[10]

Meanwhile, sometime after 5 p.m. a black man was pushing his bicycle up an incline at Snow's Mill, about two and a half miles south of Moore's Ford Bridge, when an old light blue car, filled with five or six white men he did not know, passed him very slowly as it climbed the steep hill sometime. Since he was close up, the bicyclist got a good look at the young driver, who wore a felt hat and a white shirt open at the collar. All the other men were dressed in work clothes and appeared to be farmers. The bicyclist also noted the dented, rusty left rear fender which looked as if someone had tried to straighten it. Fifteen or twenty minutes later, as the bicyclist neared another intersection, he heard gunfire coming from about two miles ahead. He thought hunters might be shooting doves. After he had ridden the remaining mile to his home, he glanced at his watch and noted that it was 5:45 p.m.[11]

Earlier, a white farmhand, Ridden Farmer, was lying on a cot on his porch, fifteen yards from the road and only a quarter of a mile from the scene of the crime. At about 4 p.m., he sat up to take note of two cars passing by in the direction of the wooden bridge. The timing was at odds with that indicated by the other eyewitnesses, but Ridden said seven or eight young white men he did not see clearly because they were looking "yonderway" were crammed into the front car, a small black sedan with a flat top and cut "straight off on the back." The second dark-colored sedan followed close behind.[12] Ridden's wife, Reba, and son, Emerson, told the FBI that the first two cars were followed by Harrison driving black passengers, with a fourth dove-colored car, and, as far as they could recollect, perhaps a fifth, bringing up the rear.[13]

Minutes later, Reba heard "a bunch of shooting."[14] Ridden thought the shots were shotgun blasts, since the time between the shots was the same as the time it would take to reload a single-barreled shotgun. He guessed that someone might be shooting birds or other game. About a quarter of an hour later he walked to a neighbor's house, away from the bridge to the fork in the road, where he turned left into Good Hope Road, in the direction of a village called Good Hope, between Hestertown and the crime scene. Physically feeble and paralyzed in his right leg, yet able to work on the farm, Ridden covered the ground in fifteen minutes with the aid of a crutch.[15] The two men were sitting on the neighbor's porch when gunfire broke the silence. It sounded to Ridden "like a canebrake on fire."[16]

"What do you reckon they mean by shooting like that," the neighbor asked.

"I imagine it was a bunch of foolish boys having a good time," Ridden replied.[17]

Harrison related to the FBI that as he approached the fork in front of George's home, he glanced in his rearview mirror and noticed a car 150–200 yards behind, which seemed to be following at a slow speed because it was not kicking up dust. When he was only nine steps from the one-way bridge separating Walton and Oconee counties, he said he pulled up slightly to the right to give way to a shiny black 1940 model Ford approaching from the other end. But when it was only about a third of the way across, the Ford stopped, its doors flung open on both sides, and four or five men got out, all but one armed with shotguns and rifles. Simultaneously, men "popped up" on both sides of Harrison's vehicle.[18]

Harrison told the FBI that he thought he had been stopped specifically by agents from the Alcohol Tax Unit, even though later that night he told two of his farming friends that he suspected they were robbers.[19] The next day he offered yet another version of the story, telling the Associated Press and lawmen at the scene of the crime that he thought to himself, "Federal men."[20]

According to the account Harrison gave to the the FBI, one man put a shotgun to the back of his neck and ordered, "Put 'em up!" He immediately complied. Three or four others came up and barked identical orders to the four passengers, who also raised their hands. Harrison's account emphasized peculiarities indicating the hijackers were not from the area. He said a young man in his twenties, carrying a double-barreled shotgun and dressed in summer military fatigues without patches or insignia, and wearing an "overseas type cap," walked toward them from the car on the bridge, took up a position about twenty-seven feet away from the ambushed car, and leveled his weapon toward Harrison.[21]

The apparent leader of the mob got out of the Ford and walked unarmed toward the five people signaling surrender. A large man, six feet two inches tall and weighing over 200 pounds, he looked to be about sixty-five years old and was well built with long black hair that turned up under his wide-brimmed black felt hat. Harrison thought the man seemed to have a beach tan rather than a farmer's complexion. Dignified and distinguished-looking, with a cultured accent that was "not resembling that of a local farmer type, but clearly Southern," he wore a double-breasted suit and walked like a young man.[22]

As the leader approached the driver's door, the younger man with the shotgun pointed to Roger in the back seat.

"This is the son-of-a-bitch we want!"

Another vigilante eyeing George commanded, "We'll take you along, too, Charlie."

"This ain't Charlie. This is George," Harrison corrected.

"Shut your God damn mouth or I'll blow your God damn brains out![23] This ain't your party!" the leader snapped.

Other conspirators dragged Roger and George out of the Pontiac, binding their hands with rope before tugging them through the underbrush to the riverside. Harrison said he thought he heard Roger exclaim, "My time done come." The farmer told the FBI that the two wives were screaming and cursing hysterically. One of them, apparently Dorothy, cried out, "Don't take him out![24] You goddamn sons-of-bitches can't do this to my husband!" Then, Harrison said, she named one of the abductors, yelling, "_____ you can't do this!" She said a name Harrison repeatedly claimed he could not remember.[25] Immediately, the leader of the gang ordered, "You, and you, and you, get those bitches!" The subordinates yanked the women out of the Pontiac, across the road, and down to their tethered husbands.

"Get out of your car!" a man on the bridge ordered Harrison, who noticed that the Ford facing him had disappeared while the black Chevrolet that had been behind him was moving across to the Oconee side. Then he said he heard someone counting three times, "One, two, three," a ritual that some believe to have preceded executions carried out by members of the Ku Klux Klan.[26] Ragged volleys of fire followed each count. This account differed from what Harrison told the Associated Press. In that account, he said, "I'd turn my head sideways and I could see the men line 'em up. I could see the negroes four abreast. I could see the back of the men's heads. I heard the leader of the group say, 'One, two, three,' and then boom! He did that three times. There were three volleys."[27]

Around the time these events were taking place, a man fishing on the Apalachee River half a mile away thought he heard cars crossing the wooden bridge, followed by the sound of shots being fired. Investigators would soon confirm that the noise of even a single car crossing the bridge at a slow rate could be heard easily at this distance.[28]

According to Harrison, the mob's leader came back and told the armed guard, "You know what to do."

"Let's destroy the evidence," the guard replied.

"Do you recognize anyone here?" the leader asked Harrison.

"No, sir, no sir. I do not."

Meanwhile the guard continued to train his shotgun on Harrison, holding it under his right shoulder in the manner of military police.

"Don't start anything funny," the guard admonished as he let Harrison lower his hands.

The leader intervened. "Get in her and turn her around," he ordered, gesturing to the Pontiac. "You can go when you get ready."

Harrison accelerated, glancing in the rearview mirror to see the guard running briskly across the bridge to a waiting car. He estimated that the entire episode had lasted six minutes.[29]

He had gone no more than a quarter of a mile when he braked in front of Farmer's house.

"Where's Ridden?" he asked Reba.

She thought he looked "frightened or mad." Transfixed, her pre-teen son, Emerson, sensed the visitor was either "very scared or very crazy."[30] When she told him Ridden was not home, Harrison drove off without saying a word.[31]

Close by, Harrison nodded to a black woman on the porch of her home a quarter mile from the fork near George Dorsey's house. She estimated twenty minutes had elapsed since she had caught sight of him driving toward the bridge with four black passengers. Now she noticed he was alone. When Harrison had gone about half a mile further, her gaze shifted to another vehicle approaching from the bridge. It turned so sharply at the intersection that it made off "in a cloud of dust."[32]

Further along the road toward Aycock's store and Highway 78, a woman saw Harrison pass by her house "driving rather pert."[33]

Meanwhile, the prying eyes of roadside busybodies were following loaded cars scattering at reckless speeds along the dusty roads. A female eyewitness, reclining on her front porch in the first house along the road to Good Hope, saw two passing cars traveling so fast as they took the fork that she stood up, expecting one would overturn.[34]

Further along the route, a black man dusting cotton to rid it of boll weevils had just driven his tractor to the end of a road and begun to turn it around when he saw a car coming toward him. He backed up quickly, and as the car brushed by he counted seven white males. One of the men stood on the outside of the front seat with his right arm clinging to the top of the vehicle. Inside, there was a passenger dressed conspicuously in a military uniform and cap, while another wore a dress shirt and a dove-colored felt hat.[35]

About an hour before sundown, another observer, the black "jack-leg" auto mechanic skilled in identifying makes and models of vehicles, instantly recognized a 1938 black Chevrolet moving "at a high rate of speed" on the road from Good Hope toward Hestertown. He had time to count seven or eight white men packed inside.[36]

The woman who had stared hard at two passing cars loaded with white men as she stood in her neighbor's front yard on Good Hope Road, some fifteen to twenty minutes earlier, looked hard as the same vehicles returned, veering left at the intersection and continuing directly in front of her home on High Shoals Road, northeast of Good Hope.[37]

Another black witness was more specific about the three cars filled with white men that he saw in the same general area, traveling close to one another between 5:45 and 6:00 p.m. He told the FBI that the driver and a passenger in a black Ford were both dressed in soldier's uniforms. The second car was dove colored, as if bleached by the sun, and the third a 1939 black Chevrolet.[38]

Harrison braked outside Aycock's store and service station on the Athens Highway, a place he visited regularly. Mrs. Carl Aycock, whom the FBI thought "above average intelligence,"[39] was used to reporting emergencies, but nothing more serious than traffic accidents. Now it was multiple murder. When Harrison burst in, blurting, "Mrs Aycock, call sheriff for me quick! They took all my negroes from me and I suppose they shot them!" she looked at her watch. It was 5:40 p.m. Bypassing the sheriff because he was difficult to find in an emergency, she placed the call to his deputy's residence in the county jail and handed the receiver to Harrison.[40]

Within hours the airwaves were crackling with the story on *The Ten o'Clock Wire* in the Pacific Northwest. "Two young men and their young wives are on coroner's slabs down in Georgia tonight. Georgia is one of the forty-eight states of the Union, a Union which in 1776 electrified the whole world with the assertion that all men are created equal, that a man is innocent until proved guilty, that each shall have a fair trial by his peers.

"These four people had names: Mr. and Mrs. Roger Malcolm and Mr. and Mrs. George Dorsey. George was a veteran, spent five years overseas. Roger was in trouble. He had a fight with a man a few days ago and stabbed the man with a knife, putting him in the hospital. Bail was arranged this morning and a kind farmer, Mr. Harrison, had fixed it all up and was taking Roger to his farm. Roger's wife and George Dorsey and his wife came along in the car.

"As the long shadows of the jack pines were slanting across the red earth, they came to a bridge. Men with shotguns and rifles and pistols surrounded Mr. Harrison's car and dragged George and Roger into the road. Dorothy called out the name of one of the men and thereby added to the tragedy. The men returned, forced Mae and Dorothy from the car and dragged them down the dusty road with their husbands. They were lined up and then three volleys from the self-appointed firing squad. The men climbed in their cars and dispersed."[41]

It was taut and rapid, the kind of copy that radio thrived on. But they had rushed to broadcast and got it wrong. The listening public had been monstrously misled. Only the criminals with smoking guns knew that much of the broadcast was false. It would require tireless work before listeners could change their minds.

The FBI Steps In

O n the same day the nation learned of the slaughter in Georgia, allied prosecutors at war crimes trials in Germany demanded death sentences for those guilty of "the doctrine of hatred" that permitted murder "conducted like some mass production industry."[1] Disclosure of Nazi atrocities, which had drenched Europe in blood on a scale unsurpassed in history, had filled Americans with disbelief and revulsion. The outrage and horror now turned inward as Americans asked how such barbarity could have taken place in the land of the victors.

Public opinion erupted as soon as the Associated Press alerted the nation to the lynchings. Black protestors picketed the White House, holding placards reading "Down with Lynching In Georgia" and "President Truman, We Need Your Help." Thirty thousand letters and telegrams of condemnation arrived at the White House, the Justice Department, and the FBI.[2]

Civilians were aghast that one of the slain, George Dorsey, was a veteran of World War II. Ex-servicemen clamored for justice to avenge the loss of one of their own, a former private first class in an engineers battalion with the US Army, who had served in North Africa and Australia[3] and been awarded the American Defense Service Medal, the Asiatic-Pacific Service Medal, and the Good Conduct Medal.[4] His mother said she had received his discharge button the same week he was slain.[5] "How can we prosecute German and Japanese war criminals for crimes against humanity while condoning the same terror applied to our citizens in Georgia?" one American asked of the Justice Department.[6] In distant San Francisco, men and women of both races marched down Market Street in silent outrage. One banner described their common feeling: "Guadalcanal '42 North Africa '43 Germany '44 Okinawa '45 Monroe, Ga. USA '46. We Veterans Are Still Being Killed By Racists." Four coffins represented the victims, and muffled drums were the only sounds in the quiet procession.

Another man who had worn the uniform of the US military, wrote the Director of the FBI, J. Edgar Hoover, "As a member of the negro race and a veteran of World War II, I, as well as my race, are beginning to doubt very seriously whether our sacrifices were worth that which we were fighting for."[7] His outrage was taken up far and wide. Crew aboard the SS *Fred E. Joyce*, anchored off Genoa, Italy, wrote to the attorney general, "The mark of the beast of Hitler has reared its ugly head in the form of lynching, on the State of Georgia, and on the entire United States. We move to the front with all the peoples that demand justice be brought to all people."[8] Dismayed Jewish war veterans, insisting there was "no place in America for those who would spread the venom of intolerance," reminded the attorney general, "you have it in your power to show that justice takes no holiday when negroes are involved."[9]

Much of the fury was channeled toward Hoover in the expectation that his legendary agency would round up the nameless gunmen. The FBI stood high in public opinion after a series of spectacular seizures and killings of the most wanted gangsters, bank robbers, and kidnappers. Writing anonymously, one correspondent declared, "You gotta prove to the whole round world right now that the FBI means business. If it can get [gangster Al] Capone and [bank robber John] Dillinger, then it can get those mobsters down in Georgia if it wants to."[10] From the far northwest, ex-servicemen wired Hoover: "Veterans of World War Two refuse to permit such occurrences here. Further bloodshed inevitable if justice cannot prevail."[11] Pennsylvania veterans protested, "We don't want this crime whitewashed as other lynchings have been in the South."[12]

The NAACP issued a call for action to the president and attorney general. The preeminent organization devoted to the fight for the rights of African Americans urged President Truman to take to the radio and authorize an immediate investigation of the lynching. "Unless this is done we are certain that very dark days are ahead," it warned.[13] Eight weeks later the president met with six individuals, drawn from the NAACP, churches, and trade unionists. After he heard their anguish over recent lynchings and crude diatribes of the offenders, Truman said, "My God! I had no idea it was as terrible as that! We've got to do something!"[14]

This meeting led to the creation of the President's Commission on Civil Rights less than three months later, and eventually to many innovations, including desegregation of the federal work force and the armed services, as well as the creation of a civil rights division in the Justice Department.

In a separate cable to Attorney General Tom Clark, the NAACP reported that just prior to the crimes, local police ordered all blacks off the streets, "which clearly indicates at very least that Monroe county officials had knowledge lynchings were to take place."[15]

The tenor of the correspondence was sharp and scalding. The issue was as clear as it had been to those galvanized against the uncivilized regimes ground down in World War II. Protests from unionized labor deluged authorities. Detroit auto workers demanded that "Nazi methods in America must be stopped before Americans lose faith in their government."[16] Aggrieved New York fur and shipping clerks lamented, "Negro veterans, in the uniforms they wore so proudly, are killed because they happen to be black, and their killers run free."[17] Postal authorities heaved sack-loads of letters and telegrams from home and abroad. Some expressed their outrage through derision, like the insurance agent in the State of Washington, who wrote, "This incident undoubtedly makes fine reading material to the Russians and the Nazis still left in Germany."[18] A Californian suggested sarcastically, "The lynching that occurred in Georgia was the American way of showing their appreciation to their negro veterans."[19]

Even the very young spoke out, bewildered by the wrong. Writing from Kansas City, Missouri, a twelve-year-old girl pleaded with President Harry Truman, "I think that someone up there in Washington, D.C. ought to put a stop to these murders & slavery because it is getting terrible to walk down the street any moore and someone ought to do something."[20] Another youngster identifying herself as "A negro girl from San Diego, California," and addressing her carefully scripted letter to E. Hoover, White House, Washington, DC, noted almost apologetically, "I am not trying to complain but the negroes fought and died for America as well as any other tribe."[21]

Letters spewing fury inundated postal authorities in Washington, DC, many directed to the attorney general, though Hoover also continued to get long forms with scores of incensed co-signatories. Those barely able to express themselves grammatically also took pen to paper to vent their private anguish. An African American, signing off as "a citizen," wrote the FBI chief, "I am not afraid of dieng got to die some day any way But the only thing I can say if any of the Hitler minded people get me I am only sorry I dont have 14 million lives an I would not mind dieing that many times if it would good is making America A better place all the people to live in."[22] Another letter from a black person in Cincinnati urged, "It's time for America to find out how we got more Hitlers than Americans."[23]

A self-identified white man from Yellowstone Park, Wyoming, clearly hurt and grieving, entreated Hoover, "I am from the deep South myself but I am 100 [sic] American and believe in justice and fair play. I hope sincerely that you and your men will do what you can to bring to justice the dastardly cowards who murdered the four Georgia negroes. It is only a step to killing whites in the same way."[24] Identification by race seemed important to many protestors, with one white man in Dearborn, Michigan, confessing, "I myself am a Southerner but things like that only tend to make our country like the countries we have just defeated in the terrible, bloody war. No, I don't want a 'negro' in every block, nor do I think they want in [sic] every block, but they certainly are deserving of the rights of Americans."[25] When the news reached New Jersey, a resident implored the FBI: "Bring these dogs to justice."[26]

The level of outrage aroused cries of protest from religious communities as well. They sounded an amen to condemnation. The Ohio Baptists, for instance, decried "one of the most hideous crimes committed against our group."[27] A cluster of California churches prophesied that "Christian civilization will be a thing of the past unless such outrages are brought to an end."[28]

Conspicuous for its counterattack, a letter from a Georgian signing off "Your friend in Jesus Christ" bristled at the rage against his state. "Please help us here in Georgia," the Southerner pleaded with Hoover. "The lynching of the negroes looks like a rehearsed job, and it looks like a job to further blacken Georgia in the eyes of the nation. We and the negroes have got along very fine till outsiders have come in and stired [sic] up the race issue."[29]

Angry reaction also flared up in the august US Senate. When a colleague from California asked to have an Associated Press account of the mass lynchings inserted into the Congressional Record, Georgia Senator Richard Russell rose with embattled vigor. While deploring the crime, especially since it took place in his state, he demanded similar publicity in the record of Senate proceedings for "other crimes of equal brutality in other states." With undisguised indignation and disgust, he charged that murders of all kinds were committed in other states, sometimes by more than two or three people. Russell, who remained a lifelong segregationist even as others considered him for the presidency, would have none of what he saw as the politicization of the lynchings. "There is no element of politics in these crimes unless they involve a difference in races and happen in the South," he declared, expressing sentiments backed up by other senators from the so-called Bible Belt. "There seems to be an effort to make political capital out of crimes in which negroes are the victims if they are committed in the South, and we hear a clamor for federal intervention, which is never raised in the case of similar crimes committed in other sections of the country."[30]

Washington was in no need of second thoughts. President Truman expressed "horror" at the crime.[31] He would soon tell Attorney General Tom Clark, in strict confidence, that he was "very much alarmed at the increased racial feeling all over the country" that would require "some sort of policy to prevent such happenings."[32] Clark, who would later be appointed to the Supreme Court, launched an immediate investigation by the FBI. In Georgia, lame-duck Governor Ellis Arnall said the mob had perpetrated an "outrage" and had to be discovered and punished.[33] He told the NAACP that he would use "every resource at his command" to see that members of the mob were brought to justice.[34]

But these intentions were instantly hobbled by the clumsy ineptness of the federal agent who would take charge of the investigation.

John Trost, thirty-five, the FBI's Special Agent in Charge (SAC) of the Atlanta, Georgia, field division, had racked up a roller-coaster performance since being accepted into the agency eight years earlier, quickly winning praise from a supervisor as "one of the best in the class."[35] The plaudits had been tempered with an assessment that he was "slightly slow and need[ed] to acquire additional effervescence, enthusiasm or ambition."[36] Just three years later, his career was almost scuttled when he recklessly disclosed the name of a superior who had taken a colleague to task, then openly attacked FBI overtime policies. In demoting Trost from number two man in the Washington field office,[37] Hoover had scrawled, "Either this man is just plain stupid or has a definitely bad attitude. Get him out of Washington and do not assign him to executive duties."[38] But Trost had rebounded, with his boss in Buffalo admiring "the calm, intelligent and deliberate way in which he conducts himself."[39] Transferred during World War II to Jamaica, he was reprimanded by Hoover after colonial British censors intercepted a letter from a female acquaintance quoting an offhand reference by Trost to one of his informants. "You are directed to use the utmost discretion in your contacts in Jamaica and to refrain from discussing the Bureau's work with individuals who have no legitimate interest therein," Hoover rebuked.[40] The "indiscretion"[41] led to his repatriation, but Trost redeemed himself in Providence, Rhode Island, where the SAC rated him "far above average."[42]

He had been SAC in Atlanta for only six months when a highly sensitive memo from the Department of Justice was read to him over the phone approximately twenty-four hours after the lynchings.[43] A Washington FBI supervisor, J. C. Strickland, read it slowly, giving Trost time to take it down verbatim, unaware that the field office chief was merely scribbling rough notes.[44] The memo, sent at the command of the attorney general, called for an immediate investigation of the atrocities. In unequivocal language it called for "every effort" to be made to find out how the mob was formed, who tipped them off, how they became aware that the victims were being transported to Loy Harrison's farm, and whether any state officials were involved, a factor that might establish a conspiracy. It included instructions for close cooperation with the Georgia Bureau of Investigation (GBI) and ordered the Atlanta office to contact US Attorney John Cowart at Macon, Georgia, for possible additional "lines of investigation."[45]

Trost did not realize that the attorney general wanted a complete and thorough investigation. His skimpy notes make it clear that he thought he had to focus on possible federal jurisdiction for breach of civil rights. He did not even remember being told to cooperate with the Georgia Bureau of Investigation, nor that he had to get the names of those in the mob.[46] His negligence led to a full day passing by without a single FBI agent at the crime scene to collect evidence and protect the site.

The following afternoon, Assistant FBI Director Edward Tamm called Trost at his Atlanta home in response to mounting public pressure for decisive federal action. FBI field offices had warned of delegations preparing to call on the president and the attorney general and of groups planning protest rallies in the nation's capital and elsewhere.[47] Tamm wanted to make sure Trost understood the gravity of his task.

The field office chief, however, could not make out who was calling, even though the connection seemed clear and the high-ranking official carefully spelled out his name. Still, Trost did not realize he was speaking with one of the members of Hoover's inner circle. Rather than being professional and courteous, Trost became offhand, testy, and bellicose. When Tamm said the Bureau was concerned about the potential criticism if it did not conduct a complete and thorough probe, Trost interrupted to say his agents were running out leads that the assistant US attorneys believed were essential to establish that a violation of civil rights had occurred. Tamm corrected him, saying the Bureau wanted a thorough investigation to get the identities of the gunmen. Combatively, as if dressing down an underling, Trost repeated his mistaken goal. Incredulous, Tamm said the US attorneys did not have responsibility for the investigation, nor would they have to face criticism by the media or civil liberties groups and others. The FBI would be left "holding the bag" if the case was not brought to a "proper solution."

Still unaware of the rank and identity of his caller, the agent charged with hunting down the most wanted men in America raised his voice, insisting he was conducting only such investigation as Cowart desired.

"Who is Cowart?" Tamm asked.

"He just happens to be the United States Attorney," Trost shouted. Aghast, Tamm tried three more times to get Trost to conduct a complete investigation. "Each time," Tamm later explained to Hoover, "Trost roared into the telephone that he 'didn't see how I could countermand Strick's [sic] instructions.' Doing my utmost to keep from losing my temper, I asked Trost if he were telling the Bureau what investigation he was going to conduct in this case and he roared, 'Yes, I am!'"

When he asked for an estimate of the time it might take to complete the probe, Trost replied dismissively, "Absolutely no idea." He repeated the answer when Tamm queried whether it might take three or six weeks.

"It was impossible for me to say more than six or seven words at any time," Tamm recalled, "since Mr. Trost would interrupt to state that the Departmental memorandum had been read to him, that the assistant US attorneys were directing the investigation, etc."

Exasperated, Tamm told the intemperate subordinate that it was "futile" to continue, but that the Bureau would be in touch. Then the assistant director of the FBI hung up.[48]

Soon after, Trost took another call from Washington. It was Strickland, who had originally given him the instructions for the investigation. This time he insisted on immediate compliance for a complete and thorough investigation, chiding Trost for failing to understand the consequences for the FBI if this were not done. He ordered Trost to leave without delay for Monroe, forty-five miles east, and to send daily updates by teletype. Chastened and now obedient, Trost said he would leave within ten minutes.[49]

Tamm's four-page complaint landed on Hoover's desk. "I don't think that a special agent in charge should be as rude, arrogant and nasty to anyone who contacts him from the Bureau. I think he is a misfit not only as a special agent in charge, but as a Bureau employee," Tamm raged. "He is both stupid and has a bad character." Recommending a letter of reprimand, he added, "I think it is bad to let a man get by with 'telling the Bureau off.'"

"I certainly agree," Hoover appended. "I want an early inspection of Atlanta and I want Trost to thoroughly understand his responsibilities and how to play on a team."[50]

Then the feared head of the FBI dictated a letter to the unruly SAC. "I must express to you my extreme displeasure at the unsatisfactory manner in which you discussed with a Bureau official the handling of the investigation. It is presumptuous of you to challenge the Bureau's authority to issue instructions to you. The Bureau cannot tolerate a repetition of this kind of conduct."[51]

He waited to impose the penalty until reports came in from inspectors detailed to interrogate Trost. One of them branded Trost's judgment "atrocious,"[52] and both recommended that he be dismissed from his position as agent in charge.[53] Hoover, ever protective of the cohesion and reputation of the agency he had nurtured and led for two decades, did not hesitate. "In view of the extremely poor judgment displayed by you in connection with your official responsibilities, this is to advise you that orders have been issued transferring you to Cincinnati and reducing you in grade and salary." As a measure of his chagrin, the director growled, "It is not necessary for you to await the arrival of your successor prior to your departure for Cincinnati."[54] Two days later Trost wired his resignation, surrendered his revolver and FBI handbook, and was gone.[55]

Trost's unexplained departure provided an opportunity for rabble-rousers and others wondering why the killers had not been captured. A Bureau official had warned Hoover that transferring Trost out of Atlanta "would probably give rise to conjecture and questionable publicity, due to the widespread interest in the case."[56]

As if on cue, the Associated Negro Press filed a wildly speculative and mischievously provocative story to its subscribers nationwide. "Although the white press refused to delve into the reasons for Mr. Trost's sudden decision to enter private business, it was believed that there was something deep and mysterious in the act. Did Trost know the lynchers, and pressure kept his office from revealing that information? Did the pressure for his resignation come from the Georgia Bureau of Investigation? Did the pressure come from forces of Gov.-nominee Eugene Talmadge, who will have the power to appoint a new GBI chieftain and subordinates after January 5? Did he and his FBI move too fast for GBI and local investigation officials, stepping on the toes of somebody 'too big to be touched' in middle Georgia?"[57]

The story served only to exacerbate tension between the FBI and a restive public impatient for arrests. Only those investigating on site could appreciate the monumental task that lay ahead.

Hostility and Fear

Even before Trost's banishment, FBI Director Hoover had brought in a substitute agent from New Orleans to take charge.[1] Charles Weeks, thirty-eight, had been so intent on a career with the prestigious Bureau that he had signed up sixteen years earlier as a lowly messenger with the FBI while still in law school at George Washington University in the nation's capital.

The South Dakotan was soon recognized as "a quick and accurate thinker, conscientious but just a trifle methodical."[2] He had conducted himself well in armed surveillance of bank robber John Dillinger's family, getting a nod for "a satisfactory attitude when facing danger," though his superior also passed on that "he is a man of rather slight, personal appearance and not such as would necessarily impress others."[3] Fond of tennis, swimming, and reading history and biographies,[4] the slightly crossed-eyed and knock-kneed Weeks[5] had only once fallen afoul of the ever-watchful Hoover, after an instructor caught him gazing out the window during a fingerprint course for rookie agents. "I don't like this indifference," the director penned to the lecturer's report, though he took no further action.[6]

Just two years before the slaughter at Moore's Ford, Hoover had met with Weeks and reevaluated him with singular praise: "I have always considered him to be lacking in animation and enthusiasm and to have what I have characterized at times as a 'dead fish' expression," Hoover wrote his deputy, Clyde Tolson. "I was extremely surprised yesterday to note a marked change in his manner and personality. He has acquired enthusiasm and I believe can now be considered for additional respon-sibilities in the Bureau."[7] Within ten days, Weeks had been elevated to acting SAC in Cincinnati.[8] He was SAC New Orleans when assigned amid the glare of national attention to take charge of the hunt for the murderers. Not long after he arrived in Georgia, he had to let those he had left behind probe the slaying of a black man dragged out of a jail in Minden, Louisiana.[9]

Weeks tried manfully to control disarray in the makeshift head-quarters, set up in room 310 of the Monroe Hotel at a daily rental rate of two dollars. It was cramped[10] and uncomfortable as the squad quickly swelled to twenty special agents with supporting stenographers, the equivalent of a middle-sized FBI field office.[11] It was a clear indication of how much priority the Justice Department had given to a quick resolution of the case.[12]

Charles Weeks worked with almost sleepless zeal, shaping the probe, directing his team, interviewing suspects, tracking leads, assessing informants, and filing daily updates to Washington. "Weeks has an excellent grasp of the situation," a top aide to Hoover enthused on a special mission to Monroe. "He impressed me as having his feet on the ground and being thoroughly capable of handling this investigation which is, of course, very delicate."[13]

But the Monroe headquarters immediately had problems communicating securely with Washington and Atlanta. With no direct line to Atlanta, they had to install a private dial telephone, though toll calls had to be placed through the local operator until 6:00 p.m. After 6:00 p.m., they were directed through another switchboard operator ten miles away.[14] To avoid the possibility of operators eavesdropping, the FBI censored teletypes to Atlanta, erasing the names of all informants and other highly confidential data.[15]

Agents worked grueling hours by day and by night, logging extensive overtime.[16] Some interviews began in the afternoon and stretched through 4:00 a.m., with agents relentlessly pressing for breakthroughs.[17] They interrogated so many blacks and whites in the rural and urban areas that eventually the tally would reach 2,790.[18] The squad gathered frequently to debrief and pool information, mostly on weekdays at 8:00 p.m. and on Saturdays for afternoon sessions.[19]

While the FBI was settling in, the Georgia Bureau of Investigation noted disturbing racist remarks from a former Atlanta fireman visiting downtown Monroe only two days after the massacre. They thought

Charles Towler, fifty-three, then unemployed, might have been the leader of the lynch mob, after he said in the presence of a GBI operative and others, "It looks like mister negro has been put in his place, and that it should be a lesson to the rest of them." Unchecked, he "felt sure no one would ever find out anything regarding the persons who did commit the crime." Towler was instantly recognizable at six feet tall, weighing about 230 pounds, with a heavy build, rimless glasses, and a vivid half-inch scar over his upper lip. A quick background check showed he was always armed, formerly belonged to the Ku Klux Klan, and was not opposed to lynching blacks. He went into a "tirade against negroes" when questioned by FBI agents, who spoke to dozens of people, including Harrison, who said the leader of the mob was twenty pounds heavier. This piece of evidence finally allowed the suspect to go free.[20]

However, the Georgia Public Safety conceded blockage early on. "We just can't cope," said a dejected chief. "The best people in town won't talk." He disclosed that unnamed local authorities had been uncooperative. "We've been out on things like this before, but never anything like this." However, he thought the crime might have been planned since Roger Malcolm had first been confined to jail. In a stunning revelation, he also said Harrison had told him George Dorsey and his sister, Dorothy Malcolm, had come very close to escaping.[21]

The FBI scrambled to stay ahead of the nationwide fury demanding rapid results. A week after the lynching, forty-five women from the National Association of Colored Women, representing forty-three states, met with an aide to the attorney general to deplore mob violence. They demanded federal legislation to outlaw lynching, saying "the barbarities have reached such a tragically alarming state that women are now being lynched with impunity."[22] More than 200 NACW members marched on the White House, hoping to influence the highest elected official in the land.[23] Many more blacks, almost 2,000, assembled in Washington to protest the killings.[24]

The clamor intensified as the probe dragged on without arrests. Only those agents in the field knew how many obstacles had to be overcome to identify and seize the killers. They jumped on every opportunity to mollify critics. When a telegram arrived at FBI head-quarters from Fort Valley, Georgia, it stated tersely, *Investigate Fort Valley.* Hoover dashed off an order to the head of the Atlanta bureau directing an interview with the sender, adding, "He may have information of value."[25] The reply came back from Atlanta saying the telegram had been misdirected. It should have been sent to the Office of Price Administration, since it was a complaint about the high cost of lard and other food.[26]

Farmers and their hired hands clammed up or recounted in detail what had preoccupied them on the relevant dates. One man told of fishing for turtles far from Moore's Ford Bridge.[27] Another offered an alibi of repairing an automobile under an oak tree in the front yard.[28] A first cousin of the man who was stabbed said he knew nothing of the incident until the next day because he was busy putting brick sidings on the house of his mother-in-law.[29]

Whites in the Monroe area openly resented the FBI presence and raged against outsiders meddling in local affairs.[31] As if defensively circling wagons, they were tight-lipped and refused to cooperate. Blacks kept their distance from investigators, fearing they might suffer the same fate as those found lifeless by the banks of the Apalachee River if anyone discovered they had snitched.

Meanwhile Harrison stood above the fray, in complete command of himself, though the same could not be said of his wife. She had suffered in the past from mental problems but since the lynchings had become visibly nervous. Harrison consulted a doctor, who had treated his family and sharecroppers for twenty years, and was given a six-ounce bottle of medication for his spouse.[31]

The FBI had gotten off to a feeble start through the incompetence of John Trost, soon to be ousted as head of the unit. As a result, about thirty-nine hours had elapsed before a pair of agents made their first appearance at the densely foliaged crime scene.[32] It was immediately apparent from footprints, flattened brush, and tire tracks that "hundreds" of people had tramped over the unprotected site since the executions.[33] How much evidence had been pilfered for souvenirs or carried away by curiosity seekers was a matter of conjecture. Regardless, the agents crouched down, ignoring a falling snake,[34] looking for spent cartridge slugs, shotgun pellets and shell wadding, empty shell cases, and pieces of rope cut from the two dead men. The search for such small objects was made more difficult by a long pile of pine brush spread over the ground where the gunmen were believed to have stood.[35]

The land grudgingly gave up some of its secrets during painstaking sifting. Five slugs, whether from rifles or pistols, were dug up from what appeared to be a bloodstained section where the victims had fallen. Close by, agents spotted a 20-gauge shell and a piece of shotgun shell wadding. One of the shells found near where the bodies lay was later identified as having come from Deputy Sheriff Lewis Howard's .38-caliber revolver, but agents could not be sure if the weapon had been fired during a period when it was periodically loaned out. The sheriff was also known to have teamed up with the Georgia Bureau of Investigation for practice firings in the vicinity.[36]

Meanwhile, officials from the GBI dredged the bed of the river about twenty feet east of the bridge and scooped up three twelve-gauge reddish shotgun shell hulls and a 20-gauge shotgun shell case. From mid-stream they brought up four pistol shells, which might also have come from the practice firings by local law enforcement officers.[37]

So little was recovered from the surface that the FBI dug up patches of ground and brought in contractors' sieves to examine the contents. They test-fired identical caliber bullets into the earth from various angles to see how deep they might penetrate but, with rare exceptions, the ammunition ricocheted off. Only a few specimens were discovered from the digs and it was unclear whether they could be linked to the murders.[38] As agents scoured the area they glanced at four rough crosses, which anonymous memorialists had carved into tree trunks,[39] standing upright like motionless honor guards.

With laudable efficiency, the FBI contacted reporters and photographers from news agencies and newspapers, hoping they or their photographs might prove the presence of any physical evidence since removed from the site of the killings, but every time they came up empty-handed, even from a journalist who visited the day after the shooting.[40]

A parade of about fifty cars with delegates from the Negro National Baptist Convention in Atlanta held a memorial service for the slain quartet at the scene of the crime, where a preacher asked whether the lynching was white supremacy or white savagery. In the six weeks since the massacre, they had raised approximately $12,000 for those who wanted to leave Walton County because they feared for their lives. The *Walton Tribune* commented drily that "their conduct was above reproach."[41]

There was no letup in hostility toward the FBI, who were looked upon as dangerous interlopers. Some of the resentment was so crude and overt that squad members were ordered to work in pairs to guard against physical injury. Only when they interviewed in Monroe did they work alone. A trusted top aide to Hoover reported to Washington during a fleeting visit that "the white people in the area are illiterate, uncooperative, feel no crime has been committed and resent Federal interference."[42] Ten months earlier an FBI agent had been given a rapturous welcome by more than 100 veterans of World War II in Monroe's American Legion Hall, where he spoke of the Bureau's exploits in tracking down spies and foreign agents.[43] Now agents from the same Bureau were shunned as unwelcome outsiders and slandered for ruffling an isolated and fixed way of life. In a daily briefing to Washington, Weeks warned, "There is some element of danger to the agents working on this case in backwoods sections, encountering irresponsible and excitable people." Before setting out each morning, agents had to sign out automobiles so they could be rescued or aided "in the event anything should happen."[44]

Before his dismissal, Trost had alerted Washington, "majority of white people in sympathy with shooting of victims."[45] Weeks was quick to elaborate. "Our chief disadvantage in making interviews with suspects and other white people is that we must do it on their own grounds, frequently in the presence of a large family, as many of them refuse to budge off the porch, even to come to an automobile, and even those believed not to be involved are mistrustful and frequently sullen or hostile."[46]

In one instance a suspect was approached as he sat on the front porch with family members but refused to accompany an investigator to a car to be interviewed away from the group, claiming he had rheumatism and could not get out of his swing. Eventually he walked to the car but would not get in. Visibly ill at ease and high-strung, he was resentful at being interviewed and railed against interference by blacks in Alabama and New York, whom he accused of orchestrating the probe. Investigators, he charged, must have come from northern states, making them, in his opinion, automatically sympathetic to anything done by blacks.[47]

Though faced with a widespread conspiracy of silence and glaring antipathy, Weeks reported dispassionately to Hoover, "The community in the part of Walton County, where the people we must interview live, is of a type strange to all of us, but which is understandable. These people are highly sensitive and suspicious. They are unread and their views regarding negroes are very different. They feel they treat negroes fairly and their acts should not be subject to inquiry by outsiders. Most of them refuse to sign statements, to show their guns, or otherwise cooperate in the investigation."[48]

Few disguised their rigid adherence to white dominance or tempered their feelings with ambivalence. It was normal, correct, and established. An unidentified black man passed on what he'd heard his employer say on the farm at the outbreak of World War II: "Hitler cuts off the heads of people, and we lynch them over here."[49] A pair of farmers told Weeks shortly after his arrival that "lynching negroes was a good thing as it kept them in their place." Even though they did not approve of the killing of the three "innocent" victims, they thought blacks were getting a little "sassy."[50] A white justice of the peace flouted constitutional protections by openly bragging to the FBI that he hoped the murders would not be solved "because up until the lynching, the negroes in Walton County were getting out of line and the lynching had a deterrent effect upon belligerent and uppity negroes."[51] Another resident was equally candid. "If Roger Malcolm had been killed at the stabbing nothing would have been done or said about it."[52] But others appeared to disagree. "It sho wuz bad," mused Harrison's father-in-law.[53]

The Monroe Klavern of the Ku Klux Klan was dissolved about 1936 when their meeting hall burned,[54] but FBI trackers soon learned that the notorious KKK, apparently quiescent or moribund for years, had been making tentative inroads during the racially charged primary election campaign. A few individuals in the vicinity had solicited white supremacists to join the KKK or renew lapsed memberships.[55] Little was known of its influence or numerical strength in the area since fledgling bands of hooded civilians had begun spreading fear and terror in the late nineteenth century. It was a violation of the oath of a klansman to reveal the identity of any Klan member,[56] and its roster of members and rites of brotherhood were closely guarded by initiates sworn to secrecy.[57] An outsider would have to be familiar with Congressional hearings in Washington, DC, seventy-five years earlier to know that members recognized each other by closing four fingers of the right hand, then drawing the open forefinger across the forehead toward the right temple, while the other acknowledged the code by answering in the same manner with the left hand.[58] While membership did not enhance feelings of racial superiority, it bound these individuals closer together, solidifying their common commitment to violent acts in unison, principally against defenseless blacks. The Ku Klux Klan was lauded as "a good organization" by a local who had farmed near Moore's Ford a decade earlier, even though he said he quit the organization because it "ceased to function."[59] Others, including Harrison, professed to have let their memberships expire, but it had not diminished their domineering attitude toward blacks.

Many whites dismissed the agents' overtures with snide rebukes and snarling insults. One man publicly huffed time and again that "the FBI had no business being here investigating the case and wished they would leave."[60] Another brushed aside all questions, saying, "I ain't looking to hear nothing." For good measure he told investigators that those who committed the crime "will not be talking."[61] There were telltale signs of guilt or evasion. One man was so upset during his appearance before agents that his mouth became dry while being questioned.[62] An older white resident dismissed interrogators, insisting, "if anyone would be fool enough to talk about the lynching they would also be killed."[63] A white man told the agents, "I thank God I don't know a thing in the world about it. I'd stand on a stack of Bibles as high as that post and swear on that, and I got witnesses to prove where I was."[64]

A black servant volunteered that she had overheard her white male employer curse his wife for the first time in memory after the spouse said she would talk to the agents. "Shut your damn mouth!" she quoted the husband rebuking his wife. "You don't have to tell them a damn thing. You have been running your mouth off ever since this mess got started. Just shut your mouth!"[65]

Though many interviews drew blanks, they revealed telling insights into the community's makeup. After questioning one couple and the woman's mother, an agent wrote, "they appeared very stupid and illiterate. They all stated they do not have a radio, do not read the newspapers, and have not heard the case discussed."[66] One white man who agreed to be an informant nevertheless said he would refuse to testify if called upon, for fear his house or barn would be burned down in retaliation.[67] A white truck driver for the state highway department denied knowing anything about the murders but advised that if he accidentally overheard anything relevant he would have second thoughts about disclosing it.[68] Loy Harrison's estranged older brother apologized for his mean behavior yet, doggedly refused to sign anything, not even "for the Salvation Army."[69]

One of the Hester clan parried questions with the taut rejoinder, "I haven't heard a thing about nothing."[70] Another Hester relative willingly joined the agents in the vehicle but although friendly, was obdurate, refusing to discuss the lynchings, even if he subsequently learned something, explaining that "it was not a fair question."[71] When the agents arrived at the home of yet another Hester father and son, the wife of the older man turned angrily on the visitors and ordered them to leave, reprimanding, "they have already been questioned and didn't know nothing else."[72] Unsurprisingly, one man turned on his inquisitors and grumbled that he did not meddle in other people's business "and that is what the FBI should do."[73] A farmer described as "belligerent" was not only offended at being interviewed on suspicion of being part of the lynch mob, but said he resented his black farmhands being interrogated because it interfered with the harvesting of his crop.[74] Yet another defiantly told the inquisitors that even if he knew anything he "damn well wouldn't tell it to the law."[75] An equally aggressive farmer declared he was too busy to talk, chiding, "You've got to work if you make a living."[76]

Upset at having been called out of a store to sit with agents in their car, another man decried public visibility of the interviews. He thought they should be conducted more secretively because blacks believed any white man contacted by the FBI must have participated in the killings. With pointed candor, he confessed, "I would not tell if I knew anything about the lynching. I would be afraid for my personal safety."[77] Most whites rudely objected to signing their statements. One man ranted, "I just don't care nothing about signing, but it is the damn truth."[78]

In their attempts to pry subjects away from eavesdropping relatives, the FBI sometimes succeeded in luring them away from their homes. One congenial distant relative of the Hesters was quizzed in the yard of a vacant house near his home.[79] But many were driven to the distant enclosure of the federal courthouse in Athens, far from observation by neighbors and would-be tattlers, where it was believed they would "talk more freely."[80]

A couple who spoke more openly than any of the other Hester relatives were somewhat emotional, even though they denied any knowledge of the murders. Ever alert to personal characteristics, the agents noted that whenever the man smiled the back of his top lip was visible. His wife thought the killers would be identified and arrested and said she was "sorry for them." Her husband agreed, but added, "nobody made 'em do it."[81]

Some disgruntled whites, who had already been interviewed, smeared the investigators, claiming the FBI had threatened them. They even spread false rumors that their federal adversaries were encouraging blacks to "burn out white people in retaliation for the lynching,"[82] and that interrogators had barged into homes of partially-clothed women and searched homes in a roughshod manner while threatening occupants.[83]

The rumors subsided only after agents tracked down the sources, who quickly withdrew the allegations, claiming they had been misunderstood and that there was no truth to any of them. But there was no weakening in the solidarity of the farmers, even though their interrogators had followed orders and been purposefully tactful and discreet.[84]

The FBI were so thorough in interviewing as many as possible that they even talked to a white man who had served in the garbage detail in the African and Italian theaters. Stammering and apparently mentally impaired, he said he did not bring back a souvenir pistol from abroad but he did own a revolver, last used almost a year before.[85] When a veteran was interviewed after rising to the rank of sergeant at a general hospital in Texas during the war, he said he didn't know anyone who took part in the murders, and even if he could identify them, he would not mention it because, said an agent, "he is afraid they might do the same thing to him that they did to the negroes."[86] Another former soldier with allied forces in Europe said about twenty men from Walton County were attached to his division and he had brought back a Luger 9-mm pistol, without ammunition, but it was in his sister's possession.[87]

One farmer stood out among all the locals by suggesting to the FBI that blacks might have been involved in the lynch mob because of George Dorsey's reputed closeness to a family of white girls.[88] In contradiction, a war veteran, wounded and hospitalized within three hours of combat in Europe, said he had not heard anything about Dorsey and the females, or that blacks "were more smart" than they had been before the war.[89]

The combative stand of the community won influential backing from the *Walton Tribune* weekly newspaper, which alleged, without proof, that outsiders might be the guilty parties. Offended by the blaze of negative publicity, the paper struck back, editorializing, "Walton County is made up of law-abiding people. It is unfair to stigmatize twenty thousand people with a crime committed by a handful of outlaws, some of whom no doubt came from other counties."[90] Governor-elect Talmadge also tried to dim the spotlight on Walton County, declaring, "that black boy just got liquored up and almost killed his boss. It's liable to happen anywhere. The rest of the country can't seem to understand these things down here."[91]

The truculence of the white residents did not surprise Hoover, who told the Committee on Civil Rights, set up by President Truman, that the FBI was usually faced with "an iron curtain" in these investigations. "We are absolutely powerless, as investigators, unless the citizens of a community come forward with information. Our function is to go out and get the evidence. We have to have sources of information. We have got to be able to go to citizens and have them talk freely and frankly to us, so that we may prepare the case for the prosecuting attorney."[92]

The FBI was confronted with an equally stiff standoff by black sharecroppers and household employees in the Hestertown and neighboring areas. One longtime black observer sensed that the entire county was "in a stir" because of the FBI's wide reach.[93] "The negro residents of that territory are frightened and even terrified when approached for information," Weeks reported to Washington in a confidential memo sent by airmail special delivery. "One negro informant, who gave some valuable information, fled when agents approached him and had to be practically run down in the cotton patch for an interview. When he gave the information, he advised that white folks have been warning him against helping the investigation."[94]

Blacks were so overcome by the paralyzing message of the lynchings that they feared identical reprisals if it became known they had met with the FBI.[95] Many of those who told what they knew pleaded for anonymity. A black tenant who informed on weapons owned by his landlord refused to sign his statement, concluding that he would never be able to bring himself to testify in court.[96] In another interview, the agent carefully wrote down the sounds of words spoken by an informant: "We sho hopes the FBI stays here until us get our crops gathered, 'cause the white folks sure is scared good, and we gotta go when the FBI goes."[97]

A farmhand who arrived to milk cows was accused by his boss man of probably having met with the FBI. He was also told that he and "all the other niggers had been talking too much."[98] A female house servant, who had earlier in the day met with the FBI, returned to work to be censured by her employer's wife and told that she "had better not be running her mouth off."[99]

Informants among the black community were hard to come by, with one man saying he could not learn anything about the killings because "the white folks were not talking since the FBI came to town."[100]

To build confidence among potential informants, the agents tried to interview every black resident in a specific locality so that no individual would stand out as a suspected collaborator. But even though some were quizzed four or five times, Weeks passed on that "they are not relating all they know (and) if these negroes do come through with the story it is doubtful they will ever agree to testify."[101] Convinced that the black community was fearful of being beaten or killed by whites if seen as informants, Weeks decided it would be futile trying to talk with them in their homes. Somehow the agents would have to meet with them clandestinely in Monroe.[102] While some blacks cringed when asked to be informants, others had reached a breaking point. A black male was overheard threatening, "If the FBI keeps on talking to me I am going to kill hell out of one of them." [103]

The community was rife with intimidation by white overseers. In the weeks that followed the murders, several farmhands secretively disclosed to Hoover's men in the field the extent of Harrison's threats. Huddling with agents, a middle-aged black man said it began within a day or two of the lynchings. "He said if any of us did tell anything, folks would find us scattered about dead." Harrison instilled fear by stating he could find out anything confided to the FBI. "Mr. Loy told me he had a secret man in the FBI who was telling him what was going on and what they were doing every day," the informant declared.[104] With chilling directness, Harrison warned another laborer, "Boy, you need not tell everything to the FBI. Don't tell them anything. Everything you tell them, they tell me."[105] And to other farmhands living on his land, Harrison suggested they tell the FBI the truth, but whatever they said would be passed on to his lawyer, who would in turn disclose everything to him.[106]

One day a federal agent and an officer with the Georgia Bureau of Investigation followed a black man they wanted to interview passing by in a truck. They trailed it to a farm where Harrison got out of the front seat and, without any questions being asked, began a long discussion of the case. He said he had consulted his attorney about his black employees "who were very much upset and he was unable to get them to work steadily." He said his attorney counseled him to tell his black farmhands to give statements in writing to the FBI; then they could refuse to answer any other questions.[107]

The agents were so exacting that they even quizzed pre-teen children. Three siblings, fourth and fifth graders at a school for blacks, were interviewed separately and away from their home, but all "appeared to have been coached" to say they knew nothing about the killings, or anything about Loy Harrison's conversations with their father. This was a reversal of their earlier admissions that Harrison had threatened their father that the same mob would come after him if he said anything to the FBI.[108]

The FBI were ever alert to having wool pulled over their eyes. One black man who claimed to know a lot about Harrison was said to be "very illiterate and ignorant." In comments appended to his statement, an agent wrote, "It is not deemed advisable to utilize his services as a witness," because whenever he was "caught in a lie . . . he feigned that his mind was bad, and he could not recall events."[109]

Even the announcement of reward money failed to attract informants. The National Association for the Advancement of Colored People offered $10,000 for the arrest and conviction of the killers. The National Maritime Union held out a promise of $5,000, the Georgia State Patrol pledged $12,500, and the retiring governor $10,000.[110] Fear of exposure kept many from coming forward. On one occasion a white man approached a black man shortly after seeing him confer with the FBI and warned that anyone who told anything for money would never live to enjoy the use of it because "something would happen to him."[111]

Weeks had already offered limited amounts of reward money to some informants, but he was hamstrung because he could never guarantee payment that was beyond his control.[112] He reported that most of those in the know were so closely tied to the community that they would not think of going to live elsewhere, and would never be able to explain possession of or spend such lavish amounts if they stayed put.[113]

At the same time, secretary Walter White of the NAACP alerted all southern branches of the organization to reports of the "mysterious disappearances" of blacks, especially veterans in the deep South. Some might be explained by individuals fleeing after conflict with whites, "but there have been other cases where there is reason to believe that the persons who disappeared have been taken out and lynched, and the news suppressed." He asked the branches to check out all rumors of disappearances.[114]

Washington had been given early warning to expect an "improbability of (an) early solution."[115] But by mid-August the pressure increased to interview as many as possible because of the imminence of Labor Day, when farmers concentrated on the harvest and farmhands returned to the fields to pick cotton and bale the hay.

The investigation had weighed heavily on the overworked squad, and the special agent in charge reported laconically to Washington that the process was "detailed and tedious." However, he added, the hundreds of transcribed interviews had begun to throw the spotlight on "some good suspects."[116]

Major Suspect

Suspicion quickly focused on Loy Harrison, forty-two, whom a radio broadcast had glorified as the "kind farmer" who arranged bail for Roger Malcolm.[1] An offended reader in New Jersey hurried to denounce the broadcaster's description. Writing anonymously to J. Edgar Hoover, he insisted, "You no [sic] as well as I do if a Negro do anything to a white in the South, no other white man is going to bail him out for no good reason. The nice man that went bail for the decesed [sic] in that lynch mob in Georgia did it in order to help kill him. You no that. Everybody in fifty miles no each other by name. If you don't lock him up you will never solve that case because he is your man."[2]

He was backed up by others who knew Harrison intimately. An Atlanta attorney scoffed at Harrison's claim not to have recognized any of the abductors and killers. The lawyer told the FBI he had known Harrison since he was a little boy, even employing him to help out in a sawmill during World War I. "Harrison knows more people in Walton, Oconee, and Morgan Counties than any other man," he charged. And, he insisted, "Harrison feared no man."[3] Corroboration came from a black man who had worked for Harrison four years earlier. Describing him as "a big man and tough," the former employee said "even the sheriff of Walton County does not dare to enter on Harrison's property unless he has received permission." He noted that the wealthy landowner always carried a gun and was known and feared throughout both Oconee and Walton Counties. As for the farmer's tale of being stopped by others at Moore's Ford Bridge, he countered, "no one would dare stop an automobile" in which Harrison was traveling, unless he was acquainted with them and knew they were not targeting him. Otherwise, the informant asserted, "It would simply result in Harrison drawing his gun and shooting at those attempting to stop him."[4]

The police chief of nearby Watkinsville, willing to speak out, said Harrison was "capable of entering into any kind of a conspiracy to kill negroes."[5] Soon the FBI had compelling evidence that the "kind farmer" was as unsavory as anyone with murderous tendencies.

Pot-bellied Harrison, 240 pounds and five feet eleven,[6] had a criminal record stretching back twenty-three years, when he was convicted of shooting a federal internal revenue officer to death during a raid on a liquor still in South Carolina. Though the verdict was later reversed, he served more than a year in the penitentiary for the first of a number of liquor law violations. Over the years, alcohol tax unit officials had "cut down" about twenty illegal stills on his farms,[7] in an area known as Dark Corner for the frequent presence of federal agents.[8]

Loy Harrison was amiable, congenial, talkative, and even cooperative with FBI agents who interviewed him for long sessions. Unlike most suspects, he was neither uptight nor antagonistic. He professed to be good-natured and benevolent toward his farmhands, claiming this exemplary relationship with blacks should have eliminated him from being linked to the multiple murders. "He gave the impression he was extremely good to his negro employees; that he had no difficulties with any except Robert Lee Elder," one agent reported, "and that his past record was such that would not stand him to be involved in anything of this nature."[9] He answered every allegation of violence toward his farmhands and tenants by turning the tables and accusing each of them of having been drunk or provocative at the time.

Importantly, Harrison finally admitted to his interrogators that he had gone into Monroe on the morning of the lynching. He had not owned up to this before because "no one had asked him." And anyway, he said, he had only gone in to get 800 pounds of arsenic to dust his cotton, and returned home as soon as possible to hop on his tractor and get on with the job.[10]

He kept his composure even when denying accusations that he had bad-mouthed investigators to blacken their image among locals. The owner of a prominent fertilizer plant in Monroe said Harrison told him FBI agents had questioned him for fifty consecutive hours, driving all over the county as they replaced one another in relay shifts. The businessman quoted Harrison telling him agents had taken him into a church, listened to the sermon, then accompanied him outside and prayed with him to tell the truth. In a bizarre addition, Harrison related that the FBI had even given him a "truth pill." Additionally, Harrison mentioned that no interrogator had tried to intimidate him by pointing out a jail.[11]

Sometimes Harrison paid his laborers with a gallon of whiskey in lieu of cash.[12] Once he bailed a drunken worker out of jail for four dollars, then told the black man it was thirty dollars, which he would be expected to work off through unpaid labor.[13] One of his black female employees, a twenty-two-year-old illiterate, told the FBI, while "in great fear of her life," that Harrison often did not pay her wages of one dollar fifty per day for housework and cooking when it became due at the end of the week. She and her husband left the farm when he withheld payment for picking cotton.[14]

With no more than a seventh grade education, Harrison owned 722 acres of farmland straddling Walton and Oconee counties[15] and operated untrammeled, much like a feudal lord swaggering over peasants as docile as serfs. He was so overbearing that his brother had not spoken to him in over a year, after accusing Loy of snatching a black laborer from his farm where he was the only one available to pick cotton in a particular field. The feud was so intense that when the house of a black man burned down on Loy's farm, he fingered his sibling as the likely culprit.[16]

A self-confessed member of the Ku Klux Klan for about fifteen years until his klavern broke up about 1939 or 1940,[17] Harrison felt a visceral resentment against black war veterans, like George Dorsey who lived on his farm, for receiving unemployment compensation, which he and other critics denounced as "rocking chair money."[18] Dorsey's uncle, Robert Lee Elder, also a veteran of World War II drawing unemployment compensation, was jumped upon while walking along a country road, blindfolded, and beaten bloody and unconscious. He told rescuers that he recognized the voice of Harrison who had said contemptuously, "All these damn niggers been to the Army and come back and think themselves something."[19]

Over the weeks, as a handful of scared and reluctant informers braced to tell all they knew in secret liaisons with FBI agents, a portrait of Harrison emerged as a ruthless landowner with a record of frenzied violence and repetitive brutality toward black men and women. One fall weekend during hog-killing time in 1944, Harrison ordered Moena's younger brother, Anderson Elder, who had served in the army,[20] to get to work immediately. "Boss man," Anderson answered, "you'll have to take me home to change clothes because I was going to town." Harrison cut in, "I'm going to beat hell out of you!" The farmer jumped off his porch and reached unsuccessfully for a yard broom as Anderson ran off. Then he drew a pistol from his pocket, shouting that if Anderson didn't stop he would open fire. As Anderson halted, Harrison picked up a brick and slammed it so hard against the black man's head that the building block shattered. He continued beating him with the pistol and stomping on him as Harrison's daughter ran screaming into the house. Then her father knocked Anderson down by swinging a length of wood against his head. He kicked, pummeled, and whipped the black man with a rubber hose while he was down and told an eyewitness, "If the damn nigger had started to work, I never would have hit him." Blood ran down Anderson's head and into his eyes as Harrison warned employees who had witnessed the assault that if they said anything about it, the same thing would happen to them.[21]

Harrison did not deny assaulting Anderson when questioned by the FBI but claimed the black man was drunk when told to build a fire and had picked up a rock. "I knocked him down and hit him with the rock," Harrison explained.[22]

That same day Harrison set a trap for a ferocious attack on another farmhand, Willie Adams, thirty-one, then the common-law husband of Moena's sister, Grace. As Willie approached the house, Harrison told him to go into the barn. Once inside, Harrison pulled a gun on him as four black men punched Willie and knocked him down with swipes from a plank and a rubber hose. When he tried to get up Harrison kicked him in the face and shouted, "God damn you! Lay still!" They knocked him unconscious. When he came to he was missing two lower front teeth.

Grace had heard the screams from inside the house and started for the barn, defying Mrs. Harrison's warning, "Grace, don't go out there!" Harrison, standing by the barn door, yelled out, "Go back in the house with the women!" Some twenty minutes later the farmer came in the house and she watched him take a revolver from the inside of his shirt and place it in a drawer. As she wept, he turned and asked, "What are you worrying about? We heard he beat you up a lot. Now you have to nurse him a while."

"No, he never has nursed me," she said. "I'm sorry you all did that, Mr. Loy."

"You all!" he railed. "Hell, them niggers done that!" He put an end to the talk, yelling, "You all get the hell out of here! Go on home!"

When she caught sight of Willie he was staggering out of the barn, barely advancing as he dragged a leg and limped with one shoulder higher than the other. His mouth was swollen and his eyes were puffy.

She overheard Harrison telling someone to take Willie home and clean him up. Harrison said before it was all over it was going to cost Willie fifty dollars, as well as the beating, because he had stolen a sack of sugar worth ten dollars.[23] But half an hour later, Harrison and a white employee came to Willie's house, put him in the vehicle, and drove behind the farmer's house to a well. All three got out. Harrison looked down the well.

"Come on, jump in that well!"

Willie backed away.

"I ought to make you!" Harrison threatened. Willie could see the revolver protruding from his employer's pocket, but Harrison got back in the car and drove off with the white man. Willie stumbled back to his own home.

Four or five days later, when Grace could finally make out his mumblings, she asked why he stole the sugar. He told her Harrison owed him $15 and wouldn't pay, so he made off with the sack of sugar and sold it for $10 because he needed the money to buy himself a pair of overalls and a shirt.

About two weeks later, "Mr. Loy" went over to Willie and asked if he wanted to leave the farm. Willie replied, "Yes." Harrison gave him four dollars and Willie left for New Jersey.[24] Willie's fear was so ingrained, even several years after the savage beating, that he told the FBI he would not go down to Georgia if compelled to testify about the lynchings unless he was guaranteed protection, nor would he board a train unless assured that an FBI agent would meet him on arrival.[25]

On another occasion Grace ran to Harrison's house for help when a group of rowdy drunks tried to break into her home while her new common-law husband was absent.

"Mr. Loy," she pleaded from the porch as he lay in bed, "get up, please, and go stop those colored boys that are trying to break into my house!"

"Didn't I tell you awhile ago about coming here and worrying me!" he shouted.

"You told me to come and get you if anything happened," she said apologetically.

Harrison, now facing her, bellowed, "Yes, I told you that, but damn it, now get home!" He hit her so hard that it knocked loose a front tooth, leaving a permanent scar on the inside of her upper lip, and she fell over backwards, landing three or four feet below the porch. He stormed down the steps, kicked her on the leg, told her to get up and shouted, "I wish to God you'd quit worrying me at night!"[26]

The following day Harrison apologized for slapping her but warned, "If you ever tell anybody about me slapping you I'm going to kill you."

Obediently, she replied, "Yes, sir." Grace kept her word, but when she eventually ran away she did not tell him beforehand "because I was afraid he would not let me go away."[27]

Disputing her version of the assault, Harrison told FBI agents that he had pushed her off the porch while she was drunk and refused to leave. "I don't think I hit her," he added.[28]

A black man, employed by Harrison as a farmhand by day and an illegal liquor still operator by night, was eating dinner on the landowner's porch when the white man's pet dog tried to drink out of the glass of milk. "I knocked him off the porch and his little boy told Mr. Harrison I had hit the dog," the laborer told FBI agents. "He came out on the porch, picked up a heavy work shoe with a steel plate on the heel and hit me on the head with it several times. Then he kicked me in the chest. I was pretty sore from it the next day."[29]

A few days before the lynchings, a friend asked Moena's younger brother, Robert Lee Elder, thirty-two, "if that boy what done the cutting was still in jail." Robert replied, "Yeah, he is still in jail."[30] Then he said he himself had taken a beating when he decided to leave Harrison's employ. Harrison had claimed that the man owed him sixty dollars.[31] While he was waiting to catch a bus into Monroe, Harrison drove up, forced him into the vehicle, and drove to Moore's Ford. There, Harrison beat him mercilessly with a car crank. He tried to escape but froze when Harrison threatened to shoot, thinking it preferable to take the whipping. When it was over, Harrison warned he didn't want any trouble out of him for the rest of the year. An eyewitness who saw Elder get out of the vehicle at Harrison's house said "the upper part of his nose was mashed in. He had a cut by his right eye and on the right side of his chin, and holes pecked in the upper part of his right arm." Telling a bystander he had "just beat the hell" out of Elder, Harrison told him to wash the battered man and dress him in clean clothes so he could take him to a doctor. His wounds were stitched but he was bedridden for two weeks.[32]

Harrison did not deny knocking down Elder with the swipe of an ice maul but told the FBI he acted after a black woman told him Robert had stolen eight dollars from her and was leaving the farm. Denying he had forcibly abducted Elder, he said the victim voluntarily got into the vehicle and en route back to the farm "said he wanted to get with me and for me to stop. I hit him with a bolt in the car," the burly farmer told federal agents.[33]

Two months later, on the Fourth of July, Harrison again unleashed a furious attack on Elder, this time beating him with a black jack.[34]

Harrison was also named as the culprit who beat up a black woman for saying anyone who voted for Eugene Talmadge was "trash." Word got back to Harrison, who had named his youngest son Talmadge, that she made the comment to colleagues while working in the field. That night, while she was cleaning up in the kitchen after supper, he stormed in and hit her, leaving an ugly bump on her forehead.[35]

A former black employee on Harrison's farm was unexpectedly bold with the agents, telling them, "All the colored people are afraid of Mr. Harrison and not many of them will stay with him over one or two years. I have heard that all the folks on Mr. Harrison's place go to him as soon as the FBI leaves, and tell him everything."[36]

Only five days before vigilantes murdered the two black couples by the banks of the Apalachee River, Harrison had chased one of the victims, George Dorsey, through the countryside and caught him at Moore's Ford, where he punched him and stamped on his chest. That same day Dorsey's younger brother, Charlie Boy, sprinted through the fields ahead of the enraged farmer, who fired five shots at his elusive target. Harrison's explosive temperament had ignited when the Dorsey brothers and their mother's brother, Robert Lee Elder, arrived back several hours later than arranged with Harrison, who had loaned them his truck to drive to Watkinsville and collect their "rocking chair money." Instead of returning immediately, they had cruised the country roads before returning to George's house. Harrison drove by, recognized his truck, and got out.

"Mr. Loy walked up into the yard. I hid behind the crib because I was afraid he would get on me because I kept the truck out late," Charlie Boy recounted. "When Mr. Loy got out by the fig bushes I lit out running down the road and across the bridge and then I taken the field. William Jackson was plowing his field and I told him I thought Mr. Loy was after me. I told him I wanted to spend the night there as I was scared to go home." Charlie Boy, panting and wet with sweat, was so out of breath he collapsed. He begged Jackson to take him to the residences of relatives because he was afraid to go home, but Jackson's truck was broken down.[37] Jackson told him not to stay and talk if he was being pursued, so Charlie Boy set off down the road.[38] About an hour later Harrison and two men drove by Jackson's house, looking for the fugitive. When darkness set in, George stopped by Jackson's house. He'd taken a beating and his pants were shredded. He said that Harrison assaulted him because he had tried to stop the farmer from catching Charlie Boy.

For the next four days Charlie Boy stayed out of sight, but when he returned to George's house his brother warned, "If I was you I would not go back over there as I heard Mr. Loy say that if you come back he was going to kill you."

Charlie Boy stayed out of Harrison's reach for more than a week. The day before the funerals of George and Dorothy, their mother, Moena, was being driven by Harrison in search of Charlie Boy. They pulled up beside a car driven by one of her friends, who told them Charlie Boy was staying at his house.

"They done killed all of my children," Moena wailed. "They killed all of them for nuthin'."

Harrison interjected. "I wouldn't have gotten him out [of jail] except George and Dorothy asked me to get out Roger."

"It was no harm in getting him out," said Moena.

"He would have come out better if he had stayed in," said Harrison.

"I know if he ever put his feet on the ground they were going to kill him," Moena replied.

"They were not intending to kill Dorothy and Mae," said Harrison. "But one of them knowed one of the men and they killed them, too."

Harrison told them he was lucky to get home alive. He said he had called up law enforcement officials and they had guarded him until he got home.[39]

When they arrived at the friend's house Charlie Boy stayed concealed until Moena told him his brother and sister had been murdered. Then he came out of hiding, and mother and son went home to grieve together.[40]

Within two months of the murders, Weeks had enough background on the fearsome farmer to record "indications of involuntary servitude on the part of negroes working for Loy Harrison."[41] But Harrison eluded arrest because nobody could crack his story about being ambushed while driving the victims home. There were no independent witnesses and Harrison's account, according to Weeks, was by no means outlandish or far-fetched.[42] His tale of a group of twenty to twenty-five men making up the mob had been accepted by all, even the media, who repeated it in their retelling of the tragedy. Harrison teetered on the edge of disbelief, but there was no definitive proof of his guilt.

He did not seem to care. A month after telling the FBI that he only had trouble with Robert Lee Elder, he shrugged off the litany of violence against others by saying that the incidents had taken place "so long ago."[43]

Prime Suspects

Exhaustive interrogations of whites and blacks within a wide radius of the crime singled out dozens of resident suspects, but ten merited special scrutiny. However much they shifted and squirmed, they could not wriggle free of incriminating evidence. The files bulged with their own entangling statements and the audacious accusations of others.

Foremost among them was Weldon Hester, thirty-eight, brother of the white man stabbed by a black. One day a pair of hardened agents looked on aghast as they stood in Weldon's yard hoping to interview him. In silent disgust they watched the infuriated man run after several terrified hound puppies scampering for cover. Weldon caught one, picked up a stick and whacked its head so hard and repetitively that the weapon broke. "Get me a goodun!" he shouted to his wife, who brought him a replacement stick. But it also splintered as he beat the whimpering little dogs. All the while his wife and mother-in-law looked on, apparently "quite pleased." After the second stick broke apart, Weldon explained to the agents that the puppies had killed several chickens. Now it was his turn to punish them. They had to be disciplined and learn who was master.

When he got through with thrashing the puppies, he told the dumbfounded agents he would not have time to talk as he had "other plans."[1] Filled with revulsion, they reported to their superiors that what they had witnessed was "a possible indication of the character of this suspect."[2]

Damning evidence linked Weldon to the tragedy, not from his widespread notoriety as a violent white supremacist, but because of one black man's remarks. He said he and his wife were eating breakfast very early in Powell Adcock's kitchen when Mrs. Adcock told them about the lynching the evening before. She said the two women had been killed "because they recognized Mr. Weldon Hester and called him by name."[3] She might have picked up gossip, but it was also likely that her husband had blabbed what he'd witnessed.

To most people Weldon played the simpleton. He said he first learned of the killing of four blacks at work the morning after it happened. "I didn't even know nothing about it," he said of the stabbing.[4] He told Sheriff Emory Gordon that he had "practically raised" Roger, who had "surprised" him by stabbing Barnett Hester.[5] But according to an eyewitness, an emboldened Weldon had previously said he wanted to kill Roger. He even admitted he planned to lynch him.[6] Weldon told the agents, "I don't know what I said about Roger. I was so damn mad I don't know what I said. I did not say anything about killing him—not as I know of," he recalled. "I don't know what I went down there to do. I'll just be fair with you."[7] Weldon claimed he had been interrupted by his hysterical mother. "Mama came out and told me to go to the hospital and see how my brother was," he said.[8]

Later, FBI agents perked up when a relative of Weldon's family said the mass killing of four people was unjustified, but "if any revenge was necessary, the killing of Roger Malcolm would have satisfied him."[9] It was one more indication of the vengeful mood following the stabbing of Weldon's brother.

His cruelty toward animals was only one reason why Weldon Hester shot to the top of the list of those thought to be linked to the lynch mob. He was also Barnett's older, protective sibling. Additionally, his life was a succession of short-tempered fury and inhumanity toward blacks. Time and again black men and women timidly informed the FBI that Weldon had lashed out at Roger. The victim's first wife related that when her baby was just two days old, Weldon had berated the farmhand for breaking a wagon tongue. She thought someone would be severely injured when Roger armed himself with an axe, but the white man's mother stepped in and put an end to the fracas.[10] On another occasion Weldon had told Roger and his late grandfather to pick more cotton, but the confrontation ended when the white overseer picked up a rock and threatened, "I'll knock your God-damn brains out!"[11]

Weldon denied ever having hit or shot at Roger, who he said had worked for him about a decade and was "a pretty good worker."[12] Yet Roger's colleagues told a different story to the men sent by Washington.

They said Weldon had railed against Roger, accusing him of being an incompetent farmhand. Once he had thrown Coca Cola bottles at the tormented laborer for refusing to haul wheat on a Sunday, and the black man, younger by thirteen years, had tangled with him briefly before running off to avoid another whipping.[13] Roger, they said in strict confidence, was more vulnerable when Weldon had too much to drink and went looking for a fight. In one exceptional instance many years back, Roger had stood up to Weldon to prevent him from whipping the black man's grandmother, who had been accused of not working hard enough.[14]

For years Roger had endured Weldon's sudden outbursts until one day he disappeared to escape another assault for allegedly hoeing a cornfield badly. But half a year later Weldon located his hiding place and brought him back.[15] "I went down there to get him," Weldon said defensively. "He was ready to come back and work for me."[16]

While being quizzed by the two agents, Weldon, blind in one eye, appeared to resent the questioning. Wrote one interrogator, "He appears unable to look the agents in the eye when talking to them, and cast his good eye about when talking."[17]

Weldon protested his innocence, claiming, "I have never discussed with anyone killing Roger." He told the FBI he did not know Loy Harrison or Moore's Ford. "I have never been to the place the negroes were killed," he insisted. "I don't know where it is. I have never been there, as I know of."[18]

He told the FBI that on the day of the lynchings he drove alone to work. He said that he didn't ride with his wife, who worked identical hours at the same place and always lunched with him, because he had to go in early. Also, he noted, the front passenger seat of his two-door black 1934 Ford sedan was in bad shape. "I don't know nothing at all about the killing of the negroes," he stonewalled.

Weldon stuck to his story of being ignorant of the killings. By his account he got home between 5:00 and 5:30 p.m., before his wife, and visited his "Papa" after supper. Then he returned home to change and set off for the revival meeting at the Union Chapel United Methodist church about 7:30 p.m. He said he stayed there until almost 10:00 p.m. and then went straight home.[19] In his mind this would eliminate him from being part of the pack of men who had gunned down the black couples.

But his alibi was undercut on two fronts. His wife agreed with everything he had volunteered but unwittingly denied he had gone out again that day or night.[20] And a black man swore that on the evening of the lynching he had seen the suspect driving past his basketball court, en route from the bridge, when it was too dark to continue playing ball. His passenger, whom he also knew personally, was Alvin Adcock.[21] Weldon did not care what they said. He exasperated the agents, telling them, "I don't know nothing at all about the killing of the negroes. I do not know of any of the person [sic] who were in the mob that killed them."[22]

After the lynchings, employees at the Monroe Manufacturing Company, where Weldon worked on a bradding machine, surrounded him and asked if the news was true. Confidently, he replied that he did not know anything about it. "You all know I worked yesterday," he said, indicating it would have been impossible for him to know anything about the slayings.[23]

*

James Verner lied over and over to the FBI, showing neither guilt nor shame when changing his story. He stunned Hoover's men by stating he could not remember going to the ice plant on the day of the lynching, even though he was seen there by others. The most reputable eyewitness was Louis Malcolm, a serving member of the Monroe Police Department, born and raised in the county. He told the FBI that almost immediately after returning home from a fire about 4:30 p.m., he had driven to the plant to buy ice. There he saw Harrison, Vivian Tillman, and Verner conferring together. The officer thought no more of it until the following day when he learned of the lynchings and recollected what he had seen close to that time frame on the preceding day.[24]

A black teenager, Lamar Howard, employed for the past four months making ice and helping out with the plant's delivery truck, also reported seeing Harrison deep in conversation with Verner and Tillman on the afternoon of the murders.[25] Lamar said Harrison had driven into the yard and shortly afterwards James Verner arrived in his LaSalle coupe. Lamar described how Verner and someone else walked over to Harrison's vehicle, where they conversed for about half an hour. Lamar told the FBI that he was unable to overhear anything.

Another black man, employed by the City Water and Light Company, also saw Harrison talking with Tillman at the ice plant within two hours of the lynching.[26] Agents knew that Verner visited the ice plant frequently, where he loitered around with Tillman. Despite these sightings, Harrison and Verner vigorously denied knowing each other, let alone being together on the day of the lynchings.[27] Harrison stated emphatically, "I have never talked to James Verner as far I know. I know definitely I did not talk to him at the ice plant in Monroe the day of the lynching."[28]

When first interviewed, Verner was certain of his facts, which he offered with comfortable ease.[29] He flatly denied knowing Loy Harrison.[30] Later he brazenly denied even being an acquaintance of Harrison. He could not even tell the difference between Loy and his brother. But in the same breath he softened his tone, allowing that "he could not recall ever having talked to Loy." And even though he said he did not even know Loy by reputation, he obviously knew Harrison was a disreputable liquor dealer when he stated, "I sold red whiskey and he sold corn whiskey." Yet he refused to admit speaking with Harrison at the ice plant that afternoon.[31]

When quizzed by the FBI, a "semi-hostile" Tillman steadfastly insisted that Verner and Harrison were not together at the ice plant the day of the lynching.[32] But just two days later Verner reversed himself, telling the agents that he had just spoken with Tillman, who reminded him that he had indeed stopped by the ice plant in the afternoon and again late in the evening of the murders. Verner justified his turnaround by announcing that his memory was befuddled by drinking a fifth of whiskey on July 25.[33] If he did go to the ice plant, he suggested, it must have been several hours after the lynching, after he had already driven out to look at the corpses.[34]

His shifting positions were nothing new. Many suspects did the same thing, citing forgetfulness. Nobody seemed unsettled by contradictory evidence from the same person. Aware of this, the Special Agent in Charge passed on to Washington that whites changed accounts of their whereabouts "in order that their stories might coincide upon re-interview."[35]

Narrating his whereabouts on July 25, Verner claimed to have gone into Monroe about 4:00 p.m. and stayed about a quarter of an hour at the filling station owned by Malcolm Marcus, who recently had solicited him for membership in the Ku Klux Klan. He had filled in the application form, though he was not yet a member.[36] From there he said he stopped for about two hours in a pair of beer-drinking "joints" on the Social Circle highway south of Monroe. He accounted for the next two hours with a stop at another filling station on the Monroe-Athens Highway and a return home for dinner. He claimed that he found out about the mass killings only after calling again at Malcolm's filling station.[37] He told investigators that after Malcolm gave him directions to get to Moore's Ford, he picked up his girlfriend in Monroe and drove out to the crime scene.[38]

He had been drinking heavily. His girlfriend said they had no difficulty in finding their way to the bridge over "a little bitty road." She waited behind the green coupe, near four other vehicles, while he walked down to see the bloodied bodies during the inquest, his path lit by the headlights from his car. Minutes later he came back.

As they drove to his uncle's home, Verner mentioned that he had seen someone at the crime scene taking pieces of rope that had bound the male victims.[39] The uncle, a brother of Verner's mother, and owner of a large farm and general store, told investigators that Verner said that when he got to the cadavers he turned down an invitation to be on the coroner's jury. The uncle did not believe that Verner did not know Loy Harrison, telling the FBI, "I don't know why they wouldn't know each other. They were both born and raised around here."[40]

Verner's girlfriend said they stayed at his uncle's home until about 11:00 p.m., then drove back to the ice plant in Monroe. There they had "a couple of drinks" and talked with Tillman before he took her home.[41]

Three weeks would pass before Verner lied again. Now he said he knew Harrison, but he still insisted he had never spoken to him.[42]

During the interview with the FBI, the agents noted, James Verner's demeanor under questioning was "very cool." He answered questions readily and did not seem disturbed. Verner also skillfully deflected opinions on his racist views by saying he "is not, and never had been a member of the Ku Klux Klan," even though he had completed paperwork for membership.[43] He told the G-men that even if he knew anything about the lynchings, "I don't believe I would tell you. I'll be fair with you. I just don't want to get mixed up in it."[44]

Voluntarily, he handed over his German Mauser and his .32 revolver to the FBI. They were rushed to the laboratory in Washington, examined, and test-fired. On October 1, the results came back. The weapons could not have been used to fire any of the lethal ammunition because they did not match specimens found at the site or in the corpses. Confounded, the FBI had no choice but to return the weapons.[45]

Verner had avoided conclusive identification as one of the mob. For the moment he was safe. However, he remained a strong suspect because of his admitted falsehoods, his acquaintance with Weldon Hester, his shifting stance on knowing Harrison,[46] and the firearms he kept in his green LaSalle coupe or army jeep.[47]

When agents questioned a gunsmith in Good Hope, he told them that James Verner, and others unknown to him, had tried to trade a six-inch barrel revolver for a four-inch barrel Smith & Wesson revolver the day before the killings. But the gunsmith refused to deal with him, suspecting that something might be wrong with the weapon because, he said, Verner was "a crook, bootlegger, and gambler."[48]

*

B. H. "Bob" Hester, father of George, Weldon, and Barnett, strenuously fabricated his movements. Even when a white deputy sheriff spoke out against him, he refused to change his mind. But he flummoxed the FBI. Bob was seventy years old, gray, balding, and slightly stooped,[49] though in good health, yet the agents thought it unlikely he would have "actively participated" in the lynchings because of his advanced age.[50] But they could not be sure. They were open-minded because he was the desperate father of a man hospitalized with life-threatening stab wounds.

Time and again, Bob crossed swords with Deputy Sheriff Lewis Howard. The lawman would not budge from his declaration that Bob had talked to him outside his home in the county jail in the early morning of the day of the lynchings. He was adamant this had taken place on the same day the victims were slain. And a passing black bicyclist said he had also seen Bob talking with the lawman at the same time, on the same day.[51] The bicyclist knew it was Bob because they had lived in the same neighborhood for twenty-four years.[52]

According to the deputy sheriff, he was standing in his yard, waiting to be picked up at 8:00 a.m., when Bob drove up and inquired about the bond that would be necessary for Roger's release. The lawman did not recall who was with Hester at the time but thought it might have been one of Bob's sons. The deputy sheriff advised that he had already obtained a warrant. That was when he said Bob Hester wanted the bond set large enough so that Roger would have to appear in court. He also wanted Roger put on a chain gang.[53]

Bob refused to back down and agree. He said everything the deputy sheriff had remembered took place a few days earlier, before the killings.[54] No matter that two people said one thing and Bob Hester another, the elderly man staunchly resisted and said they were mistaken.

Bob's stubbornness would almost certainly exclude the deputy sheriff as a suspect, for Howard had now taken a stand against a prime suspect, who was white. And Howard, his colleague, "Doc" Sorrells, and even Sheriff Gordon, said they had not passed on to anyone, except Loy Harrison, information about Roger's imminent release from prison.[55] Howard was "emphatic" that when he met Bob on the morning of the killings he had told him that no one, up until then, had inquired about a bond for Roger.[56] Harrison himself would not yield in claiming he never tattled about Roger's bond. The FBI concluded that "they have denied any knowledge, nor have any logical suggestions been advanced, which would tend to explain how the assailants learned of Roger Malcolm's release in time to organize and ambush him, approximately 30 minutes after his release."[57]

Nobody would admit that the three lawmen, or Harrison, might be lying, which made the task of frustrated interrogators even more challenging. Excluding the sheriff and his deputies from suspicion, combined with Harrison's intransigence, made it almost impossible to prove state collusion in a conspiracy—an essential requirement for federal jurisdiction.

When two agents called at Bob Hester's home, they found him sitting on the porch. Summoned to meet them, his wife, Ida, locked the front screen door and bridled at their questions. She would not buckle under questioning. "I don't know nothing anyhow," she snapped. All she knew was that her son Barnett had been stabbed by Roger Malcolm. Then she sputtered, "If the election had gone the way the big people wanted it there would have been more trouble than they have already had."[58]

Bob maintained he had spent every day in his youngest son's hospital room, arriving at 8:00 a.m. and leaving at 6:00 p.m. And on the day of the lynching he arrived on time with his oldest son, George, who always drove straight home alone. Then suddenly, three weeks after the killings, he altered this line. Now he was just as sure that he had spent the night of July 24 in the hospital, returning to his home on the morning of the day the four were shot dead. His change of stance might have deflected guilt from himself but it implicated his son, because Bob remembered being driven back to the hospital by his nephew, not his son George. And he told the FBI that George had stayed at home all day, giving him enough time to have taken part in the lynching.[59]

George, forty-five, added to the murkiness even as he continued to dispute the deputy sheriff. Originally he told the FBI that on the day of the lynchings he had gone to the hospital to take the night nurse back to her residence. Then he had gone home until the early afternoon, when he drove his parents to the hospital. He stayed there until about 6:00 p.m., then returned home and stayed there all night.[60]

A few weeks later he, too, flip-flopped. Now he said he had discussed the events with his parents, who had "refreshed his memory." What he had already put in evidence was no longer true. Now he said the day the two black couples fell dead by Moore's Ford he had really driven his mother to the hospital about 8:00 a.m. He stayed there until approximately 9:30 a.m., long after the deputy sheriff said his father was talking to him outside the jail. Then he took his father home, after stopping in Monroe only to make a brief purchase. That crucial day he never stopped by the county jail so his father could talk to the lawman.

He recalled that in mid-afternoon he picked butterbeans and then shelled beans, milked his cows, and fed the stock until ninety minutes before midnight. That would have given him no time to go out to Moore's Ford.[61]

But even this was doubted when the middle-aged son related how he had driven the night nurse to the hospital about 5:00 p.m. and left there with his father and Barnett's wife between 5:30 and 6:00 p.m. They had all driven directly home and stayed there through the night.[62] The sun had not yet gone down when they arrived, and George said he was able to take care of the stock and remove the cows before dark.[63]

It was a confusing tale of switched facts and jumbled events. The agents were skeptical but powerless to do anything, especially when those being questioned referred to incidents shrouded by the growing distance of time. Attempts to quiz Bob's and Barnett's wives were equally fruitless because the women would not take questions. "You have already run this thing in the ground," rebuked one.[64]

But the FBI already knew how George had bragged that he would have killed Roger immediately after the stabbing—if only a gun had been available. The informant had been none other than George himself.[65]

*

The FBI targeted the Malcolm brothers, Grady and Wayman, for close attention because they had chased Roger to a cornfield and caught him after the stabbing. They were also the knifing victim's first cousins, their mother being the sister of Barnett's father. Nobody doubted that they had the motive and energy to kill Roger.

Grady, the older of the two at fifty-three, was six feet tall, weighing 160 pounds, with a distinctive flat nose and heavily lined face. Interviewed in his home, only half a mile from Barnett's house, he could not stop trembling at his first meeting with the FBI, though he was at all times friendly and cooperative.[66] Grady stuck to his account that on the day the four African Americans were violently done away with, he had stayed home all day and night, going outside for only half an hour to get roasting ears from a nearby field. There was no question that he had all the time necessary to go out and commit murder near the river.

He said he heard about what had happened near Moore's Ford Bridge when he tuned into the noon broadcast the following day. This squared with an FBI check that none of the radio stations in the Atlanta area carried reports of the massacre until 11:00 a.m., although a white man was sure he had heard the news at 7:45 a.m. while listening to the Griffin Shoe Polish program.[67] But Grady persistently denied knowing any of the killers, or Loy Harrison. And he looked to be excluded from suspicion by telling the attentive agents that he owned neither a gun nor a car.[68]

At the end of the session the special agents handed him the statement for his signature, but he declined to sign it, indicating that "he would if he had to, but didn't want to."[69]

Wayman, forty-nine, was more talkative when interviewed on two successive days soon after news of the killings shocked the world. Younger by two years but a strapping six feet two inches tall and twenty pounds heavier than his sibling, Wayman was notable for the right eye being smaller than the left and a prominent one-inch scar over his upper lip. He, too, was forthcoming and amiable when interviewed by Hoover's men.[70]

On July 25, he said he dropped off his wife at work at the Monroe Manufacturing Plant at 8:00 a.m. He picked up some shirts for his adult son, then stayed home until 9:30 a.m., when he took his son into Monroe to report to the local draft board. He said he and his son "sat around in the courthouse yard visiting, and also went to one of the local drug stores." An FBI check of the draft board confirmed that the young man had boarded a bus at 12:30 p.m. with other inductees going for a physical examination at Fort McPherson in Atlanta. But no explicit explanation was given for his activities before the bus left for Atlanta.

Wayman said after the bus left he spent the next couple of hours going into a store, having a flat tire fixed, and visiting "various people" in Monroe, but could not remember who they were. He related that he got home about 3:00 p.m. and for approximately the next two hours picked vegetables in the field, fed the hogs, and took care of his cows. Obviously, he had time in Monroe to learn of the mob's plans and then to drive out to Moore's Ford and join the gunmen. But he fudged that critical later time frame, leaving in doubt whether his farm work lasted until after sundown, when the killings would be over. Wayman told his interrogators that he had supped at home with his wife and children, then gone with them "to his wife's daddy's place" south of town until 10:00 p.m.

He admitted owning a .16-gauge shotgun, but when he showed it to the interviewers it was rusty and covered in cobwebs and dust, suggesting it could not have been fired for some time.[71]

Grady and Wayman agreed that they had motored out to Moore's Ford three or four days after the lynchings, but they pointedly said they had to ask for directions. When they arrived they saw two armed men working with tools, and two other white men they did not know. None of them found anything to take away as souvenirs though they later heard that someone had found a piece of a cartridge.[72] Significantly, the brothers, raised in the small community, denied knowing the landowner Loy Harrison, even though they all visited Monroe regularly to buy supplies, service their vehicles, and have haircuts.

Again, the siblings seemed to have stymied the loathsome outsiders.

*

Alvin Adcock, forty, a first cousin of the stabbing victim,[73] sounded like a bare-faced liar when he denied that he had gone to Moore's Ford, even when contradicted by a white man who said he drove him there in a car. "I don't know where Moore's Ford is," said Alvin. "I sure don't. I have never been there. I said I was going over there where they were killed if I could get someone to show me the way and go with me, but I never did go."[74]

Undeterred, a white man working at the Little Sandwich Shop in Monroe told the FBI that he had seen Alvin and his brother, Leonius, both of whom he had known all his life, and who lived within three miles of him, talking to each other near a drug store the morning after the lynchings. He had given the brothers a ride to Moore's Ford, where they stayed about forty minutes. "I was driving the car and I do not recall specifically what was said while we were going and coming but some general remarks were made about the lynching," he remembered. "I recall seeing Mr. Loy Harrison out there at the time. I do not recall seeing anyone in our crowd talking to him. [We] went to the spot where there appeared to be several patches of blood on the ground. I noticed several pieces of rope near these patches, and I also saw a short piece of rope on the ground nearby. We all arrived back within an hour from the time we left. The two Adcock boys, Leonius and Alvin, got out at the same time."[75]

Alvin easily blocked this, saying he wouldn't know Loy Harrison if he saw him. And he was mule-like in resisting evidence against him. "I haven't heard nothing to amount to nothing about the lynching. I ain't heard nobody say nothing about it. I have no idea who it was."[76]

When the FBI interviewed Alvin they noticed that he was so ill-disposed, unfriendly, and ruffled that his hands trembled excessively and he licked his lips continuously. He refused to allow the agents to take his photograph.[77]

His innocence claim was further tarnished by a day laborer on his father's farm, who said he witnessed a tense stand-off between Roger Malcolm and the younger Adcock about two weeks before the stabbing. He told Hoover's men that Roger, then drunk, had thrown something at Alvin's dog. Alvin had stormed out of his house shouting, "What the hell you doing throwing at the dog!" Roger had fired back that he was trying to stop the dog from barking. "You black SOB. I'll kill you!" Alvin roared. Roger made things worse by taunting, "You ain't going to do a goddamned thing to me." Infuriated, Alvin ordered him to "stand there until I get back" and disappeared inside. As Roger ran down the road, Alvin reappeared with a double-barreled shotgun, but by then his quarry had fled and Alvin lowered the weapon. The unidentified hired hand said that because of this Alvin hated Roger.[78]

Alvin's older sibling, Leonius, forty-one, was also a suspect because they had gone together to the site of the killings even though he insisted, "I have never been to Moore's Ford. I don't know where it is." He could remember what happened years ago, by stating he had known Roger "ever since he was a little old thing," but he was unable to recall what he had done on the day of the killings, even though he said he had gone to a revival meeting that night at the Union Chapel Church.[79]

He, too, was "abnormally nervous" when interviewed by the FBI. Leonius refused to get in the agents' car when questioned and was "hostile and resentful."[80] He allowed the interrogators to take his photograph,[81] but when it was shown to Loy Harrison he did not identify Leonius and said "to the best of his recollection he had never seen the man." It was a startling remark because Leonius was hard to forget, with missing teeth on the upper and lower jaw on the right side, and because Leonius had known Harrison for several years, even going to his home.[82]

Leonius said that at the time of the stabbing he was milking cows and did not go to the Barnett Hester house nor to the hospital. Neither of the Adcock brothers could remember precisely what they had done on the day of the lynchings, but their mother, looking "nervous and worried," suddenly declared to the FBI that she was "never so glad of anything in her life as the fact that her two boys spent the afternoon the lynchings occurred with her on the porch" of her home.[83]

One employee described to the agents how he had been in Leonius Adcock's home when several people ate there a few days after the stabbing. "I heard somebody say 'Roger will never stab anybody else.' Leonius had piped up, 'I don't think he will ever stab anybody else.'"[84]

Another black informant was convinced of Leonius's guilt. "Mr. Leonius jumps from place to place and he looks and acts scared ever since the FBI has been here," he confidentially told the overworked government officials.[85]

*

Powell Adcock, father of Alvin and Leonius, came naturally into the focus of investigators because of his sons' links to Moore's Ford. He had also married a sister of Bob Hester's wife and lived only a quarter mile from the stabbing victim.[86] In addition, Powell had bailed out the man who had earlier sold his pistol to Deputy Sheriff Howard[87] and would not allow his farmhands to keep any type of firearms, going so far as to confiscate several small arms from his tenants.[88]

A written comment by an agent conceded that "Powell appears to be more intelligent than his sons." However, he was described as "unfriendly" during the meeting and, though not particularly upset, "appeared to resent the interview, and gave no indication that he made any real effort to recall his activities on the day of the lynching."[89]

He said he had been home all day when the lynchings took place and that day had gone to the revival meeting at the Union Chapel Church about 8:00 p.m.[90] The first he heard of the killings was on a radio news broadcast the following day. This claim of innocence suffered a setback when a black informant shook off his fear to divulge what he knew. He told Hoover's men that he had gone to Powell's house two months after the four bodies were found by the riverside. When Powell asked where the man had been he replied that he was visiting a friend. Angrily, the farmer turned on him and snorted, "Probably been talking to the FBI." He accused the man and all the other "niggers" of talking too much. When the man asked Powell to pay him money owed for picking cotton, the irate white man ordered him first to pay money loaned for a car and then picked up a knife and charged the hapless servant.[91]

The same farmhand, who had worked for Powell Adcock in the Hestertown area, said the boss man beat him at Christmas the year

Loy Harrison (right) stands with the one-armed coroner W.T. Brown (center) and Oconee County Sheriff J.M. Bond (left) on the Moore's Ford Bridge, close to where four African Americans were lynched on July 25, 1946.

Loy Harrison (left), Oconee County Sheriff J.M. Bond (center), and coroner W. T. Brown (right) stand at the site of the lynching in Monroe, Georgia.

In 1946, a car could pass through the built-up area of downtown Monroe, Georgia, in not much longer than it took to fill the tank with gas.

Investigators from the FBI or the GBI question a farmer beside a cotton field and homes in rural Georgia after the lynching.

Mourners pay final respects to World War II veteran George Dorsey, as others file past the coffin of his sister, Dorothy Malcolm. George and Dorothy were two of the four victims lynched on July 25, 1946.

Copyright AP, Atlanta-Journal Constitution. Courtesy of Georgia State University

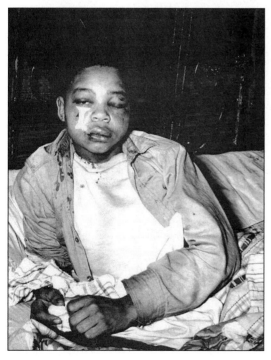

Lamar Howard, nineteen, resembles a battered boxer after being beaten by two white men for daring to testify before a grand jury looking into the lynching.

Copyright William A. Scott III and Atlanta Daily World. Courtesy of M. Alexis Scott, his daughter

Cartoonists all over the nation mocked the FBI for the lack of arrests in the case. Prominent cartoonist Bill Mauldin summed up the public's impatience in this devastating artwork three months after the crime.

88 Sherman P.
Jersey City 7, N.J.

Atty. Gen'l Tom C. Clark
Washington, D.C.

Dear Sir,

I wish to register the strong protest of an American citizen against the lynchings of Negro Americans. This is contrary to all rights and liberties guaranteed in our constitution.

Sincerely
Mrs. A. Willie Lefkowitz

Many protesters deluged the nation's capital with furious letters. This woman wrote to the attorney general that the lynchings were "contrary to all rights and liberties guaranteed in our constitution."

Courtesy of National Archives and Records Administration, College Park, Maryland

RECEIVED
RESPECTFULLY REFERRED SEP 4 - 1946
FOR CONSIDERATION
AND ACKNOWLEDGMENT CRIMINAL DIVISION
Aug. 21.
William D. Hassett
Secretary to the President

Dear President Truman
I am a little girl
about 12 year old
and I think that
someone up there
in Washington D.C
ought to put a stop
to these murders
+ slavery because
it is getting terrible
to walk down the
street any more
And someone ought to
do something

DEPARTMENT
SEP 4 6
CRIM.-CIVIL RIGHTS SEC.

RECORD
Sincerely
Miss Virginia Ann
8962 Jackson K.C. Mo

A twelve-year-old girl wrote to President Truman after the lynchings, saying "someone up there in Washington D.C. ought to put a stop to these <u>murders & slavery because</u> it is getting terrible to walk down the street."

Courtesy of National Archives and Records Administration, College Park, Maryland

Dear Mr. Clark:

It has been over a month now since the lynchings in Monroe, Ga., and the F.B.I., who were supposed to investigate, have as far as I know accomplished nothing.

I am beginning to think that "F.B.I." stands for "Finagles (with) Blithe Indifference" where the rights of colored citizens are concerned.

DO SOMETHING ABOUT IT!

J 7 McDuole

233/S. Hermitage Ave.
Trenton, 8, N. J.

Attorney General Tom Clark, together with the White House and the FBI, received some thirty thousand letters from protesters all over the country. In this letter, a scornful New Jersey resident writes, "I am beginning to think that 'F.B.I.' stands for 'Finagles (with) Blithe Indifference.'"

Courtesy of National Archives and Records Administration, College Park, Maryland

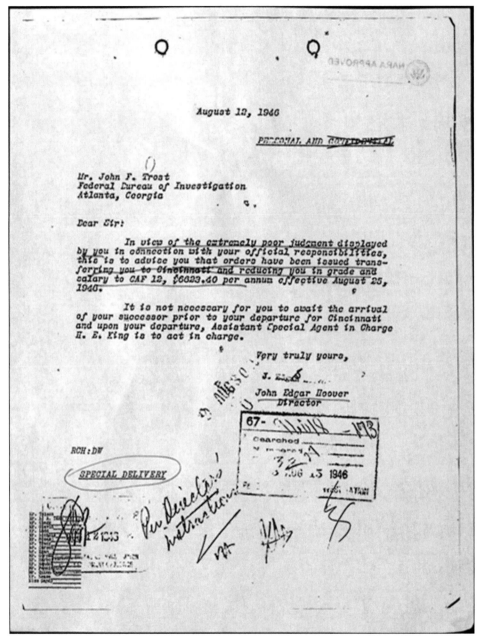

With controlled fury, FBI Director J. Edgar Hoover dismisses his inept top agent from further investigation of the murder of four African Americans in Georgia. Here he demonstrates his iron grip over subordinates.

Courtesy of National Archives and Records Administration, College Park, Maryland

before. He fled to Decatur, Illinois, and stayed with his father until the assailant appeared and took him back to the farm.[92]

The FBI had no legal right to demand weapons from any of those they investigated until they had shown a conspiracy involving a state official. They could only rely on suspects voluntarily handing over their guns. Powell owned a .32 Smith & Wesson special revolver but told the FBI it had not been fired in over a year.[93]

An offhand remark by Powell's wife to a black servant also piqued the interest of federal investigators. Only a week before gunshots took the lives of the four victims, Mrs. Adcock reportedly said there was no point in Roger's foster father taking clothes to him in jail because "he won't be able to wear them. He won't be able to walk around any more, because he stabbed that man for nothing."[94]

*

Melvin and Clarence Hester varied their tales to such an extent that the FBI had to run through their transcripts to make sense of what they might have done. Melvin met the agents at his home and immediately after they identified themselves blurted out, "I don't know a damn thing about it!"[95]

Initially he pretended to have had no time to go out and lynch people. Taking umbrage and markedly confrontational, he told the inquisitors he had definitely stayed home all day in the presence of his wife and daughter.[96] But the agents remained on guard. They knew that Melvin, who lived across the road from Barnett, to whom he was distantly related, was in Monroe on the last day of the victims' lives. What he now claimed was flatly at odds with Clarence Hester's insistence that the two of them arrived in Monroe about 3:00 p.m.[97] It also conflicted with an eyewitness who had known them for at least three years. He "positively" identified both men talking on a Monroe street in mid-afternoon the same day.[98]

It did not bother either Melvin or Clarence. They got together to wipe out inconsistences in their stories and present something of a united front.[99] Just three days after his first interview, Melvin was interrogated again, going to the agents' car outside his home without objecting. Although he was fairly friendly, he was as usual profane. Nevertheless, he refused to say whether he would hand over the names of the lynchers if he learned who they were.[100] He had not made a good impression on the agents and one of them would later dismiss him as "almost illiterate and states that he does not know his exact age but thinks he is about fifty."[101]

Yet this time Melvin, with noticeably false teeth, a square face, and high forehead,[102] admitted giving false evidence. It forced him to alter his fictional account. Now he acknowledged going to Monroe with Clarence between 3:00 and 4:00 p.m. on the day the four were found dead. "I just forgot," he shrugged.[103]

But he still clung to his position that he had neither seen Loy Harrison nor been to Moore's Ford in some fifteen years.[104]

Clarence Hester, a first cousin of the stabbed farmer, spoke out of both sides of his mouth when discussing whether he had enough time to join in killing the four. At first he said he got home after dark.[105] The next day he told the FBI another tale. His wife had just arrived home when he walked in soon after 5:00 p.m.[106] An alert FBI agent perked up. "During that particular season of the year (it) represents a difference of several hours," the agent noted.[107]

Clarence was questioned intensively but he would not yield, asserting "I have never been to Moore's Ford and I don't know where it is. No person approached me at any time and said anything to me about this lynching before it happened. I heard no talk at all in this vicinity or anywhere else regarding any revenge against Roger." He refused to concede anything, saying "I do not know Loy Harrison and I do not think I have ever heard of him."[108]

A large man at six feet two inches tall,[109] the thirty-six-year-old with long black hair, false teeth, a "sharp" face, and only a seventh grade education was so jittery at his interview with FBI agents that his hands shook and his voice broke several times.

His attempt to wriggle out of his involvement broke down after an acquaintance who knew him well said he had insured Clarence and

Melvin's cotton crops for years. He left his office the day of the lynchings to go to a poolroom for a glass of water. When he returned, he saw both men talking on North Broad Street about two hours before gunfire broke the quiet near Moore's Ford Bridge. He spoke to Melvin and recognized Clarence.[110]

Unfazed, Clarence replied that he could not remember being on that street that memorable day.[111] Instead, he recounted poisoning cotton until 3:00 p.m., when he drove into Monroe with Melvin. Clarence maintained he had gone to Thompson's barber shop for a haircut and then all of the men had drunk beers at Herbert Jackson's filling station until late afternoon, when he returned home. But Clarence was caught in a trap about the drinking when the man in charge of Jackson's beer place firmly denied any of them were there that afternoon.[112]

All the while Clarence was uncooperative, wanting to end the interview as quickly as possible, and admitted only reluctantly that he was accompanied by Melvin. Like many others he refused to sign the statement, covering more than five handwritten pages, even though he insisted it was true.[113]

*

There was much to sift through. Agents stayed late into the night trying to piece together a credible narrative of events and identities of the armed gang. They had transcribed the interviews of several thousand but dismissed much of it as imaginative and designed to mislead. None of the admissions or contradictions proved that the suspects were killers. And the mob still remained anonymous. Many suspects said they either did not own guns or did not possess them.[114] Nearly all of those who did own weapons would not surrender them. Others, who brought back pistols from the conflict in Europe, said they were either old or lacking ammunition.[115] One World War II veteran said they were banned from bringing ammunition back from Europe,[116] but another said he smuggled in a clip of bullets taken from a dead enemy soldier.[117] More importantly, there was still no legal basis for federal intervention.

There had to be other angles. The stabbing related to a white man alleged to have had sex with a black woman. Perhaps they should look more carefully at the sexual overtones. It might explain why Roger was not the only one to lose his life.

Sexual Relations

Straining under public pressure to capture the murderers, FBI agents concluded that sexual relations across the contemporary color divisions might have driven unnamed gunmen to snuff out the life of George Dorsey, the World War II veteran. After the handicapped farmhand, Ridden Farmer, saw him flirting with white girls, he cautioned Moena Williams, George's mother, to tell him that unless he stopped "he is liable to get his neck broken, or they might wake up some morning and find him missing."[1]

George had also offended whites by being, in the words of an informant, "uppity and mouthy," bragging about associating with white girls while in the army.[2] Farmer told the FBI that "he had heard it talked" that George and Robert Lee Elder said they had associated with white girls up north and they were going to keep on going with them.[3] Someone had overheard it said in his store that George "was going to get him some good clothes and ride the buses with the white girls." The middle-aged white man with missing teeth added reflectively, "I hope they catch who [sic] killed the negroes. They were negroes, but it was bad."[4]

George and his younger brother, Charlie Boy, had been socializing with the white Adams sisters, Ruth, seventeen, Effie Mae, fifteen, and Burice, eleven, and a white girl living with them, one and a half miles from Farmer's house, on a farm owned by Loy Harrison.[5] That year the tearful and homeless stranger was allowed to stay with the family when they saw her at a bus station and she blubbered that she had just buried her mother and her father had abandoned her. Mrs. Adams invited her to live with them on condition she acted like her daughters and did not run around with boys. "If you go as one of my daughters you won't have to pay no rent, but could help on the farm."[6] It was not long before she began flirting like the other girls. She showed an interest in George, telling the sisters how good looking he was. "I also heard her say she wished George Dorsey was a white boy instead of a nigger," said one of the sisters.[7]

The young women had few inhibitions. Even Loy's nephew claimed that he had sexual intercourse with Ruth Adams on a few occasions, though his contact was short-lived because he considered the family "a sorry lot."[8] But Charlie Boy and George, who had both been arrested earlier that year for drunk and disorderly behavior,[9] were not judgmental. They might have agreed that they were opportunists. The girls "got to acting sort of fresh around me and George. They used to say that they did not have no boy friends and that they wished they had some good-looking boys like me and George," Charlie Boy said. "They told us that they were just like colored women. [Redacted name] told my wife, Ruby, that if she was a colored woman she would take me away from her."

He told investigators that "several times their Mama sent them up to my house to borrow the smoothing iron and stuff. When they came they would hang around until their mother called them. They liked my brother George better than me as he was not married and I was." He recollected that his brother would go down to the Adams house and "play around" with the girls. At first he would go during the day, then he started going at night. George had told one of them that he wished she was black. She said she did, too. "I've seen them wink at one another and whisper to each other. I've seen George pat her several times and she did not object."

Speaking candidly to the FBI, Charlie Boy said the white girl living with the Adams family started playing around with George. "I saw him dance with [redacted name] twice at the Adams house and I have seen him feeling her up a little bit. I have heard her say that she wished she was black. She told my Mama this. About a week and a half after she came, George told me that he had had sex relations with her one night in a shed just across from the Adams house. He never did tell me whether or not he had had such relations with [redacted names], though I know that either of us could if we had wanted to."[10]

One of the sisters told the federal agents that Harrison's brother-in-law, Alvin Parrish, had come round once and asked her to go to the theater with him but she had refused. She also mentioned Robert Lee Elder, saying he had flirted with her several times and had tried to get her to go out to his Oldsmobile. She also accused him of trying to get Farmer's daughters to accompany him into the woods on several occasions.[11]

Charlie Boy said Harrison had come by and told George he had better stay away from the Adamses' house because the Ku Klux Klan would come and that he was a Ku Klux himself. He said the Ku Klux would get him and beat him and he might not be able to come back home when they got through with him. "But," said Charlie Boy, "George did not act like he was scared as he kept right on seeing these girls as he had before."[12]

Charlie Boy, also a veteran of the recent global conflict, had so impressed the FBI with his demeanor and statements that one of the agents reported he "appears to be intelligent, and in the absence of fear would make a satisfactory witness."[13]

An unidentified sister told Hoover's men that the only trouble came from the black men's uncle, Robert Lee Elder, who had tried to get her sister to go for a ride. Mrs. Martie Adams said she would see Harrison about it and he "would straighten it out."[14]

Elder, a World War II veteran, had also caught the censorious eye of Ridden Farmer. Just a few months earlier he had seen Elder twice drive by his house and call out to his daughters, "Hey, honey." On another occasion, he said, Elder had whistled at his wife. Farmer wrote a letter of complaint to the property's owner, Loy Harrison, whom he later met up with on the road and warned that "if it happened again he was going to find him as full of shots as would stick." Harrison promised to talk to Elder, following which he never again molested the family.[15]

The day after the lynchings a woman at the scene of the crime said Ridden Farmer appeared and volunteered that whoever had slain the four victims "had saved him a lot of trouble because they had done something he was going to have to do." He told those assembled by the Apalachee River that George Dorsey and other black men had passed by his house and hollered at his daughters. Only a day or two before the slayings, Farmer said he had lain on his front porch armed with a shotgun, waiting for George to come by, when he would kill him. When George did appear, Farmer asked what he meant by hailing his daughters. George denied he had done this, explaining that it must have been Robert Elder or Charlie Boy. Farmer then let George go, after threatening to shoot anyone who yelled at his daughters in the future.[16]

In a surprising twist, Mrs. Adams and her daughters then accused Harrison of making unwanted advances. The daughters told investigators that Harrison had tried about six times in the past year to get them to ride with him. "I will give you whatever you ask," they quoted him. They always declined, saying they had been told by someone living on his farm that he could not be trusted. One time, they had been told, Harrison waited for the husband to leave, then broke down the door and entered against the wife's wishes. "We told our Papa that he had been trying to get us to go to ride with him, and he spoke to Mr. Harrison about it. Mr. Harrison told him he didn't mean no harm."[17]

Mrs. Adams told the FBI that on February 4 that year her husband, George, had committed suicide by hanging himself. He did not leave a suicide note because all he could write was his name.[18] She passed on a rumor that Harrison had told her husband that she was intimate with a neighboring farmer. The rumor had apparently been the final straw in Adams's mental condition, the implication being it was the cause of his suicide.[19]

Before he took his own life, the sick man had passed along to Farmer that George Dorsey had spent three nights in the Adams home in the preceding fall. Adams had been ill and bedridden, but he suspected that George was merely helping out around the house. However, George Adams could not help noticing that the Dorsey brothers maintained relations with his daughters "closer than normally held" between blacks and white women. He had, after all, seen his daughters dancing while George played a guitar. But he had not seen the relationship go further. Farmer himself said he did not know whether George had sex with the girls, but the general belief was that he had.[20]

Mrs. Adams said that after her husband's death Harrison called by to say he would give her food and shelter. Three weeks later he suggested she move out, as the neighbors might accuse him of keeping a woman other than his wife on his property. She immediately left but just two weeks later she told agents that Harrison called to see her and asked for a date. She refused and was so livid that she packed up and moved out of this place as well.

Her late husband had been quite friendly with Harrison, and she said that she learned from both of them that Loy had been abusive to his black farmhands, frequently beating them.[21]

Now that they had insight into the sexual mores and illicit subterfuges of the area, it was time for the FBI director to save the reputation of his beleaguered Bureau. For much of the time he had been reacting to public pressure. Now his opponents cried out for arrests, and their voices grew more strident by the day.

Hoover Offensive

J. Edgar Hoover could have taken his cue from Abraham Lincoln's advice to a Civil War general when giving him command of the Armies of the Potomac: "Beware of rashness, but with energy, and sleepless vigilance, go forward and give us victories."[1] The longtime director of the FBI was never more energetic than when flushing out critics and protecting the good name of the Bureau, which he commanded with a father's devotion and the iron grip of a dictator. Keenly aware of his power and sensitive to his protective mission, Hoover exerted authority surpassed by few others beyond the walls of the White House.

Only four days after the Moore's Ford murders, he alerted Attorney General Tom Clark to plots that would exploit tensions over the racist murders. Reports had come onto Hoover's desk of Communists planning widespread protests and demonstrations that would give them an opportunity to influence and co-opt support from rank and file trade unionists. "Communists in the Philadelphia area are planning to demand your removal on the alleged basis that you, as a Southern Texas Democrat, will not follow through and prosecute the men responsible for the shooting," he warned. "The Party in this activity is seeking to obtain the cooperation and assistance of various trade unions."[2] He followed up with the names of "Communist elements and other organizations" said to be instigating and pressuring others to agitate. Among them were the "Communist" head of the National Negro Congress, the Southern Conference for Human Welfare, "reported to be under Communist influence," and the "Communist-controlled" American Youth for Democracy.[3]

Hoover's sword was always at the ready to duel against Communists, and he would shortly warn Americans of the contagious nature of their foremost foe. "Communism, in reality, is not a political party," he explained to a rapt and respectful House of Representatives Committee on Un-American Activities. "It is a way of life—an evil and malignant way of life. It reveals a condition akin to disease that spreads like an epidemic, and like an epidemic a quarantine is necessary to keep it from affecting the nation." In Hoover's eyes, the most vulnerable institutions were the trade unions. "I do fear," he told the legislators, "so long as American labor groups are infiltrated, dominated, or saturated with the virus of Communism. I do fear the palliation and weasel-worded gestures against Communism indulged in by some of our labor leaders, who should know better, but who have become pawns in the hands of sinister but astute manipulations for the Communist cause."[4]

Foremost among those to congratulate Hoover on his stand against Communists was a former vicious foe, Senator Kenneth McKellar (D-TN), who now said he was "delighted" with the director's views. "We must get rid of Communists in this country," he agreed enthusiastically.[5] Only eleven years earlier, while serving as chairman of the Subcommittee of the US Senate Committee on Appropriations, McKellar had tried unsuccessfully to reduce Hoover's budget, tearing into him with a personal fury, even questioning his background, including his admission that he had never made an arrest.[6] While Hoover had his underlings build up a file on his adversary, he had simultaneously courted the senator's friendship and succeeded so well that years later Charles Weeks, then SAC Memphis, Tennessee, wrote the director, "He [McKellar] expressed the opinion that you are the most honorable public official in Washington."[7]

Hoover was always stoked for a counterpunch when learning of slurs against his Bureau. His weapons were compromising files built up over years of elaborate surveillance. Then it was vintage Hoover, who unleashed the full reach of his wrath as if spewing dragon-like fire. Two weeks after the riverside slaughter, the Washington edition of the *Afro-American* newspaper published a cartoon lampooning the FBI over its futile hunt for the Georgia killers. Captioned, *Who're You Trying to Kid?* the cartoon portrayed an FBI sleuth promising, "We are leaving no stone unturned to bring the lynchers to justice!" as he peered through a magnifying glass while lifting stones, even as armed white men took cover behind his cloak. The Bureau's secret dossier on the cartoonist, Ralph Matthews, had already marked him as a Communist who had rhapsodized four years earlier that "the salvation of Russia was the only hope of the democracies."

Notwithstanding his political tilt, Matthews had been accredited a year later to the White House as a representative of the Baltimore *Afro-American*.[8] Angered by the cartoonist's "left-handed attack upon the Bureau," Hoover instantly ordered a "discreet investigation."[9] Ten days later the findings branded Matthews as "woman and whiskey crazy, possessing poor character and one who runs with a fast set." Wiretaps of Communist Party headquarters confirmed past telephone contacts with Matthews, but he had since reversed his political bias, and reportedly was now "very anti-Russian and hates the Communists."[10]

When Hoover learned that Paul Robeson, the internationally renowned black singer, actor, civil rights activist, and suspected Communist, would be highlighting a meeting in Massachusetts to protest the lynchings, he reacted with predictable irritation and harsh criticism of the attorney general for failure to tell the public how the FBI's hands were tied. Hoover and Justice Department lawyers had sensed early on that unless the sheriff's office or other Georgia state officials could be implicated in the murder, there might be no grounds for federal jurisdiction. This could hobble and possibly disqualify the FBI's involvement. Failure to tie state employees to the mob, suggesting a conspiracy to "injure and oppress" the slain four "in the exercise of their right to due process of law," would probably strip the Bureau of legal standing, and disallow its hope for federal search warrants to locate the weapons used.[11] Hoover's ever-sensitive antennae detected a grim scenario in which his Bureau would be unfairly condemned, by a public ignorant of the strict limitations of the law.

He bared his frustration in the usual manner of communicating with aides, by filling in blank spaces on official documents with his bold and untidy scribble. He scratched his scorn on the memo requesting his opinion for the attorney general on whether a Justice Department official should attend the meeting in Boston to explain the narrow jurisdiction of the federal government in civil rights cases. The attendance of the governor of Massachusetts would inevitably be overshadowed by the formidable presence of Robeson, who had never confirmed suspicions of being an advocate if not an ardent apologist for Soviet Communism.

"The storm developing is inevitable when Dept. (of Justice) waltzes into every kind of case merely to appease a minority, particularly when no jurisdiction exists," Hoover scrawled. "I think it height of folly to participate in public meetings and forums of kind in Mass., for questions are bound to be asked of a leading character. The sooner the A.G. issues a statement on the limitations of the law, so as to inform the public of fact it is lack of law and not the lack of interest—the better." Then, in a corner still blank, he signed off, "You may advise A.G. of all three of these observations by me."[12]

The attorney general did all he could to defuse the situation. When he received a letter from Robeson saying 3,000 Americans would meet in conference to end lynching, and requesting a meeting with Clark, he replied that September 23 "happens to be my birthday" but arranged to meet a small delegation that day.[13]

Hoover's disgruntlement at critics led him to counterattack in kind. As soon as he learned that the *New York Post's* eminent crime reporter, Victor Riesel, had savaged the Bureau for failing to hunt down the killers in Georgia, Hoover whipped his inner circle into action. "I fear it is just the beginning of a series of editorials which will appear in various papers of the country unless we do two things," he warned. "It is imperative that the civil rights cases be very promptly and vigorously handled and most carefully supervised, both in the field and at Washington."

Then he outlined a plan to infiltrate the media by syndicating a planted feature favorable to the FBI. Preferably, it would be written by someone unconnected with the FBI, who would laud its accomplishments in investigating civil rights cases. "We have over a period of years handled very effectively peonage cases and various other cases involving the interests of minorities," he wrote in a confidential memo. "Nothing has been said about these types of cases but a great deal of emphasis has been

placed upon any one of these cases on which we do not 'click.'" To drive
home his point he added, "the need is now more pressing than ever, particularly in view of the criticism which is now starting of the Bureau for
its failure to obtain prompt results in the Malcolm case."[14]

But the media offensive intensified as the weeks passed by without
an arrest. A syndicated story by Scripps-Howard cited the FBI's "fruitless efforts" to crack the crime. The article quoted the nationally circulated black weekly *Pittsburgh Courier*, questioning "how so many detec-
tives could have failed to uncover one single clue. How is it," the *Courier*
asked, "that men who could catch the most elusive criminals are unable
to track down a few back-country Georgia murderers?"[15]

Though the article explained the narrow scope for federal intervention, Hoover scribbled his simmering discomfort at the bottom. "This is
just what I feared would be the reaction. We had no business to allow
State police to jockey us into such a position. I again and again expressed
my concern re the setup in Georgia of Weeks' squad, but both he and the
supervisory staff here *failed* to sense the ultimate reaction."[16]

The Georgia Bureau of Investigation had ceded nearly all of the
investigation to the FBI, deferring to its superior skills and welcoming its
enviable resources. In the process, it all but withdrew from the probe, an
official saying, "The best people in town won't talk about this."[17] Barely a
month after the lynchings, the GBI cut its assistance to a single operative.
GBI input had been insignificant, but its vanishing role had saddled the
Bureau with sole responsibility for the outcome of the investigation, a
situation Hoover was anxious to avert.[18]

His reservations surfaced again after he learned that the sole GBI
operative was not only incompetent and untrustworthy, but also insen-
sitive to the need for discretion. The operative told Weeks that an
unnamed organization of blacks had offered him $1,000 to help solve
the case. He said he planned to use the money to pay off black maids
working for white suspects so that they could smuggle weapons out of
their employers' homes. GBI would then be able to test-fire them for
possible links to the crime. Weeks had also advised Hoover that the GBI
operative was "very talkative" and even though he would not be given

confidential information, an FBI agent should be assigned to be with him at all times to prevent him from jeopardizing the probe.

"Why do we have to chaperone [redacted name]?" Hoover asked. "He is not of FBI and we are not chargable [sic] with his derelictions."[19]

When told that Weeks wanted the lone GBI operative paired with an FBI agent because the latter might pick up valuable information and could prevent the careless operative from passing on sensitive material to "ignorant and illiterate" blacks, Hoover grudgingly consented, even as he sensed pitfalls.

"OK," he wrote on the document from a top aide, "but I fear by doing so FBI assumes responsibility we shouldn't have. Georgia can certainly claim no move was made by it without knowledge and acquiescence of FBI, and that all [redacted] was, was a liaison for FBI and that FBI was making the investigation and not Georgia."[20]

In delicate maneuvering to overcome doubtful federal jurisdiction, Weeks pressed for close collaboration with the GBI. He suggested that once the identity of suspects had been fairly well established, the GBI should get search warrants to look for personal weapons in each of their homes. But to prevent suspects from being tipped off beforehand and then rushing to hide their guns, Weeks proposed that FBI agents be inside the homes, interviewing each of the suspects, at the moment the search warrants were served. It would then be impossible for suspects to run off and conceal their shotguns, rifles, and pistols.

Again, Hoover reacted with misgivings. "I am concerned about the way this is developing," he wrote in his familiar bold handwriting that sloped left and right. "Apparently we are doing *all* or *most* of the work and yet when case is to be broken some Georgia politician is to do *all* or *most* of the talking. In other words if case is lost FBI will get the brickbats but if won FBI will be out of the picture."[21]

Nevertheless, he was cautious about ceding powers to the GBI while the Bureau remained in charge. Hoover had no objection when a top aide counseled, "an effort will be made to find some legal basis upon which the Bureau can obtain search warrants enabling us to keep this matter completely bottled up within the Bureau." The director appended his usual reaction at the base of the document: "I agree. We ought to be able to handle this ourselves."[22]

Meanwhile, the daily flow of teletypes from Weeks sustained Hoover's confidence. Some leads looked promising. Informants continued to be coaxed and cultivated. Periodically a breakthrough seemed imminent, particularly when the supervising agent in Monroe declared, "Believe two participants fairly certain."[23] Two days later Weeks wrote, "Progress in obtaining some valuable informants whose identities must be protected carefully."[24] A week later the field office informed Washington, "It is believed we are nearing some good results."[25]

But encouraging reports were dashed by harsh realities. Reluctantly, Weeks had to admit, "The stories related by Harrison and by the sheriff and his deputies have stood up this far and are all plausible."[26] Even though he noted with confidence that "re-interviews are frequently much more productive than the originals and some of the hostility has been dissipated," the stubborn front held firm among the phalanx of suspects.[27] Aware of the slow progress, Weeks asked if Hoover still required a daily teletype. The answer, marked Urgent, came back affirmatively.[28] But time was running out, forcing the agents to speed up their enquiries as the season to pick cotton was almost at hand.[29] The farmhands, however, were no sooner out in the fields than heavy rains slowed down the investigation.[30] Almost two months into the case, Weeks had no option but to advise the Bureau, "Harrison is so cold that the probability of breaking him is very remote."[31]

Stymied by the resistance of suspects within the unified white community, Weeks considered bugging private homes. Listening devices had proven unusable in the rural areas. Now he suggested installing electronic surveillance in the Atlanta home of a person of interest and that "he be agitated" into talking about the case through interviews. "The purpose of this surveillance would, of course, be merely to find out what these people are talking about in private, this being a matter we have never been able to develop through interviews," he elaborated.[32]

Weeks would not give up on his hunt for the weapons. Because pistols represented the best possibility of identifying the firearms, a special effort was made to locate them. Agents descended on pawn shops and second-hand stores from Atlanta to Athens, as well as scattered outlets selling ammunition. But once more Weeks had to convey the discouraging news that "a number of the suspects are definitely lying about their possession of such weapons and considerable investigation will be required."[33]

However, the relentlessly methodical head of the Monroe squad had succeeded in narrowing the geographic area from where the killers originated. He had drawn up a map [never located] covering an area in all directions within twenty miles of Monroe. On it he had marked every dwelling, with the identities of all owners and occupants on roads leading to and from the crime scene.[34] It showed clearly that the killers came from, and returned to, the direction of Good Hope, south of which lay Hestertown. Its residents were the most logical suspects because, as he relayed to Washington, they were related to the victim of the stabbing and had a common motive to kill. Other suspects lived in the vicinity of Harrison's farm in Oconee County. Some, most notably James Bradley Verner, lived a mile from Gratis, northwest of Moore's Ford.[35]

But Hoover was impatient. No evidence had been found to link Georgia state officials or law enforcement officers with the killers, and nothing had been found to establish a violation of federal statutes. Almost two months had elapsed since the victims fell by the river, yet few of the suspects had voluntarily delivered up personal weapons, and none had implicated their owners. Hoover had been advised that as matters stood no court would authorize search warrants for the FBI. Even in the unlikely event that a court approved the request, Hoover estimated that at least 100 agents would simultaneously have to search the homes, barns, outbuildings, and other premises of a considerable number of whites in the vicinity of Monroe. Inevitably, he foresaw a backlash for this type of "mass action" by the FBI, given the probability that nothing would be found in many of the targeted buildings.

Having highlighted the negatives, the squat head of the Bureau signed off to his superior, Attorney General Tom Clark, with a transparent appeal for agreement to terminate FBI involvement. "I would, therefore, appreciate your advising me specifically what your desires are with reference to the continuation of the investigation at Monroe, Georgia," he wrote.[36]

The attorney general would make up his mind, and Hoover had no choice but to bow to rank.

Pre-Grand Jury

Attorney General Tom Clark had handwritten to the head of the FBI, "Let's have a G.J. (grand jury) real quick."[1] It was a decree that Hoover had to accept. But he signaled his real feelings when Weeks suggested reducing the number of agents working on the case if a grand jury did not come into being. Penning his own dictate on the document, Hoover ordered, "Be certain to do this."[2]

As the grand jury prepared to meet, nobody seemed to know for certain whether the federal government had any right to go forward with the case. By now hostility toward the FBI had diminished because agents had followed orders to take "scrupulous care" in their conduct.[3] But Hoover regretted the FBI's entanglement. Accumulated evidence tended to show that it should have been treated as a state murder, investigated solely by the Georgia Bureau of Investigation. A month after ordering his lead investigator in Monroe to cut back on staff, he intervened again. "I have always doubted wisdom of Dept [of Justice] ordering us into this case because of lack of jurisdiction. Try to reduce our squad on it as soon as possible," he again demanded of Weeks.[4]

Yet the autocratic head of the Bureau harbored second thoughts. Perhaps a grand jury might lead to deeper questioning of suspects, determining whether Harrison or the sheriff's office had leaked information to the gunmen. This might indeed justify calling in a grand jury. He suggested "witnesses before the grand jury could be questioned as to any possible notice given by Lewis Howard that Roger Malcolm was being released on bond." Hoover let it be known that he had information that the deputy sheriff was married to a distant relative of the Hester family, "who are regarded as strong suspects."[5]

He did not argue when the attorney general wrote, "Dear Edgar, I think our activity in Monroe, Georgia case should continue until we find out who did it—what do you think?"[6] Quickly, Hoover told his representative on the spot that "a grand jury has been ordered."[7]

It satisfied the FBI man in charge at Monroe. Charles Weeks was still hopeful that the weapons were key to a breakthrough, reporting to his director, "Our only possibility of arriving at a solution of the case is locating one of the weapons used and securing a firearms identification."[8] He told Hoover that the only large project facing them was a check among the area's veterans, who might have brought back ammunition from European battlefields and later used it to slay the Moore's Ford victims. Weeks estimated there were about two thousand discharged veterans in the three counties surrounding the murder site. Initially, inquiries were directed solely at white veterans discharged from the European theater who might have imported 9-mm. bullets. Some bullets found at the crime scene, "undoubtedly of German manufacture," could have been fired at the two couples.[9] "Care is being taken to avoid an appearance of our making a general investigation of veterans, which might bring some criticism upon us," Weeks was careful to note.[10] However, he soon reported that questioning had been "unproductive."[11]

On the eve of the grand jury hearing, more than forty weapons, or test specimens fired from weapons of all of the principal suspects, would be in the hands of the FBI, but, a dejected Weeks noted, "no identification has been effected." And ownership of guns used in the crime would probably "not be admitted."[12] On the other hand, a hearing might allow search warrants for elusive guns, which suspects denied they possessed.[13] Hoover shared this optimism. "If some of the suspects' guns could be obtained . . . it is possible that a positive identification might be made by the Bureau's laboratory to show that some of the bullets now in our possession were fired from some of these guns," he confided to the attorney general.[14] Weeks had always believed that the weapons might have been permanently disposed of, or secreted only for the time being. Experience had convinced him not to expect quick results, especially since it was unlikely anyone would voluntarily give up their guns.[15] Hoover, too, was hopeful of securing federal search warrants for guns possessed by suspects, if evidence cast strong suspicion on the sheriff's office.[16]

Sixteen years with the FBI had taught Weeks the many ways of flushing out a suspect. Now he hoped professional lawyers would enmesh Harrison, "who had obviously lied to us." Slyly deceptive, Harrison had pretended not to know the Hester clan, but the Bureau learned that his wife was related to some of them, and that a number of Hesters had shot birds and barbequed on his farm.[17]

The Justice Department was doubtful witnesses would reveal any more than they had already told the FBI. However, they too left open the faint possibility that, faced with a grand jury, witnesses might give details they had up to then withheld. It was hoped that the closed inquiry would entice recalcitrant witnesses to open up. Vivian Tillman and James Verner could be asked why Harrison had spent so much time at the ice plant shortly before the killings. It might even allow sharp questioning under oath of Bob Hester and Deputy Sheriff Howard about their meeting on the morning of the lynchings. Weeks thought suspects "should be questioned along the lines of whether Lewis Howard, or any other member of the sheriff's office, advised them in any way that Roger was being taken out on bond." He told Hoover, "Other than this point, there would probably be little grounds for taking suspects before the grand jury."[18]

Even though Hoover was a hardened realist, he understood the power of an oath. He thought some witnesses might be so fearful of the consequences of lying under oath that they would tell the truth, even if they felt uncomfortable in doing so. Suspects would also be questioned about alibis that had proven to be false. But, he cautioned, it would be inadvisable to call most black informants if it could be avoided. If named, their lives would be endangered. Instead, agents would repeat their testimony, especially that of roadside observers watching suspects in passing cars, contradictions notwithstanding.[19]

Witnesses would also be encouraged to waive immunity, though it was unlikely they would agree to this. If it were to happen, Hoover decreed that only Harrison, representatives of the sheriff's office, and those who incriminated themselves would be asked to sign waivers of immunity. "Loy Harrison has consistently claimed that he was perfectly innocent of any complicity in the lynching and had nothing to do with notifying the members of the mob," he wrote the attorney general. "The only other logical source of information to the members of the mob appears to be the sheriff's office."[20]

Even US Attorney John Cowart cast a damper by insisting there was no evidence to connect the sheriff's office to the lynching. He was well aware that the attorney general outranked him, and he would call a grand jury if ordered to. Yet he would not amend his stance, finding there was no legal justification for the FBI making any investigation, and it might be advisable to withdraw. However, he knew Harrison personally, having prosecuted him before, and thought he was the kind of person who would "fight every case to the end." But there was a chance, he thought, that Harrison was the type who might make a deal to name the members of the mob if he could be persuaded that otherwise he would be convicted on internal revenue charges.[21]

A lot of hopes hinged on what might happen in the secret session. According to the outgoing governor, the names of as many as fifteen to seventeen of the mob were known to insiders, but so far it had been difficult to get evidence to convict them.[22]

As the date neared for jurors to take their seats, Hoover ordered Weeks to prepare summaries reflecting witness discrepancies and the possibility of getting them to divulge more than they had already outlined.[23] There would be much material to absorb. The FBI had interrogated more than 2,790 witnesses since the lynchings.[24]

Weeks was a meticulous planner, a trait recognized from his earliest days at the FBI.[25] One of the first witnesses would be a person who admitted to some knowledge of what took place at Towler's Woods, only hours before the primaries. Were they really planning a jailbreak to grab Roger and lynch him? If so, it would surely compromise some of the suspects. Others with a fair knowledge of what happened in the woods would also be called to testify. Hopefully someone would answer the question. It would then put the sheriff's office on the defensive because both deputies had sworn they knew nothing about a plot to storm the jail and did not pass on news of the timing of Roger's release.[26]

Weeks also wanted to summon a few of the incarcerated, even though their sullied reputations would weaken them and cast doubt on the testimony of convicts. In deference to Hoover, he expected members of the sheriff's office to be examined once more, only this time to be grilled relentlessly. The case might crack wide open if only those who knew, or perhaps saw, the killers would be brave enough to tell the truth. Shrewd prosecution could ease or even entrap the facts out of Harrison's sons, his farmhands, and swimmers who might have been near the bloodbath. There was no telling what they would say under rigorous questioning.[27]

Nonetheless, the case might still flounder on jurisdiction. An aide close to the director was adamant that there was no evidence to link any state official to the crime. He was fortified by five reports ranging in length from 80 to 757 pages that had come in, none of which had proven this connection.[28] The head of the FBI agreed. "The investigation conducted so far has failed to indicate a federal violation," he concluded.[29] However, contradictions in witnesses' statements had to be addressed. Perhaps new facts might emerge under questioning.[30]

As the date approached for momentous hearings before the grand jury, Weeks told Hoover his entire squad of agents would be needed until its conclusion. Only then should the number be "greatly reduced."[31]

Both the Justice Department and federal judge T. Hoyt Davis of the Middle District of Georgia, who would preside over the grand jury, favored having it meet at Athens rather than at Macon because it was closer to the homes of the suspects, and Georgians would be in charge rather than appointees from Washington. "It would have been done by their own people and there would be less possibility of criticism, and a better impression would be made during a subsequent trial," the FBI agent in charge of the field office reported.[32] He preferred holding the grand jury in Macon because a panel drawn in Athens "would undoubtedly include representatives from Walton County" and witnesses might be confronted by people they knew, making them less inclined to part with secret information.[33]

Eventually the date of December 3 was set for the grand jury to meet in Athens.[34] No one thought it would stretch longer than a week. Witnesses would surely be done by then.[35]

The twenty-three jurors comprised thirteen farmers, two merchants, two coal dealers, a barber, a cotton gin operator, a banker, a laundry manager, a clerk, and one "retired farmer."[36] But, as if to underscore the grand jury faults, Weeks said sixty names of prospective jurors had been drawn and "a few of these are from the vicinity of Monroe."[37] Clearly, he expected the jury to be tainted.

Apart from the jurors, only three journalists were allowed in the courtroom during the twenty-five-minute instruction by the judge.[38] He told those empanelled to inquire "fearlessly and fairly."[39]

Grand Jury

Testimony was only into its sixth day when the stunned lead investigator, Charles Weeks, passed on that "most of the witnesses for the grand jury are lying."[1] Disheartened, he told Washington that it was not acquiring any evidence of value. Even the government's main backers despaired of a breakthrough. The deflated attorney general told Hoover by telephone that the grand jury had "almost broken down."[2] Disliking a policy of straddling the fence, the FBI director decided to cut his losses and salvage whatever he could. Always thoughtful and never impulsive, Hoover thought that further "agitation" would be caused by letting the matter hang in mid-air rather than closing it. To his top aides he remarked, "I want to bring this to an early termination."[3] The attorney general agreed, saying very little had been achieved and that "he believed he would close the case."[4]

Events had spun out of control. Just before the federal grand jury assembled, Theron Caudle, assistant attorney general in the Department of Justice criminal division, had told Hoover that a federal violation could not be excluded until the identities of the mob had been established. And, he said, conferences between the FBI and lead prosecution lawyers would eliminate the need for a summary report. To which an indignant Hoover replied with characteristic pique, which many of his critics would call vindictive. "I am surprised we took position we would not prepare a summary report irrespective of what the facts developed showed," Hoover pounced. "Such an attitude puts me in an untenable position. It can certainly be misconstrued by our enemies," whom he did not name.[5]

Weeks, who had rented an office with a private telephone at the Holman Hotel in Athens,[6] wanted to use a lie detector in court on at least three people. The US attorney supported him, even suggesting the machines should be turned on before the grand jury. But the desperate idea of a beleaguered FBI underling was quickly scuttled by Washington, which argued that the Bureau would be accused of using "coercive force" against the witnesses. "I concur," Hoover signed off.[7]

A tall but pale, weak, and gaunt Barnett Hester appeared before the jurors when the grand jury assembled early in the hearings.[8] His serious stab wound and almost three-week hospitalization had taken their toll on his formerly robust spirits.[9] It would be many months before he could remove the tube inserted into his side to drain the wound under his heart, which he told reporters he wore when testifying.[10] He was followed in strict secrecy by Loy Harrison, who emerged after three and a half hours in the witness room[11] to shout back at inquisitive reporters, "I don't know a damn thing!"[12] None of their testimony leaked out to the media.

An even more dangerous incident erupted when Walton County bailiff Ray Flanigan tried to eject reporters from a room not far from where jurors were listening to evidence. He suddenly grabbed a license to carry a pistol, which a gunsmith had given a newspaperman, and screamed at anyone within earshot, "I'm Ray Flanigan! Don't you men talk to these newspapermen! They just came over here to write a pack of lies!" When a journalist asked Flanigan, who had been a member of the coroner's jury, if he were a federal marshal, the bailiff answered, "It's none of your damn business who I am!" Before being forcibly removed by federal officers from the third floor, Flanigan roared at the journalists, "Get out and stay out! I don't care if (President) Truman said you could stay!" As Flanigan was taken away, lawmen reassured the reporters that they had the right to be there.[13]

Standing by in the wings was Mrs. Jesse Warwick, whose Methodist missionary husband told newsmen she would testify that she was returning from missionary work in Monroe when she saw three carloads of men talking at Towler's Woods when there were known to be people meeting there the night before the primaries. Her husband noted that it was not far from where the four victims were shot to death.[14]

By the third day it was clear the jurors would be seated long past an anticipated week. Few witnesses were quizzed each day, while those still to be heard overflowed the courthouse waiting rooms. None of them were summoned at the opening and only two were called the next day.[15]

Weeks had interviewed a prisoner in the Walton County jail, but the inmate had been "scared to death" and nothing of value had been extracted from him. The SAC thought the man might be lynched, and an aide to Hoover said this would cause "a great hue and cry" because the Bureau would not have safeguarded him and would be charged with not protecting the prisoner. He told Weeks to discuss the sensitive issue with the US attorney and bow to his feelings. The aide was unimpressed by the manner in which the grand jury was developing and believed that the majority of the witnesses had lied. He recommended that as soon as the hearings ended, assuming nothing of value arose, the squad of FBI agents could be slashed to one or two men from the Atlanta office.[16]

Under the final paragraph Hoover had written, "I want to bring this to an early termination, with of course proper regard to the thorough handling of the case."[17]

The day before the hearings closed, an internal document circulating among the FBI's top echelon said the Bureau "considered it a serious mistake to have any recommendation which would require further investigation of this case, because the facts had failed to disclose any violation of a federal statute within the Bureau's jurisdiction." The finding was passed down to Weeks.[18]

Hoover himself had determined that the grand jury should be halted because it had considered "very little." As it would have to be closed sometime, it might as well be now. He advised the attorney general to stop the investigation as soon as the grand jury ended. This would avoid "further agitation and exploitation" of the lynchings.[19]

During the sixteen days of hearings, an impartial observer would have agreed with Weeks's impression that there was a "strong conspiracy of silence" among those who must have known about the bloodletting. The SAC in charge of the probe was in no doubt that many of the witnesses were "lying." Others who should have given evidence were not even called because they said they would "not feel secure" if they testified. Some were even embarrassed before the grand jury, adding to their animosity. Weeks thought the suspects were demonstratively "hostile, very nervous, and frightened, and absolutely unwilling to tell anything they knew."[20] Worse still, one witness was thought by the US attorney to have "lied palpably."[21] Many witnesses even retracted their statements and claimed never to have intended them to mean what they originally said. Perhaps the most egregious example of bias in favor of the suspects was that one of the jurors was reportedly related to most of those thought to have been part of the mob. Two other jurors were apparently interested in protecting witnesses, who were thought to be lying rather than telling the truth.[22]

Some of the blacks had testified, but only after they said they felt safe enough to do so. Officials still worried about their well-being, but it was doubted that any of them would actually be lynched. The federal government backed away from accepting responsibility for these blacks, other than determining whether they wanted to testify. "Many of them were not called because they stated they would not feel secure if they testified," Weeks reported to Hoover.[23]

Testimony from jail trustee Major Jones would have been devastating for Deputy Sheriff Howard had the jury believed him. The inmate said he overheard Howard saying in the jail office, "The reason they killed George Dorsey was because when he was in the army overseas he took a white girl away from a white soldier from Oconee County."[24]

The convict, Major Jones, repeated that he was picking beans in a garden when Howard came out to see him and seemed convinced that a jailbreak was imminent. "He told me a mob wanted to come get Roger out of jail." In the testimony heard by the closed court, Jones claimed he was visited in the jail by Howard, who said they were going to subpoena the trustee. "He then said 'Let's go out here and talk this over.' We went out to Mr. Howard's car. Mr. [Deputy Sheriff] "Doc" Sorrells was sitting in the front seat. I got in the back. Mr. Howard said the reason he had me sleep upstairs was because it was around election time and he was afraid 'they' might do something to scare the negroes, and also there was a toilet up there, which the run-around did not have. He told me to say, if they ask me before the grand jury, that I had taken some medicine and asked him to let me sleep upstairs."[25]

But jurors would have to weigh the word of a jailed felon, serving a sentence for murder, against the vehement denials of a lawman distantly related to the Hesters.

To top it all, Police Chief Ben Dickinson changed his story during the hearing. Earlier he had told the FBI that the meeting at Towler's Woods the night before the primary election was to plan for Roger's abduction from jail.[26] Now he told jurors that he had never received a report of a meeting at Towler's Woods. To make matters worse, the mayor of Monroe said he thought the police chief might have said something about it, but he could not remember the exact words.[27]

Both lawyers agreed with Weeks that there was now no point in continuing with the investigation of the shootings because it was unlikely that anything new would transpire.[28] Hoover gave the nod, prophesying that "the most sound finding which the current grand jury could make would be that the thorough and complete investigation by the FBI, as presented to the grand jury, fails to disclose any evidence of a violation of a federal statute."[29]

Understandably, the jury of twenty-three men, made up of twenty-one whites and two blacks, was apparently "somewhat divided" over the investigation.[30] But when the formal findings were handed down on December 19, the statement was agreed to by everyone and unsurprising in its content.

"We, the grand jury, have carefully and patiently, during the past three weeks investigated the killing of four Negroes in Walton County, Georgia, which occurred on July 25, 1946.

"Numerous witnesses called as a result of the extensive four months investigation by the Federal Bureau of Investigation have been questioned exhaustively. Our efforts have been centered upon establishing the identities of the individuals who are responsible for these deaths.

"The members of this body are unanimous in reporting that we have been unable to establish the identity of any person or persons participating in the murders or in any violation of the Civil Rights statutes of the United States. Signed: Charley S. Rowe, Foreman."

As an appendage, they thanked the US attorney and the special assistant to the attorney general for their "untiring efforts in bringing the witnesses and evidence before this jury."[31] Hoover's prophecy had been amply fulfilled.

Assistant Attorney General Caudle contacted the FBI by telephone, hoping they would "quietly pull all the agents off the lynchings in Monroe."[32] Only nine were on the case when the grand jury shut down, a drop from a peak of twenty.[33] Within days the Department of Justice made it official. "You may discontinue the investigation in this case," it ordered the FBI.[34] Ironically, Caudle himself would be imprisoned fourteen years later, following conviction on an indictment charging conspiracy to defraud the federal government of income tax money. Paroled after five months, he was pardoned by President Lyndon Johnson in 1965.[35]

A staggering 125 witnesses had testified[36] and the grand jury was now left with three options. It could indict someone for perjury or participating in the mob. It might turn over evidence to state officials for a possible murder trial. Or finally it could take no action, leaving the matter entirely up to the state courts.[37]

They decided to issue the lone indictment against Alvin Adcock, forty, a pudgy man at five feet nine and missing all his teeth from the lower right jaw.[38] He admitted that he was lying to the FBI when he said he had not gone to Monroe on the day of the lynchings when in fact he had gone there with his father and brother. Contradicting his claim that he had not been to the crime scene, the man with bloodshot eyes[39] now said he had gone with his brother, Leonius, to Moore's Ford the following day, when he saw twenty or more men there. "I lied about this trip to Moore's Ford too when I first talked to the FBI. I want to tell the truth now," he confessed to agents. "But I don't know anything about the lynching or any plans that might have been made to kill the negroes, or anyone who was in the lynching."[40]

Leonius added to his brother's travails when he corrected his earlier story by saying that he had gone with his brother and father in a Dodge pickup truck to Monroe on the morning of the lynchings. "I denied this when the FBI talked to me before but now I wish to tell the truth," he said contritely.[41]

Alvin was indicted for perjury on two counts. He had made a false statement under oath to the grand jury, saying he did not leave his home for Monroe, and he had falsely denied going to the crime scene. He was arrested and taken before the US District Court where bond was set at $2,000.[42] Alvin was then released and the bond was returnable in June 1947. It was continued to the first week in December 1947, then to June 1948, and finally dropped in March 1949 after the US attorney told the Justice Department that a conviction would be unlikely, and that a trial would require reviewing in open court secret testimony given before the grand jury.[43]

Nobody knows why Leonius escaped indictment on similar untruths.

Judge Davis congratulated the jury for its "painstaking and thorough" work. However, the jury was not dismissed but only recessed so that if new information came to light, the same grand jury would be summoned, obviating the need to call witnesses all over again.[44]

Weeks told Hoover he would depart for New Orleans by the first available transport.[45] He also advised the director of the FBI that he understood transcripts of the testimony might have been sent to the Department of Justice for review.[46] However, more than seven decades later, the grand jury testimony could not be found despite a rigorous search of the Georgia National and State archives; the FBI in Atlanta and Washington, DC, courts in Macon, Athens, and Monroe; the archives of the US attorney appearing in the case; the National Archives in College Park, Maryland; and even requests made under the Freedom of Information Act.

The night after the calamitous end of the grand jury, Assistant Attorney General Caudle repeated himself, telling the FBI in Washington that no comment should be made to local authorities, and that the Justice Department did not want any further investigation.[47] The attorney general's office officially ordered Hoover to halt all examinations four days after the jurors went home.[48]

But confusion and a fair amount of animosity continued to bedevil relationships between the FBI and Justice Department. An agent who visited the *Washington Star* newspaper on a "friendly" visit was told that the attorney general had twice insisted the FBI would continue to investigate the lynchings, even though it was clear there was no federal jurisdiction and that it had come to an end with the termination of the grand jury. Hoover was puzzled, then angry. "I can't understand such double-talk," he seethed.[49]

When it was finished, Weeks thought it would be good for morale if the director of the FBI acknowledged the commendable service and "energy and enthusiasm" of the agents, who had worked under unpleasant and often uncomfortable conditions. "It is suggested a note of appreciation to each of them is justified," he added.[50]

The terse reply came back in Hoover's handwriting: "I recommend against letters. They did only the work normally expected of them."[51]

But the aftermath of the sixteen-day grand jury hearing was not so clear-cut for Hoover. He had to fend off ferocious criticism from Thurgood Marshall, special counsel to the National Association for the Advancement of Colored People and later an Associate Justice of the Supreme Court. Hoover was not aware of Marshall's playful sense of humor, evident in his letter from a hospital two days before Roger stabbed Barnett, when he asked that NAACP staff be told, "Give them the bad news that I'll live."[52] Then, while recuperating in the Virgin Islands, he wrote to the NAACP executive secretary, "The only exercise I have taken so far has been to lose money at poker, which, as you know, is no effort for me."[53]

Now Marshall lashed out at the FBI for treating blacks differently from whites. "The inability of the FBI to identify any members of the lynch mob in the Monroe, Georgia lynchings is the latest example of this," he accused the attorney general. In the letter, a copy of which Clark sent to Hoover, Marshall excoriated the FBI, charging it with discriminating against blacks when keeping records of crimes against victims. There would be very little use in strengthening civil rights statutes "if the FBI continues its policy of being unable to produce the names of persons guilty of such crimes," he fumed. In launching his uncompromising attack on the FBI, Marshall compared it unfavorably to the NAACP and other organizations, which had used "inexperienced investigators who have usually been able to produce the names of the members of the mobs."[54]

In a five-page reply, Tom Clark said the FBI conducted all investigations of violations of federal law in a completely unbiased manner without looking at the race, color, or religion of the person involved.[55] The same day Hoover dashed off a letter to Walter White, executive secretary of the NAACP, charging Marshall with repeatedly embarrassing the FBI and discrediting its investigation, particularly regarding the civil rights of blacks. "I don't think that the attitude and actions of Mr. Marshall and some of his legal associates measure up to the standards of cooperation which have been set by you," he hit back. For good measure Hoover said it was neither ethical nor fair to charge the Bureau with dereliction of duty.[56]

Chastened, White told Marshall to be "more temperate."[57] The lawyer agreed but was unrepentant, telling White, "I have no faith in either Mr. Hoover or his investigators and there is no use in my saying I do."[58]

But disagreements with outsiders were leap-frogged as the FBI stumbled over more obstacles ahead.

Vengeance

Lamar Howard should have been on high alert against unruly white avengers after testifying before the grand jury on December 5. An FBI agent had pointed out that he was not compelled to testify but Lamar had overcome any reservations, insisting he was not afraid.[1]

When the black teenager returned to work at the ice plant in Monroe, doubling as an assistant to the truck driver when not making ice, a white employee, Will Perry, asked why he had not come to work that day. The nineteen-year-old made no attempt to cover up the fact that he had gone to Athens to testify before the grand jury. Perry brushed aside the secrecy of the hearings, asking brashly what he had told the jurors. "Nothing," Lamar replied, because, he said, he "did not know anything to tell."[2] A local policeman, sidling up to Lamar in a grocery, also tried to pry out of him what he had said in now-sealed testimony, only to have the black teen give the same reply.[3]

He dared not say otherwise, for he had given evidence that put his life on the line. He testified that on the afternoon of the lynchings he had seen Loy Harrison deep in conversation at the ice plant with James Verner and plant employee Vivian Tillman.[4]

Perilously for himself, he also declared that James Verner had come to the ice plant with two pistols, either shortly before or soon after the lynchings.[5] One was a .32 Smith & Wesson revolver and the other a German Luger.[6]

Neither James Verner, thirty-six, nor his younger brother, Tom, twenty-five, said anything to Lamar during numerous visits they made to the ice plant following the grand jury testimony, but the black youth noticed that "they were looking hard" at him.[7] His denials were no protection against those determined to silence blacks through intimidation and reprisals. Lamar Howard was a marked man from the moment he stood before the grand jury. Now he would feel the full wrath of those he had endangered.

A few days before Christmas, the driver of the ice truck was tipped off cryptically by an acquaintance to warn Lamar "to be careful" at his workplace. Fortuitously, Lamar did not show up to collect his pay one Saturday, learning later that James Verner and Vivian Tillman had been lying in wait for him.[8]

On New Year's Day 1947, Lamar worked a seven hour shift on the ice truck before driving it back to the plant. Will Perry sent him on an errand and half an hour later he was back, shortly before the blonde-headed Verner brothers drove up in the green LaSalle Lamar knew well.

The black youth was seated on a stool in the office when Tom Verner walked over, jerked Lamar's hat off his head, threw it down and stomped on it. "Have you been a good boy?" asked Tom, a private in the US Army, on leave from Ft. Bragg, North Carolina.[9] Anyone looking straight at him would notice the half-inch-long diagonal scar between his eyes.[10]

Slow to realize they were not being playful, Lamar replied, "Yes, sir, I guess so." Tom pulled the youth's hair, threatening to cut it off, but the older brother told him to step aside.

"I'm going to beat the hell out of you!" James roared. "What did you tell them down in Athens!"

"Nothing," Lamar answered as he sought backing from Will Perry, asking if that wasn't true. Perry merely said that was what Lamar had told him.[11]

Lamar noticed a revolver tucked into James's belt but continued his denials, even as a volley of clenched fists struck his face and body. The older Verner grabbed him by the arm. "I'm here to get the truth out of you or kill you! I ought to shoot you!" declared the enraged white man, whose six-foot frame topped Lamar by a mere half inch, though at 165 pounds he was twenty-five pounds heavier than the teen.[12]

Will Perry, listening to radio commentary on the Georgia Tech ball-game, interjected, telling the Verners, "Take him out in the back. Don't beat him up in here."[13] The siblings took Lamar to a cow shed at the back of the ice plant, where they told him they were going to make him tell the truth.

"How much did they pay you for going over to Athens?" James asked.

"About forty dollars?" Tom interrupted.

"No, sir," Lamar mumbled, about four dollars and ninety cents, I think."[14]

James kept asking if he had told the grand jury that they had cleaned some guns at the ice house on the day of the lynching. Lamar, already bruised and bloodied, steadfastly denied it, gasping that he hadn't told the jurors anything regarding a gun, fearing he would be killed if he mentioned testifying about the weapon.[15] "You're telling a lie!" one of the tormentors insisted.[16] Again a fist slammed into Lamar's face. Frequently an arm swung and dazed him before he could answer their questions. The blows came so swiftly that Lamar was like a punching bag. At times his head was rammed against a wall. Lamar never struck back, for fear they would kill him.[17]

Suddenly James removed the revolver from his belt, clasped the barrel and pounded the butt over Lamar's head, blow after blow. When the cartridges fell out James stooped to put them back in, then resumed the battery. Lamar heard one of the brothers remark, "He sure has a tough head!" All the while Lamar held to his denials, afraid they would murder him if he admitted testifying about a gun.[18]

Delivering a parting blow, James ordered the groggy victim to get in his car and go back home. With his clothes now blotched red from open wounds, and barely able to see through eye sockets pummeled purple, Lamar edged himself into his box-like 1935 black Chevrolet Tudor sedan[19] and let it roll out onto the street, but it choked and died. A black passerby tried pushing, but the ignition failed until a white motorist carefully nudged Lamar's vehicle forward and it sputtered into action.[20]

His siblings were waiting for his arrival home to join them for a show downtown when Lamar drove into the yard. Paul Brice, thirty-one, who lived with the family, was setting off on foot to buy flour and thought of borrowing the car until he saw Lamar's grotesquely distorted face, and clothing splashed with blood.

"What's the matter with you boy?"

"Mr. James and Mr. Tom Verner beat me up."[21]

An older brother, Jimmy, twenty-one, looked out from the house in shock.

"I couldn't hardly know who he was because his face was so swollen up and bloody," James recalled. "I asked Mama, 'What's the matter with his face?' and Mama jumped up out of bed to see him."

When Lamar entered the house his mother, Katherine, thirty-nine, gasped, "What's wrong?"

"I got beat up while ago."

"Who done it?"

"Mr. James and Mr. Tom done it."

"Why?"

"They beat me because I wouldn't tell them what I told at the grand jury."

Lamar turned down Brice's request to borrow the Chevrolet, saying he was afraid the Verners would come after him and kill him, and he wanted to get away. "They may be coming behind me now," he fretted.

The youngest brother, Gene, fifteen, opened the door and spotted James Verner's familiar green LaSalle approaching on the country road. "Yonder they come, Lamar!" he cried out.

Quick-thinking Brice jumped in the car and sped off as a decoy, giving Lamar a chance to escape in another direction on foot. As he passed a white church the driver of the LaSalle honked several times. Brice pulled to the side of the road. The brothers got out and walked over to Lamar's vehicle.

"I thought I told you to go home!" said James.

"No, sir, not me. You ain't seen me today," Brice replied.

"No, you ain't the one," said James, fixing his gray eyes on Brice. "Where's old Lamar at?"

"Lamar done took off."

"Where's he going?"

"I don't know. He said he was going somewhere up the country."

"You go back home and tell him if he ever messes in my business anymore I'm going to kill him, and if he don't, I ain't going to bother him anymore," said James.

"I sure will tell Lamar," Brice promised.

Brice later recalled that "Mr. Tom was standing there crying and he didn't say anything, except he told Mr. James I was a pretty good nigger and that I had worked for him. I drove on up to the store but was so scared I forgot what I went after and turned around and drove back to Lamar's house. When I got there Lamar had done gone."[22]

Lamar and his younger brother Willie, seventeen, had fled out the back door as the Verner's car drew up. At first they took cover behind a pile of brush in the pasture, then cut across to hide in the woods. Minutes later his mother ran up carrying a coat Lamar had left behind, then the trio sneaked over to the house of Katherine's seventy-six-year-old mother, who lived with a son. As Lamar's mother washed the blood off his aching face, he repeated to his grandmother and uncle how he had been beaten up.

"His face was so swollen and so sore he could not eat," said the grandmother. "The next day about noon he ate some turnip soup."[23] When Jimmie arrived in Lamar's Chevrolet they cranked it up again and drove Lamar to the Walton County hospital.

Nurses in the emergency room were alarmed by Lamar's appearance. Clearly frightened, and speaking with difficulty, he managed with the help of his mother to outline the brutality of the attack. Over Lamar's feeble objections, an assistant superintendent told a nurse to call the sheriff. As soon as the doctor saw Lamar he sensed he had been assaulted with fists or a blunt instrument. There was no sign of a skull fracture although Lamar was suffering from a concussion of the brain, evident from bruises on the top of his head almost two and a half inches long. Most conspicuous were his eye sockets, both of which were bulging so much that they almost enveloped his eyes. His nose had stopped bleeding, but his lips and eyes were vivid evidence of severe blows. There were multiple contusions and abrasions on his face and head. Skin had torn open on the right cheek bone. A bandage was carefully placed over the cut below his right eye and the other wounds were painted with an antiseptic. The doctor told Lamar's sobbing mother to keep him in bed for a few days.[24]

When Deputy Sheriffs Howard and Sorrells came into the room, Lamar briefly described what had happened and why he believed he was targeted. The Verner brothers had beaten him with their fists and a pistol "because they thought I testified against James Verner before the grand jury," he uttered with difficulty as the lawmen took note of his badly bruised face, lips, and eyes.[25] A deputy sheriff said he lacked jurisdiction because the assault took place in town, but when he offered to get the city police involved both mother and son recoiled, pleading that they had known the Verner brothers a long time and did not want it reported "because they might get killed."[26]

Early the following afternoon, undertaker Dan Young picked up the phone and learned about the beating from a friend. Young, who had carried out the autopsies on the lynch victims five months earlier, immediately phoned his brother-in-law, Cornelius Adolphus "C.A." Scott, editor and general manager of the *Atlanta Daily World*,[27] the oldest black-owned newspaper in the country and a conspicuous crusader for civil rights. Within hours a pair of the newspaper's reporters were in the home of Lamar's grandmother. The swelling had subsided fractionally, but he still resembled a battered boxer. While Lamar again recalled the barrage of blows at the ice plant, one of the newspapermen snapped photos of his bloated and asymmetrical face, which would shock readers of the *Atlanta Daily World*.

Lamar at first resisted pleas to go to Atlanta but relented when told he should be examined again. After a change of clothing at Young's home they headed for the state capital. There, a noted black physician diagnosed contusion of the scalp, two cerebral contusions, a laceration on the right cheek, multiple contusions of the lips and eyes, and traumatic conjunctivitis, most marked on the left eye. He, too, recommended hospitalization.[28]

The newspapermen called in the Associated Press for nationwide coverage and once again the wounded teen relived his terror during a beating he said might have lasted ten or fifteen minutes. "I didn't tell 'em nothing because I didn't know nothing," he said.[29] His long ordeal slackened somewhat that evening when he was admitted unobtrusively into the recuperative shelter of McLendon's clinic. They were so secretive about the medical facility hiding Lamar that not even the Atlanta FBI was told of his location.[30]

The following morning, Monroe police chief Ben Dickinson was listening to the early morning radio news when he learned details of the assault. The previous afternoon a subordinate had passed on sketchy news about an unidentified black being beaten up, but Dickinson had not been able to find out anything more. The radio broadcast now named Lamar and described the anonymous assailants as white brothers. Later that morning a caller requesting confidentiality phoned the police chief to identify the assailants as James and Tom Verner.

En route to the ice plant, Dickinson and one of his officers recognized James Verner in his distinctive green LaSalle. They flagged him down and, without stepping out, told him to follow them to the ice plant. There, the police chief questioned him about the radio report.

"Yes, I beat him and I'll do it again if he tells another lie on me," Verner responded defiantly.

Dickinson advised that he would have to put Verner and his younger brother under bond. Disregarding James's claim that he acted alone, the police chief ordered Verner to find his sibling and meet the lawman at City Hall. When they got there, they each posted a $100 bond for "assault and battery on one Lamar Howard, colored." Later they were bound over to Superior Court under bonds of $500 each for a hearing on February 6.[31]

The US attorney for the Middle District of Georgia, John Cowart, simultaneously authorized separate federal charges against the brothers for conspiracy to intimidate a witness, by injuring Lamar in violation of laws shielding those who gave evidence before grand juries.[32] James, a bachelor, was arrested in his bed at the home he shared with his sister and brother-in-law. An FBI agent removed a Smith & Wesson revolver from under the pillow and another found the German Luger in a dresser drawer, but laboratory tests in Washington did not link them to the lynchings.[33] Tom Verner was taken into custody at a house in Campton. When they appeared before the US commissioner in Athens, their attorney waived a hearing and they were released on $10,000 bond each, signed by Howard Leonius Peters, fifty-nine, a prominent farmer with rimless glasses,[34] who listed as security 306 acres of land in the Hestertown area. Five months earlier the ruddy-cheeked man, who walked with a cane to support a handicapped leg, had helped report to police the stabbing of his second cousin, Barnett Hester.[35]

While the Verner brothers were being fingerprinted, James asked the US marshal to be careful as his fingers were stiff and sore. An FBI eyewitness observed torn skin on the knuckles of both hands and a swollen knuckle on his right fist. Tom had a scratch about half an inch long on his nose and ripped skin on his forehead.[36]

The following night a black employee of the Blue Room Café in Monroe walked into Marcus Malcolm's filling station to borrow a tool. As he neared the doorway he hesitated because "I didn't want to push over Mr. Malcolm." City policeman Louis Malcolm had his back to the black man and James Verner stood just inside the room. The black man overheard Verner exclaim, "I asked the son-of-a-bitch what he said and he wouldn't say anything, and I beat the hell out of him." There was a hush as they noticed the black man standing by the door. He said he only wanted to borrow a wrench to tighten his fog lights.[37]

A few days later a white farmer, Richard Beardon, entered Dan Young's funeral home with a chilling ultimatum that all blacks who had testified at the grand jury hearing, and others who were thinking of giving evidence at the Verner's trial, exile themselves from Georgia. A man who spoke to him shortly before Young returned from a funeral replied, "Let's see if I understand you right. The boy has been living around here all his life and now you don't think it advisable for him to come back home?" Beardon, just defeated in the election for the State House,[38] reacted with disdain. He said he didn't see it like that and he would come back and talk to the undertaker.[39]

Later Beardon warned Dan Young that "next time there wouldn't be a mob and the witnesses will just be found shot." He singled out Lamar, demanding he leave the state and not return to testify against the Verner brothers. Irately, he railed against the witnesses who "didn't know a damn thing about what they were talking about." The farmer said he knew Howard Leonius Peters, who had made bond for the Verners, and who lived among the Hester clan, where "nobody bothered people in that district because they would kill white as well as colored." With a parting personal threat against Young, the farmer from Hestertown warned that "he did not want this to get to the FBI."[40]

Undaunted, Young disclosed all to the federal agents, willingly signing his statement, even when cautioned that it might be made public in court.[41] But the farmer's intimidation was allowed to stand unchecked after US Attorney John Cowart, backed by the Department of Justice, decided not to confront Beardon, nor interview him, for fear it "might endanger Dan Young and other negroes in the Monroe area."[42]

The FBI stored more evidence against James Verner after a black neighbor who lived across the road said they were alone after hauling corn when the volatile white man tried to coax him into giving patently false evidence at the trial ahead. "He asked me if I remembered how Lamar used to drive that car standing on the side. I told him I remembered that. He then told me that that was what all the trouble was about, that Lamar had kicked at him and tried to run him off the road." The man refused to testify for Verner, even turning down $4 a day and mileage offered in return.[43]

However, the FBI braced for more flash violence after the Justice Department instructed the agent in charge of the Atlanta Bureau to interview Will Perry for the imminent case, even though Hoover had reported "the situation in Monroe is very tense and there is a probability that the appearance of an agent in Monroe will precipitate a riot and possible bloodshed." But Hoover refused to be deflected. "The interview will be conducted despite these circumstances," the stoic director assured the attorney general. He ordered a squad of additional agents to be present at the interview, instructing them to "remain inconspicuous" and conduct themselves "in the most unostentatious manner possible."[44]

That same day a pair of FBI agents took notes of their confrontation with Will Perry in Monroe, which remained peaceful. But Perry portrayed himself as an innocent bystander. In a series of denials, he said James Verner had never told him anything about Howard's appearance before the grand jury. He denied that either brother had mentioned it on the day of the assault. And he denied he heard of the beating immediately. Instead, he claimed two days passed before he first heard about it on the radio.[45]

But at FBI headquarters in Washington, Hoover stood tall for having pressed ahead with Perry's interrogation, despite fears of a riotous backlash. It was Hoover as his staff knew him—wary, watchful, and in total command of his domain.

Defective Juries

Meanwhile, lawlessness lurked in another quarter. City police chief Ben Dickinson passed on to the FBI a rumor from an unidentified source that James Verner had vowed to kill Lamar if the teen testified against him in the state trial for assault and battery, set to begin in a month.[1]

When the trial opened on February 24, 1947, at the superior court in Monroe, witnesses shrugged off Lamar's testimony, giving an entirely different version. White men who were present at the time the quarrel began said under oath that no one had been struck in the ice plant office. To discredit Lamar's statement that he was busy serving a customer, manager Will Perry said no ice sales had been made since noon. "It was as cold as a zip," he told the court.

In the most damaging evidence against Lamar, James and Tom charged him with lashing out at them as soon as they got behind the ice plant.[2] James had earlier said it was not true that he hit Lamar with a gun, or that he even had one with him. He said it was "probably" in his car.[3]

Jolting the teenage black's credibility, James then testified under oath that when he made bond at police headquarters he had attacked Lamar because "the nigger had run him off the road in his car" on a previous occasion.[4]

James's attorney played to the prejudices of the white jurors, whom he had helped select, posturing in his summary that it was "this nigger's word against that of the two fine white gentlemen."[5]

The jury of twelve men deliberated for two hours before astonishing Lamar's backers with a verdict of not guilty.

It was a "shocking surprise," the *Atlanta Daily World* editorialized. "Only because of the race of the victim could the jury bring in a verdict of 'Not Guilty.'" The answer to this injustice, the newspaper added, lay in giving more representation to black people on juries.[6]

The Georgia state solicitor general, Marshall Pollack, confidentially admitted that one of the reasons he lost was because of a "bad jury." Most of the jurors were from Hestertown. "You will recall that our main suspects in the lynching case were the Hesters, Peters, Adcocks and Malcolms," he wrote Cowart,[7] who passed on to the attorney general that Pollack "had a good many members of these families on the jury, and of course was unable to strike all of them off."

Cowart pulled no punches in his assessment of what went wrong. "From my general conversation with Mr. Pollack, I believe his case was lost mainly because of the type of jury which he had," Cowart declared.[8]

During the federal trial, which was heard on a single day in June,[9] James Verner offered a scenario completely different from Lamar's. He repeated what he had told the FBI after his arrest when he said he had gone to the ice plant on New Year's Day, but only to see whether Tillman had returned from a vacation in Florida. He claimed he did not even know Lamar had appeared before the grand jury. He simply brushed aside Lamar's earlier testimony to the grand jury that he had come to the ice plant with two pistols, shortly before or soon after the lynchings.[10] And he denied that Tom had taken part in the assault, though federal lawyers considered the younger brother an aider or abettor in the crime.[11]

James testified that the fight began when they argued about what had allegedly taken place between them on a road. It was not true that he or his brother were armed during the attack, an assertion backed up by the testimony of James's girlfriend. James Verner said when they got to the back of the ice house he told his brother to see that Lamar did not cut him. Questioned whether he saw the teenager holding a knife, he replied he did not, "but he knew all negroes carried knives."[12]

In new evidence, he told Lamar he was going to pummel him because "this negro had tried to run him off the road on several occasions during the last year and was running up and down the highway in his automobile in a fast manner." He had seen Lamar occasionally since the first attempt to run him off the road, and the only reason he did not thrash him during those times was because he "never caught him in the ice house."[13]

In Verner's favor, Cowart said there was "some degree of conviction" that the beating suffered by Lamar was administered because the black teen "while driving his automobile, darted out in the road" at the defendant.[14]

Jurors debated for five and a half hours before finding Tom Verner not guilty. They struggled for an extra hour on James Verner's fate but could not agree amongst themselves and a mistrial was declared.[15]

It was disastrous for the prosecution and their allies. "Informal conversations" with several jurors after the court adjourned indicated that ten of the twelve jurors had voted for James Verner's acquittal. "It is exceedingly doubtful whether we would be able to obtain as many as two jurors on a retrial of the case who would hold out for the conviction of James Verner for as long as the two men who took that position in this trial," Cowart briefed the attorney general.[16] "If this case were retried an acquittal would result without a great deal of deliberation by the jury." Tellingly, he was convinced that retrying the case "would recall the unpleasantness of the situation which resulted from the government's failure to solve the Walton County lynching case."[17] He was curt, honest, and very sure of himself.

Two years later the government withdrew all charges against James Verner. The principal witness, Police Chief Ben Dickinson, had died in January 1948, and it was not felt that a conviction could be obtained on a retrial without his testimony.[18] Again the US attorney did not think James Verner would be convicted upon retrial and the government "would lose the advantage of the moral victory" that Cowart thought had been gained by the failure of the jury to acquit. "We strongly object to the unfavorable publicity which would result from an outright acquittal, which we sincerely believe would result if the case were retried," Cowart pressured the attorney general. "A retrial of the case would serve as a reminder of the fact that the government was unable to solve to any extent the Walton County lynching case. We believe that any further publicity in this respect can only result in harm to the government."[19]

He was so persuasive that the indictment against James Verner was finally dismissed on May 5, 1949. More than two years had passed since he had admitted bashing grand jury witness Lamar Howard.[20]

Tom Verner died in a North Carolina car crash six months after the last of the 1947 trials.[21] James Verner was slain in 1952.[22]

Eyewitnesses

Forty-five years after four people were shot like wildlife at Moore's Ford, a white man said he had witnessed the lynching when he was only ten years old. Clinton Adams said he had kept silent for so long in the face of threats by the Ku Klux Klan. He was speaking out now since his left leg "was pulled slam off" when someone turned on a feed mixer while he tried to bail out water.[1] FBI special agent Jim Procopio interviewed Adams[2] and wrote to his director in 1991: "he is telling the truth."[3]

Adams laid down only three conditions for meeting with lawmen in the short time he said he had to live and relate "what he saw." He demanded an FBI agent be present at every debriefing. He insisted that the Georgia Bureau of Investigation consent, in writing, to his anonymity. He agreed to speak about the events only if his current address, and that of his family, remained unknown. Two weeks later, on April 24, 1991, the district attorney for Walton County, Alan Cooke, met with representatives of the GBI to consider Adams's pre-conditions. Cooke said he would prosecute the case "if the actual killers were still alive, and enough credible evidence could be gathered to make a prosecutable case."[4]

Clinton Adams was illiterate with only a fourth grade education. When his sharecropper father got sick, Clinton said George Dorsey would come over to their house, cut the wood, put it in the woodbox, feed the horses, and take care of everything that needed to be done. The boy was nine years old when he said his father committed suicide, leaving him "one old gray horse and fifteen cents." The boy was on such good terms with his neighbor, Dorsey, that "when my daddy died George flat ran two miles to a store to call an ambulance to come out to the house. He was that kind of man," Clinton remembered.[5]

He told the FBI that he was tending cows in a pasture with his close friend, Emerson Farmer, son of Ridden and Reba Farmer, when he heard screams and shouts coming from a hollow adjacent to the field. The boys ran to the edge of the field, lay down on their stomachs at the edge of a pine thicket, and saw a group of about a dozen white men surrounding a car, from which they had dragged out two black men and two black women.

He said he recognized his next-door neighbor, George Dorsey, who was struggling with the men and trying to fight them.

"As several of the men struggled with Dorsey, a Georgia State Trooper, whose car was blocking a small wooden bridge and caused the car in which the blacks were riding to stop, drew his revolver and struck Dorsey across the head. Dorsey, stunned by the blow to the head, was subdued by the men and his hands were tied.

"Adams recognized several of the men in the gang as local residents, among them Loy Harrison, the driver of the car," the agent wrote to his director. But the same FBI man, or a misquoted Clinton, wrongfully said Adams recognized Dorsey's wife, Mae, her sister, and husband, when he should have described George and Dorothy as brother and sister. "The women were crying and screaming and were led off into the field, along with their husbands, by the band of white men. The women recognized several of the men because they addressed them by name. Once in the field a group of four of the men drew their weapons and fired at the two black couples. All four fell to the ground mortally wounded. The rest of the gang, including Harrison, then fired their weapons at the blacks as they lay dying on the ground.

"The group of men then reassembled at the trunk of the State Trooper's patrol car, where they placed all their weapons. The group of four men who initially shot the blacks, told the rest of the group to give them one and a half hours and they would be in North Carolina. The murderers crossed the bridge to the other side of the river where their car was parked. Then the four got in the car and left. The rest of the group, whom Adams recognized to be local members of the Ku Klux Klan, remained talking for several minutes before dispersing.

"After the men left the area, Adams, choked with emotion and crying over what he had just seen, and his friend Emerson, stood up and stared for several moments at the now motionless bodies lying in the field below them. The two then left the area," Procopio wrote.[6]

Adams told the FBI agent that a day or two later the two deputy sheriffs, "Doc" Sorrells and Lewis Howard, visited him at his home to talk about the murder. No reason was given for their singling out a ten-year-old to discuss the killings. Adams volunteered that he knew who had committed the killings and named the four men he recognized.

Shocked by this confession and the fact that there had been an eye-witness to the lynchings, Sorrells warned Adams that he should never tell anyone what he had seen or else klansmen would return and kill him and his mother, Maudie. The woman, recently widowed, reportedly was so frightened that she never again spoke about the killings. Neither did either of the boys, said Adams, because the sheriff's deputies ordered them to remain silent.[7]

Sorrells, by contrast, took Adams under his wing, looking after him and above all making sure that he never divulged his secret. Adams told the FBI agent that when he turned eighteen, Sorrells advised him to join the army and leave the area. He took this advice and served a tour with the occupation forces in Germany. When he returned he thought every-thing would be forgotten. "But it wasn't that way," he remembered. "They don't ever forget."

Adams related to the FBI that over the years he had conversed with several of those involved in the lynchings. A local farmer and neighbor, Ernest Dillard, told him he parked a piece of farm machinery in the roadway leading from the main highway to the murder site so that no one would inadvertently stumble upon the scene of the crime. Dillard, he continued, also built a house on his property for Adams's mother, who lived there rent-free until her death. Adams was convinced this was done to buy his silence.

Loy Harrison had told Adams that he wanted George Dorsey killed because the World War II veteran thought he was "better than white folk." Adams said Harrison "freely admitted his role" in setting up and taking part in the lynchings. The youngster confided that "it was common knowledge" in Monroe, especially among law enforcement, who had carried out the murders. He had last seen Harrison in 1981 when he visited the burly man at his farm. He told the farmer that he was tired of the Klan stalking him. Harrison, he said, assured him that it would end. Since then Adams had not seen Harrison again.

The lynchings had so terrified Adams that he was always haunted by the threat of retribution from the Ku Klux Klan against him and his family if he ever revealed his secret. Because of this fear, he said, he had moved at least a dozen times. Eleven years after the lynchings, Sorrells suggested he leave the area, saying "I made people nervous." Adams went on the road with a carnival, setting up a rocket-ride. The following year he married a co-worker from Indiana. He told his wife what he had witnessed to help explain his nightmares and why he preferred moving all the time. When he visited Augusta in the early 1960s, he was approached by someone from Walton County who intimated he should not have returned to Georgia. It so scared him that he kept on the move.

Many years later, Adams recalled that his close friend, Emerson Farmer, had gone out one night and broken into a church. "I told him, 'Bubba, this ain't my bag of tricks. I'm out of here.'" Adams said, "I went into the Army and he went to prison."[8] In 1989 a jury convicted Emerson's sister-in-law of shooting the allegedly abusive man to death.[9]

Whether Clinton Adams told the truth is debatable. Loy Harrison was indeed a major suspect, very much under the FBI's microscope. But perhaps the most vulnerable part of Clinton Adams's many statements is the fact that Emerson Farmer declared to the FBI that he was on the porch with his father at their house when he saw Harrison in one of the cars heading toward Moore's Ford Bridge and the lynchings. Then, he asserted, he and his mother were both present when Harrison stopped by briefly after the gunmen opened fire on the four victims. An FBI agent taking the boy's evidence soon after the murder had no doubt about Emerson's mentality, describing him as "a child of average intelligence."[10] The same pre-teen could not have been at home at the same time his friend, Clinton Adams, claimed they were tending cows in a pasture. And Adams never explained why two deputy sheriffs visited him one or two days after the crime to talk about the murders. Why him, if he had not been recognized by any of the armed mob? Additionally, Adams said Emerson was ten, but the young boy told the FBI he was twelve years old at that time.[11]

However, the FBI disregarded these discrepancies. Writing to the director of the FBI, special agent Procopio insisted, "It is the opinion of the case agent who interviewed Adams and heard his dramatic story that he is telling the truth."[12]

Adams would not be deflected by accusations that he had concocted his story. "All I want is to get it off my conscience. I don't want anything else out of it," he said.[13]

But Atlanta could not check out anything to do with Clinton Adams or the lynching decades before. In May 2015, the author's startling find of a misfiled document proved that everything to do with the Moore's Ford Bridge case no longer existed in Atlanta. Agents there were stymied. They were unable to provide documentary backup for anything to do with the atrocity, which was needed to research Clinton Adams's blockbuster claim, made telephonically to the FBI on December 12, 1990, that he was an eyewitness to the murders. After drawing a blank on the unsolved horrors, the Atlanta SAC wrote to the new director of the FBI on May 1, 1991, "all of Atlanta's files have been destroyed. It will be necessary to try to construct some sort of file from data in Bureau files and other sources."[14]

People who made up the lynch mob have either died or are believed to be old and frail. Even some of their offspring are deceased, including Harrison's youngest son, Talmadge, named after the former white supremacist governor. The son served a prison sentence for drug trafficking before he was shot to death by an unknown gunman when he was a septuagenarian.[15]

If the FBI, with all its technological leaps and highly trained operatives, had failed to identify the criminals, what chance did the state have for a murder trial, if it was now dependent solely on the Georgia Bureau of Investigation, which had long since distanced itself from the case? As a result, the probe to try and identify the killers was abandoned.

Yet the search for evidence was resumed in 2008 when the FBI and GBI jointly dug on former farmland, five miles southwest of Moore's

Ford Bridge, declining to say whether they found anything, but confirming that the current residents were not part of the goal. Investigators said a judge had even sealed their search warrant.[16]

Then in 2013, a Georgia man went public with his accusation that an octogenarian uncle, living in Monroe, had taken part in the crime against the quartet. Wayne Watson, fifty-seven, named his youngest uncle, Charlie Peppers, eighty-six, and said he had decided to tell what he knew because he was tired of going through life "living with lies." In a video-recorded interview with Benjamin Jealous, then president of the National Association for the Advancement of Colored People (NAACP), Watson said that "all through my life I heard them talk about Moore's Ford and the lynching. I'm tired of it," he drawled in his native Georgia accent.

In an interview with Jon Swaine of the *Guardian*, Peppers alleged that several of the men he named were members of the Ku Klux Klan. His uncle denied the charge with a curt "Heck no" and repeated what he told FBI agents who questioned him—that he was never a member of the KKK. "Why in the world are y'all bringing stuff up that happened sixty years ago. Why didn't y'all do something about it then?" he told the *Guardian*, although it then took place sixty-seven years previously. "Back when all that happened I didn't even know where Moore's Ford was. The blacks are blaming people that didn't even know what happened back then," he said.

Watson said he had been ostracized by members of his family because he had a relationship with an African American woman. "I want it all over with the racism," he told the NAACP chief. "I told people I've dated a black woman and you can't get nothing. A white man goes around here and says he's dating a black woman, or hanging around black people, you can't get no loan, you can't go to no bank, borrow money or nothing. They turn you down."

Watson volunteered that "people tried to bribe me. They offered me money . . . $250,000 to keep my mouth shut, walk away in '99." He said that when he rejected the money, one of the men making the offer replied, "you'll be dead before you ever testify."

Interviewed while seated in an empty church, Watson outlined the fantasy of a fetus being cut out of the inside of one of the victims, Dorothy Malcolm. He said his uncle, Charlie Peppers, was laughing when he related how the killers thought she was pregnant by a black man, but, as her husband was in the military, she was pregnant by a white man. When Watson said the baby must have been dead when taken out, Peppers "cussed me out and called me every name in the book. 'Don't call me a freaking liar,'" Peppers allegedly answered, "but he used the cuss word." The uncle told him they cut the baby out, washed it off in the creek and gave it to someone who was supposed to take it to Atlanta for adoption. "That's what my uncle told me all the years I remember," Watson told the interviewer.[17]

Neither the coroner, nor the African American mortician who conducted the autopsies, and not even others who were present, including agents from the FBI and GBI, mentioned any visual evidence of Dorothy Malcolm's body having knife marks on her belly after such alleged savagery.

Watson's credibility was deflated when it was learned he had been jailed fourteen years earlier for obstructing a law enforcement officer. He said he was naked when he was handcuffed and shackled to a drain for criminal trespass. And what he claimed to have heard about the lynching was only hearsay, since he was born ten years after the crime.[18] Robbie Schwartz, managing editor of the *Walton Tribune* based in Monroe, queried Watson's allegations, suggesting he might be removed from reality. "I have to wonder if he's 100 percent there," he told the *Atlanta Journal-Constitution*. "I don't put a lot of credence in what he said. He used to come into my office spouting all kinds of government conspiracies."[19]

A copy of the recorded video was handed over by NAACP head of the Washington bureau, Hilary Shelton, to the then top man in the Civil Rights Division of the Justice Department, Thomas Perez, who later became secretary of labor. The author is awaiting the results of a Freedom of Information Act request from the Justice Department to find out its current status.

Meanwhile, the intervening years had brought dramatic change to the area. In a ceremony that would have been the ephemerae of dreams in 1946, a yellow biplane circled high over George Dorsey's grave, fifty-three years after the abomination, in tribute to the decorated World War II veteran. Mourners gathered at the little cemetery to observe a plaque at the foot of his grave, recognizing his military service and the medals he had received. After singing the "Battle Hymn of the Republic" and listening to the emotive strain of bagpipes, they looked on as two soldiers presented the neatly folded Stars and Stripes to Columbus Dorsey, the victim's nephew. Then a trumpeter sounded "Taps." George Dorsey's sister-in-law, Ruby Dorsey, was incredulous. "I didn't ever think it would happen," she mused as she stood among those in remembrance. "Thank the Lord I lived to see it." One of the invited guests was Lamar Howard, then a bespectacled septuagenarian. Since his unforgiving beating by the Verner brothers for daring to testify before the grand jury, he had moved to Atlanta, living under a pseudonym in fear of his life. The cluster of people paying homage to the serviceman had also come to honor Lamar's courage in defying brutal retaliation by telling the jurors what he knew. However, he would not comment on the unsolved atrocity.[20]

Nobody was ever held accountable for the lynching of four people near Moore's Ford Bridge, beside the Apalachee River, on July 25, 1946.

The nameless killers got away with murder.

Court Action

It seemed that the juries had spoken with finality, leaving no hope of anything new. The distance of time would work to the benefit of the killers as memories clouded, and witnesses, suspects, and investigators grew old and passed into oblivion.

Almost seventy years after the nation sickened at news of the barbarism, the author and his legal team attempted to unseal grand jury testimony from December 3 to December 19, 1946. Veteran lawyer Joseph J. Bell, assisted by his subordinates, Cheryl Capo, Michael Edwards, and Patricia Melia of Bell, Shivas & Fasolo in Rockaway, New Jersey, volunteered to help the author in this long shot at prying open more evidence.

In court papers spanning a full year, the lawyers approached the US attorney for the Middle District of Georgia. Then they filed a more lengthy legal brief with the US District Court for the same area, and finally read through the order of Judge Marc T. Treadwell.

The lawyers admitted that grand jury records could not be obtained through the Freedom of Information Act because the legislation did not apply to federal courts. And they accepted that grand jury proceedings are "protected by stringent procedural safeguards preventing disclosure under most circumstances." Grand jury secrecy had to be given great weight, and allegations of public interest alone would not normally constitute sufficient need.

The pro bono legal team even conceded that the confidentiality of grand jury proceedings prevented individuals under potential indictment from fleeing or tampering with jurors or witnesses. Secrecy would make people with information about crimes more willing to appear and speak frankly. Sealed testimony would avoid injury to the reputation of people accused of a crime, but who had not been indicted by a grand jury. The same confidentiality would enable grand jurors to investigate suspected crimes without any inhibitions and to come to conclusions "in unfettered deliberations."

However, the lawyers continued, the highest court in the land had recognized exceptions to the rule of secrecy, and even the District Court had power to disclose grand jury material. In such an event, the author would have to plead a "particularized need" and "compelling necessity" to succeed in overcoming the policy of secrecy.

In addition, the lawyers acknowledged that the author would have to show that the material sought was required to avoid a possible injustice in another proceeding; that the reason for disclosure was greater than the need for secrecy; that the request for grand jury evidence covered only the material asked for, and that this information could not be obtained through any other means. All of the requirements would have to be met, even though the grand jury had concluded its work.

These were "extraordinary hurdles," said the lead lawyer, but the documents no longer implicated any of the policy reasons for protecting them from disclosure. Because the vast majority of witnesses, government employees, and suspects would have died in the nearly seventy years since the crime, the documents ought to be released.[1]

Highly technical legal arguments followed when Bell filed a Petitioner's Memorandum of Law in the US District Court for the Middle District of Georgia. He emphasized, "A number of recent decisions have found special circumstances to exist in historically significant cases where substantial time has passed since the grand jury convened, and ordered the release of grand jury materials and testimony."

The lead lawyer summed up: "The Moore's Ford lynching remains a polarizing and historically significant event in American history. Petitioner [the author] submits that special circumstances exist and requests an Order of this court releasing the grand jury transcripts and materials from the Moore's Ford lynching federal grand jury."[2]

The US attorney would have none of it. In a stunning response he told the court that to his knowledge the transcripts did not exist. He said his office had only begun maintaining grand jury records since about 2004, some ten years earlier. Before then, he said, the Federal District Court clerk's office had them. When the same records were transferred to the US attorney's office, he added, "it did not receive, and it did not have the transcripts in question." It was apparent that if such transcripts existed they had either been lost or destroyed. It was not surprising in light of the time that had elapsed since the grand jury met and announced its findings. "The government is unaware of the existence of any transcripts of any other grand jury proceedings of such age in this district," he declared. His brief reminded the court that current policies of the US Department of Justice required transcripts to be maintained for only ten years. He asked for dismissal of the author's petition because "the traditional reasons underlying the secrecy of grand jury proceedings still exist, particularly in light of the open status of the investigation and the existence of a potential suspect." Then the US attorney appeared to slam the door shut, arguing that "the Government submits that the issue of the release of such transcripts is moot."[3]

It defied the evidence. It overlooked reason. It was implausible. Proof was there for all to see. In a letter to Director Hoover dated December 20, 1946, just a day after the grand jury's verdict, lead FBI investigator Charles Weeks wrote: "I understand transcripts of the testimony taken are being forwarded to the Department for review."[4] But on closer inspection the pivotal wording of Weeks had been: "I understand." He was not sure that transcripts had been sent to Washington. He could have been wrong. However, there is no disputing that they existed at that time, even if they were not forwarded to Washington.

The author does not accept that evidence from the grand jury has been lost or destroyed. The lynching of four African Americans in an isolated rural area of Georgia on July 25, 1946, remains unsolved. It is a cold case, with the FBI and Georgia Bureau of Investigation still hunting for evidence, as can be seen from the subsequent interviews with Clinton Adams and Charlie Peppers and the digging on land in Monroe in 2008, on which the FBI refused to elaborate, other than to absolve the current residents of any involvement. Those lawmen must have been briefed beforehand. It defies logic or common sense to think that they pursued a cold case without benefit of the massive trove of material from sixteen days of grand jury testimony. Those crucial days of hearings would have been essential to lawmen following up a cold case. Without it they would be handicapped. Citing loss or destruction of such evidence demands that reasonable people become gullible. The fact that the SAC Atlanta admitted in 1991 that all records of the aging case had been destroyed there[5] does not mean that grand jury testimony had suffered a similar fate in Washington.

An unenviable judgment was left to Judge Marc T. Treadwell of the United States District Court for the Middle District of Georgia, Macon Division. He acknowledged that the author's counsel had provided the court with some documentation suggesting that grand jury transcripts were forwarded to the FBI in 1946. But the letter Weeks wrote to Hoover, saying "I understand transcripts of the testimony taken are being forwarded to the Department for review,"[6] was insufficient. The statement was qualified. There was no certainty that they *had* been forwarded to Washington.

FBI historian Dr. John F. Fox, Jr. informed the author that the FBI did not currently have the transcripts. Some records had been located, though not apparently of the grand jury. He said redactions of the headquarters file were made "to protect grand jury testimony," and that the amount deleted was so small that he didn't believe it would change the narrative in any significant manner. At the same time he bemoaned "the lamentable loss" of historical records in Atlanta, declaring it "a shame."[7]

Tellingly, Judge Treadwell hinted at a very faint chance that the missing transcripts might still exist. He added, "Dr. Fox thinks it likely that some of the FBI's documents were not produced in response to Mr. Pitch's Freedom of Information Act request *in order to protect grand jury secrecy* [author's italics]."

The judge was able to adjudicate only on the evidence before him. He concluded, "There is no evidence that the grand jury transcripts or any other grand jury records exist. Certainly, they are not in possession of this court or the US attorney."

He was right, even though the FBI's eminent historian left the door slightly ajar because of possible secrecy concerns.

Judge Treadwell's pronouncement fell like a thud. "Neither this court nor the US attorney has possession of any documents from the grand jury's investigation into the Moore's Ford lynching," he wrote in his Order of August 19, 2014. "Accordingly Mr. Pitch's petition is dismissed without prejudice, subject to his right to renew this action in the event he discovers that the FBI has located grand jury records relating to the investigation of the Moore's Ford lynching."[8]

Undaunted, the author's legal team sent a lengthy letter to Attorney General Loretta Lynch, outlining the facts and legal arguments and asking for guidance in the search for grand jury transcripts. Despite the ruling of Judge Treadwell, attorney Bell wrote, "there is a possibility that these records exist elsewhere within the confines of the federal government, as suggested by several lines of evidence."[9]

Meanwhile, the Justice Department continues to burrow for new evidence in its quest to prosecute civil rights–era cases at the federal level, with new empowerment from the Emmett Till Unresolved Civil Rights Crimes Act of 2007. But there is a trip-wire. The Fifth Amendment's protection against double jeopardy prohibits retrial, in the same court, for the same offenses, of people who were previously found not guilty, or who were convicted but received shockingly light sentences. There is no exception to this constitutional protection, regardless of how biased the jury, how inadequate the prosecution, or misinformed the court might have been.

In the fourth annual report to Congress, the attorney general acknowledged the difficulties of all cold cases. "Subjects die, witnesses die or can no longer be located; memories become clouded; evidence is destroyed or cannot be located; and original investigations lacked the technical aid and scientific advances relied upon today." It was a clear indication that DNA technology and other scientific breakthroughs, unavailable at the time of the lynching, might have been decisive in 1946.

In unfettered language, the attorney general's report referred to "some instances where members of local law enforcement agencies were either themselves members of the Ku Klux Klan, or sympathized with Klan viewpoints, which may have impacted their investigations into racially motivated homicides." Most investigators, the report found, agreed that the first forty-eight to seventy-two hours were crucial to solving a homicide case. Witnesses were easier to locate, and their recollections generally proved more accurate soon after the incident. Investigators also agreed that if a homicide was not solved within the first year, the chance of it ever being solved plummeted.

In language echoing the cries of many and the despair of lawyers, the report offered bleak hope of a solution. "Even with our best efforts, investigations into historic cases are exceptionally difficult, and justice in few of these cases will ever be reached inside of a courtroom."[10]

Afterword

In the fall of 1997, black and white residents of Georgia formed the Moore's Ford Memorial Committee (MFMC) to remember the four people lynched near the banks of the Apalachee River on July 25, 1946. They agreed not to publicly demand the prosecution of any Moore's Ford killers who might still be living. No one would be given the opportunity to stigmatize them as a "vigilante group." Instead, they would focus on memorializing victims of the last mass lynching in America, thereby keeping the case alive.[1]

On three different occasions sympathizers had placed a marker beside the grave of Roger Malcolm, but each time it was destroyed. Undeterred, members of the memorial committee ensured that the victims would never be forgotten. In the words of their secretary, Rich Rusk, bearing an uncanny likeness to his father, former Secretary of State Dean Rusk, they wanted to "begin healing this festering sore that has blighted our counties."[2]

The MFMC kickoff event was sponsored by the Mt. Perry Baptist Church in Morgan County, where two of the victims, the siblings George Dorsey and Dorothy Malcolm, were known to be buried. "We were a little nervous when we started," Rusk told the *Athens Banner-Herald*. "There was so much anger and hatred about those lynchings. But people got the word that we were on a healing mission."[3] Almost 100 black and white volunteers cleared the rocky land from an overgrowth of weeds and long grass. Sweating and swatting away flying insects, they toiled together with a common goal of uncovering the past.[4] Finally they located the unmarked resting places of the brother and sister. "The only reason they found those graves was because a couple of people had made a determined effort to remember the sites," said an editorial in the *Athens Banner-Herald*.[5] The MFMC placed engraved markers beside each grave reading, "May Your Suffering Be Redeemed With Brotherly Love."

Seven years later civil rights activists held the first of annual reenactments, insisting that the public be confronted with the lynching. The Georgia Association of Black Elected Officials (GABEO) sponsored the activities,[6] which included gruesome scenes with fake blood to recall the horror.

Immediately the issue split the MFMC. Rusk, a staunch opponent of the reenactment, nevertheless defended those with whom he disagreed. "GABEO colleagues have every right to gather at this bridge and exercise their First Amendment rights," he wrote.[7]

Supporters of the reenactment were defiant. "We decided to do the reenactment because people don't know what lynching was all about and how horrible it was," said Reverend Benford Stellman.[8] Their aim was to concentrate on the brutality, to prevent its recurrence, and "to build pressure on prosecutors to reinvestigate the case."[9]

Demands for justice, with renewed energy, were standard fare along the route of the crime. An event coordinator and former chairperson of the Athens Area Human Relations Council, Hattie Lawson, said justice was an important part of the reenactment. But there was more to consider. "I think of those people as my family," she reflected.[10]

"For those who say leave it in the past, that may work for you. But just because you feel that way does not make it go away," added Reverend Ed Dubose, state president of the NAACP.[11] As if to acknowledge the past's hold over the present, an informed resident observer admitted, "There's still a lot of fear here. People don't want to talk about it."[12]

Opposition from both races to reenactments was just as fierce. No one objected when authorities reopened the investigation. It was universally welcomed. But there was a sense that succeeding replays of the unsolved lynchings were unnecessary. "They willfully re-traumatize participants, spectators and our entire communities," Rusk wrote as a personal commentary. "No community should reenact a hometown racial atrocity as an annual commemorative event. Their continuation threatens both the good work of this committee and the public safety."[13]

An editorial in the *Athens Banner-Herald* criticized the president of GABEO for embellishing what it felt was fabrication of a fetus being ripped out of the body of Dorothy Malcolm. "Tyrone Brooks [then a Georgia state representative] named the African American undertaker for his source for the ghoulish act. However, he acted alone in naming the fetus *Justice*. That proved too much for two of Roger Malcolm's family members, who saw Brooks's move as 'a lack of respect for the families of the victims.'"[14]

Rusk denounced Brooks even while maintaining respect for the man himself. "I personally interviewed former FBI agent Lewis Hutchison, who witnessed the autopsy in 1946. Hutchison, while sending us ten- and fifteen-dollar checks for our scholarship program, claimed he never saw a fetus or sign of pregnancy, and also said he would have remembered if he had," Rusk commented, again in his personal capacity. "The reenactments play fast and loose with standards of decency."[15]

Later the *Athens Banner-Herald* would lambaste GABEO, accusing it of agreeing to the descent "from being a moving memorial toward becoming a pitiful parody of itself."[16] The newspaper's executive editor, Jason Winders, excoriated the organization for stating that the killers slashed open the corpse of Dorothy Malcolm to haul out a fetus. "Urban legends like a pregnant victim continue to sprout from these events. They grandstand in a shameless frenzy of self-promotion. And taste suffers second only to truth," the executive editor argued. "Why not return dignity and truth to these victims just as family members are asking? Gather at the river to offer a prayer, place four wreaths at the water's edge, even solemnly march across the bridge with arms linked and heads bowed. Most importantly, get back to telling the real story of what happened. Do not muddy the waters with fiction. The lessons of what really happened at that bridge in 1946 remain powerful enough to stand on their own without embellishment or theater."[17]

While conducting research for this book, the author traveled to Monroe to witness the annual reenactment, which terminated at the site where the quartet slumped dead. This did not sanction nor give credence to what many regard as a provocative act.

Depending on whom one believes, fantasy and myth may play a major part in the reenactment. Certainly it is not portrayed factually. Prominence is given to the diabolical seizure of the fetus, but such a ghastly act would have been impossible to keep secret and would have made headlines around the world. Protests would have erupted across the country, with the president forced to express outrage. Yet nowhere in the autopsy reports, witnessed by others and condensed by the FBI from observations by Dan Young, an African American mortician highly respected by both races, is there any mention of it. There is not even a hint of such an atrocity. The author asked a daughter of the undertaker whether she had ever heard the story, or if her father, who died in 1988, had spoken of it to her. "He never did mention anything about it," said Ariel Young Sullivan, then owner of the same funeral home. "I knew nothing about it."[18]

It does not even have a cursory mention in the coroner's report, even though its jury members and lawmen were unconscionable in taking home souvenirs. Reports compiled by the NAACP shortly after the slaughter make no reference to Dorothy Malcolm's pregnancy nor to the repulsive removal of a fetus from her lifeless body.[19] The alarming allegations are also missing from a Justice Department report of a meeting of forty-three women from the National Association of Colored Women who met with a special assistant to the attorney general to discuss the lynchings a week after the crime. The NACW deplored the "barbarities" that had reached such an alarming rate "that women are now being lynched with impunity." Although they appealed for laws against lynching and mob violence, there was no talk of Dorothy Malcolm's condition, nor of her violated body.[20] Yet the chilling account of this abhorrent deed is repeated at annual reenactments.

The only references to Dorothy Malcolm's alleged pregnancy, among 2,790 transcribed interviews conducted in the year of the crime,[21] are in eleven lines out of 3,723 pages devoted to FBI activities, released under the Freedom of Information Act, and thousands more read at the National Archives. On both occasions the speakers relied on hearsay, passing on gossip and what they had overheard. FBI agents interviewed the first woman twenty-five days after the lynching and reported: "Speaking further of the victims, [redacted name] said that [redacted name] was about five months in pregnancy and that [redacted name] 'had just become that way,' according to what the people in the neighborhood had said."[22] The other woman spoke to the FBI seven weeks after the crimes and also had her name redacted. Agents quoted her telling them that "according to rumors" among her community, the day before the stabbing (erroneous) "Dorothy Malcom had run up to Mr. Hester's house, whereupon Barnett had come from the home and told Roger Malcom not to hit Dorothy as she was in no shape to be hit, meaning she was pregnant. [Redacted name] could not furnish the names of persons who had told her about this, or who could verify this."[23]

Yet hundreds of people of both races continue to congregate for the annual reenactments. They follow each other at principal stops along the way to the infamous locale of the killings. And they listen to those who promote what evidence suggests is a fable. They are unaware of what eyewitnesses saw and noted in 1946. If indeed the story is fictitious, then its proponents are no different from the legendary Pied Piper, hoodwinking many by their falsities. It seems like a mockery of the truth, inflaming untold numbers through the broad reach of social media.

I gave the principal man behind this assertion an opportunity to tell me where he found this tale, how he knew about it, and to cite its origin. GABEO President Tyrone Brooks, a longstanding civil rights activist, resigned from the Georgia House of Representatives in 2015 after thirty-five years as a legislator. He took this step just before pleading guilty to tax fraud and no contest to five counts of wire and mail fraud.[24] The US attorney said Brooks had misappropriated nearly all of more than $1 million raised through two charitable organizations for disadvantaged communities to pay personal expenses for himself and his family.[25] In his letter of resignation to the governor, Brooks made no reference to his guilty plea, but said he had decided to make the Moore's Ford Bridge lynchings his "number one priority."[26] Later he informed me that he and others were told about the ravaged dead female in 1968 by Dan Young, the undertaker who performed the autopsies. Brooks said Young even showed him a photograph of Dorothy Malcom's corpse stretched out on a table, though her belly was covered up so that he could not see it, or any knife marks. He quoted the undertaker saying she was "at least seven months pregnant," and had been seen many times by others walking in Monroe in that condition.[27] Yet nobody in a position of authority in 1946 uttered a word about her pregnancy or mutilation of her belly, on or off the record, including the African American undertaker who performed the autopsies and secretly passed on information about the lynchings to the NAACP.[28]

The MFMC is raising $200,000 to permanently endow scholarships as "living memorials" to the Malcolms and Dorseys. Every spring eight public high school seniors from Oconee, Walton, Morgan, and Athens-Clarke Counties are awarded $1,000 Moore's Ford Memorial Scholarships in a competition to promote social justice and racial healing. Finalists are given $100 Merit Awards. Students are judged on their community service, reference letters, and essays related to civil rights. Some expressed shock over learning about the "Monroe Massacre." Others expressed optimism that race relations have improved.

"Let us prosecute these killings if possible, and move forward with student scholarships, talent shows, and civil rights bus tours," said Rusk. "Let us work with schools and students, help other communities deal with their legacies of racial violence and, always, promote justice and racial healing."[29]

Rightfully, no one can dispute how the passage of time has changed outlooks. Now, at every major intersection, a Georgia state trooper or Walton County lawman was observed blocking traffic and waving participants through. This happened even though some leaders of the reenactment had called for federal intervention, claiming that local law enforcement "could not be trusted."[30]

Rusk, a witness, was quick to take note of the change that had taken hold of law enforcement officials. "Athens-Clarke County Police Chief Jack Lumpkin, Oconee County Sheriff Scott Berry, and Walton County Sheriff Lamar Palmer—and his replacement Joe Chapman—had all joined our MFMC honorary board when asked. We hear that a Walton County deputy sheriff rides around with a can of paint in his car trunk—and brushes over racial slurs whenever they appear. Providing security at the march to the bridge, Walton County Deputy Sheriff Ethaniel Rakestraw took matters a step further and walked across that bridge, linked arm in arm with the front row of marchers. Police cars escorted a motorcade of at least 125 cars with illuminated headlights and emergency flashes through Monroe, to the house where Roger Malcolm fought with Barney Hester, a white man, then to the old Walton County jail where he was held for eleven days, and finally to Moore's Ford where Malcolm, his wife and two friends all lost their lives."[31]

(Donors can send checks to Moore's Ford Memorial Scholarships, c/o Rich Rusk, 480 Stanton Way, Athens, Georgia, 30606. Tel: (706) 202–7802 E-mail: RichRusk7@gmail.com.)

Abbreviations

C—Congress
CR—Congressional Record
CRD—Civil Rights Division
DOJ—Department of Justice
FBI—Federal Bureau of Investigation
HST—President Harry S. Truman
IS—Report of the Joint Select Committee to inquire into the Conditions of Affairs in the Late Insurrectionary States, made to the two Houses of Congress, 19 Feb. 1872, Govt. Printer, Washington, D.C. 1872.
JEH – J. Edgar Hoover
LC—Library of Congress
McPF—FBI personnel file US Senator Kenneth Douglas McKellar
MF (Main File)—FBI Case File No. HQ44-1421, Unknown Subjects: Roger Malcolm and wife, Dorothy, and George Dorsey and wife, Mae, Civil Rights and Domestic Violence.
NA—National Archives
PR—Records of DOJ, CRD, classified subjects file 1930–87, case file 144–19M-14-25, boxes 506, 507, RG60, NA
RD—Unknown subjects: Racial Discrimination in Registration of Negro Voters, FBI reports, 1946, files #44-62, Case file # 44-1406, RG 65.
S—Session
TPF—FBI personnel file John Frank Trost
WPF—FBI personnel file Charles Everett Weeks

Endnotes

Background

1 Text of Senate Resolution 39, 109C 1S S6364
2 Holden-Smith, Barbara. *Lynching, Federalism, and the Intersection of Race and Gender in the Progressive Era.* Yale Journal of Law and Feminism: 1966, 44
3 CR, 75C 3S, 145–46
4 Equal Justice Initiative. *Lynching in America: Confronting the Legacy of Racial Terror.* Montgomery, Al. 2015, 5
5 Report of Marianna, Florida lynching to NAACP, NY, 20 Nov. 1934, DOJ straight numerical file #158260, box 1279, entry 112, RG 60, NA
6 Mary White Ovington to FDR, 4 Jan. 1935, DOJ straight numerical file #158260, box 1279, entry 112, box 1279, RG 60, NA
7 CR, 75C 1S, 3563
8 CR, 75C 3S, 370
9 CR, 75C 3S, 313
10 CR, 75C 3S, 1115
11 CR, 75C 3S, 374
12 CR, 75C 3S, 1101
13 CR, 75C 3S, 1102
14 CR, 75C 3S, 1115
15 CR, 75C 3S, 1105
16 CR, 75C 2S, 118
17 CR, 75C 2S, 122
18 CR, 75C 2S, 123
19 CR, 75C 3S, 305
20 Robert Wagner, *Congressional Digest,* vol. 14, 6–7, June/July 1935, 176
21 Charles Andrews (D-FL), CR, 75C 2S, 209
22 CR, 75C 2S, 208
23 CR, 75C 3S, 1687
24 CR, 75C 2S, 41
25 CR, 75C 3S, 139
26 *US Senate Election, Expulsion and Censure Cases 1793–1990,* Govt. Printing Office: Washington, D.C., 1995, 376–79
27 CR, 75C 3S, 1537
28 CR, 75C 3S, 1943
29 CR, 75C 3S, 2007
30 Senator Landrieu S6370, Senator Allen S6372 and Preamble to S. Res. 39, 109C 1S S6364

31 Resolution text 109C IS S6364
32 Senator Frist 109C 1S S6364
33 Senator Landrieu 109C 1S S6365
34 Senator Landrieu 13 June 2005, 109C 1S S6365
35 Senator Landrieu 109C 1S S6366
36 Senator Mikulski 109C IS S6386
37 Senator Mikulski 109C 1S S6386
38 Senator Kerry 109C IS S6374
39 Senator Allen 109C IS S6371
40 Senator Landrieu, 109C 1S S6365, Senator Kerry 109C 1S S6374
41 109C 1S S6373
42 *Facts on File World News Digest* 23 June 2005, copyright Roll Call, Inc.
43 Senator Kerry at press conference 13 June 2005

Chapter 1—Murder

1 Mrs. Carl Aycock statement 6 Aug. 1946, MF
2 Loy Harrison statement 2 Aug. 1946, and Howard statement 14 Aug. 1946, MF
3 Emory Gordon statement 2 Aug. 1946, MF
4 FBI record 2 Aug. 1946 in Weeks report 5 Aug. 1946, 20 MF
5 Weeks report 5 Aug. 1946, 32, MF
6 C. J. Sorrells statement 26 July 1946 in Weeks report 5 Aug. 1946, 5, 31, MF
7 Ray Flanigan statement 6 Sept. 1946, MF
8 Weeks report 5 Aug. 1946, 27, MF
9 Royce Batchelor statement 7 Aug. 1946, MF
10 Lorena Howard statement 14 Aug. 1946, MF
11 Columbus Spence undated statement in Weeks to Washington 24 Aug. 1946, MF
12 Lewis Howard statement 14 Aug. 1946, MF
13 Mrs. Carl Aycock statement 6 Aug. 1946, MF
14 J. Willie Arnold statement 2 Aug. 1946, MF
15 In Weeks report 5 Aug. 1946, 27, MF
16 Royce Batchelor statement 7 Aug. 1946, MF
17 William Matthews statement in Weeks report 5 Aug. 1946 and Weeks report 24 Aug. 1946, MF
18 W. T. Brown statement 5–9 Aug. 1946, MF
19 Weeks report 25 Nov. 1946, MF
20 Enlisted Record and Report of Separation, NAACP Group II box A413, LC
21 Coroner's report on George Dorsey 25 July 1946, Walton County Superior Court
22 Harold Boss statement 6 Aug. 1946, MF

23 FBI lab report 9 Aug. 1946, MF

24 Coroner's report on Roger Malcolm 25 July 1946, Walton County Superior Court

25 Coroner's report on Dorothy Malcolm 25 July 1946, Walton County Superior Court

26 Notes from autopsy 27 Aug. 1946 in Weeks report 5 Aug. 1946, 34, MF

27 Royce Batchelor statement 7 Aug. 1946, MF

28 Coroner's report on Mae Dorsey 25 July 1946, Walton County Superior Court

29 Redacted name undated statement, Pre-Grand Jury 153, MF

30 Coroner's reports 25 July 1946, Walton County Superior Court and Walton County Health Dept. copies of death certificates 5 Aug. 1946, MF

31 Royce Batchelor statement 7 Aug. 1946, MF

32 Harold Boss statement 6 Aug. 1946, MF

33 Royce Batchelor statement 7 Aug. 1946, MF

34 Weeks report 5 Aug. 1946, 35, MF, and Coroner's report on George Dorsey 25 July 1946, Walton County Superior Court

35 George Hearn statement in Weeks to Washington 24 Aug. 1946, MF

36 Lewis Howard statement 5 Aug. 1946 in Weeks report 5 Aug. 1946, 6, MF

37 W.T. Brown statement 5–9 Aug. 1946, MF

38 Coroner's reports 25 July 1946, Walton County Superior Court

39 Ridden Farmer statement 11 Aug. 1946, MF

40 Evelyn Patterson statement 24 Aug. 1946, MF

41 Weeks report 5 Aug. 1946, 8, and Redacted name statement 2 Aug. 1946 in Weeks report 5 Aug. 1946, 37, MF

42 Redacted name statement 8 Sept. 1946 in Weeks report 24 Sept. 1946, 25, MF

43 Clinton Adams to *Atlanta Constitution* 31 May 1992

44 Redacted name statement 9 Oct. 1946, MF

45 Redacted name of radio operator statement 19 Sept. 1946 and Joseph Bray statement 19 Sept. 1946, with FBI comment, MF

46 Joseph Bray statement in Weeks to Washington, 24 Oct. 1946, MF

47 Alvin Parrish statement 7 Aug. 1946, Jim Williams statement 20 Sept. 1946, MF

48 Jim Williams statement 20 Sept. 1946, MF

49 Harrison statement 28 July 1946 in Weeks report 5 Aug. 1946, 27, MF

50 Jim Williams statement 20 Sept. 1946, Weeks report 25 Nov. 1946, 140, MF

51 William Barnette statement 17 Aug. 1946, and Griffin Dooley statement 20 Aug. 1946, MF

52 William Barnette statement 17 Aug. 1946, MF

53 Jim Williams statement 20 Sept. 1946, MF

54 Weeks report 25 Nov. 1946, 141, MF

55 Marlon Thrasher statement 26 Aug. 1946, MF

56 William Matthews undated statement in Weeks report 5 Aug. 1946, 33, MF
57 Weeks report 5 Aug. 1946, 32, MF
58 Eugene Martin to Walter White 8 Aug. 1946, NAACP Group II box A412, LC
59 Redacted name statement 23 Aug. 1946, MF
60 Buster Malcolm statement 22 Aug. 1946, MF
61 Weeks report 5 Aug. 1946, MF
62 Judge West ruling 27 July 1946, Walton County Superior Court
63 Martin to White 28 Feb. 1947, NAACP Part IX 221, LC
64 Martin to White 24 Aug. 1946, NAACP Group II box A412, LC
65 Martin to White 8 Aug. 1946, NAACP Group II box A412, LC
66 Martin to White 24 Aug. 1946, NAACP Group II box A412, LC
67 Martin to White 27 July 1946, NAACP Group II box A412m, LC
68 Dan Young statement 24 Oct. 1946, MF
69 Weeks report 5 Aug. 1946, 8, MF
70 Walton Tribune 16 Aug. 1907 reprinted in *Walton Tribune* 11 Dec. 1968, MF
71 Martin to White 24 Aug. 1946, NAACP Group II box A412, LC
72 Notes from autopsy 27 July 1946 in Weeks report 5 Aug. 1946, 34, MF
73 Weeks summary report to Washington 25 Nov. 1946, MF
74 Martin to White 8 Aug. 1946, NAACP Group II box A412, LC
75 Weeks report 5 Aug. 1946, MF
76 See Afterword pp. 162–164
77 Mattie Louise Campbell in *Atlanta Constitution* 31 May 1992
78 Buster Malcolm statement 22 Aug. 1946, MF

Chapter 2—Monroe

1 *Walton Tribune* 16 Aug. 1907 reprinted in *Walton Tribune* 11 Dec. 1968
2 *Walton Tribune* 16 Aug. 1907 reprinted in *Walton Tribune* 11 Dec. 1968
3 *Walton Tribune* 16 Aug. 1907 reprinted in *Walton Tribune* 11 Dec. 1968
4 *Walton Tribune* 16 Aug. 1907 reprinted in *Walton Tribune* 11 Dec. 1968
5 *Pittsburgh Courier* 3 Aug. 1946
6 Ollie Harrington, NAACP public relations director, in undated article soon after the lynchings, NAACP Group II box A413, LC
7 FBI report 29 Aug. 1946, MF and Weeks to Washington Bureau 24 Aug. 1946, section IV Suspects, 210, MF
8 Leroy Bud Ramey statement 8 Sept. 1946, MF
9 Lucinda Allen statement 16 Oct. 1946 and Robert Aycock statement 16, 17 Oct. 1946, MF
10 *Walton Tribune* 29 Aug. 1946
11 *Walton Tribune* 30 Aug. 1946
12 *Walton Tribune* 11 Oct. 1946
13 *Walton Tribune* 13 Sept. 1946
14 *Walton Tribune* 6 Sept. 1946

15 *Walton Tribune* 30 Aug. 1946
16 *Walton Tribune* 16 Aug. 1946 and 11 Oct. 1946
17 *Walton Tribune* 6 Sept. 1946
18 Walton Tribune 6 Sept. 1946
19 Weeks to Washington 24 Aug. 1946, 201 disk, MF
20 Weeks to Washington 25 Nov. 1946, MF
21 Eddie Pierce Studdard statement 30 Aug. 1946, MF
22 *Walton Tribune* 12 July 1946, MF
23 Weeks report 5 Aug. 1946, 39, MF
24 Weeks report 5 Aug. 1946, 39, MF
25 Redacted name statement 29 Nov. 1946, MF
26 Redacted name statement 5 Sept. 1946, MF
27 Redacted name statement 9 Oct. 1946, MF
28 Tommie Lee Shepherd Sr. statement 12 Sept. 1946, MF
29 Weeks report 5 Aug. 1946, 38, MF
30 *Walton Tribune* 26 July 1946, MF

Chapter 3—Primary Election

1 *Atlanta Constitution* 1 June 1946
2 *Atlanta Constitution* 6 June 1946
3 C. D. Forsyth testimony 10 July 1871, vol. 6–7, 36, IS
4 P. M. Sheibley testimony 10 July 1871, vol. 6–7, 47, IS
5 *New York Times* 2 Aug. 1946
6 *Atlanta Constitution* 26 May 1946
7 *Atlanta Constitution* 26 May 1946
8 *Atlanta Constitution* 2 June 1946
9 *Atlanta Constitution* 29 May 1946
10 *Atlanta Constitution* 12 July 1946
11 Alfred Richardson testimony 7 July 1871, vol. 6–7, 3, 14; C. D. Forsyth testimony 10 July 1871 vol. 6–7, 20; George Burnett testimony 11 July 1871 vol. 6–7, 68–69; Z. B. I. Argrove testimony 12 July 1871 vol. 6–7, 75, IS
12 Alfred Richardson testimony 12 July 1871 vol. 6–7, 10, IS
13 Augustus Wright testimony 13 July 1871 vol. 6–7, 108, IS
14 Bernd, Joseph, L. *White Supremacy and the Disenfranchisement of Blacks in Georgia 1946.* The Georgia Historical Quarterly vol. 66, No. 4, 1982, 492–513.
15 Monroe County, Ladd to JEH 3 Sept. 1946, RD, file 44–123, case file 44–1406, section 4 box 95 RG 65
16 Lamar County, Cowart to Caudle 18 July 1946, RD, file 44–101, case file 44–1406, section 1 box 95, 5–6, RG 65
17 Douglas County, Ladd to JEH 3 Sept. 1946, RD, case file 44–1406, section 4 box 95, RG 65 and FBI report 22 July 1946 file 44–119, case file 44–1406, section 2 box 95, 1 RG 65

18 Meriwether County, FBI report 12 Sept. 1946, RD, file 44–116, case file 44–1406, section 8 box 96, 9–11, RG 65

19 Liberty County, Eugene Talmadge to J. Wardlow Griner 4 May 1946, FBI report 29 Aug. 1946, RD, file 44–62, case file 44–1406, section 6 box 96, 7–8, RG 65

20 Worth County, R. V. Pollard statement FBI report 24 July 1946, RD, file 44–112, case file 44–1406, section 1 box 95, 4–8, RG 65

21 Meriwether County, Robert Gilbert statement FBI report 12 Sept. 1946, RD, file 44–116, case file 44–1406, section 8 box 95, 5, 14–15, RG 65

22 Meriwether County, George Nesmith statement FBI report 12 Sept. 1946, RD, file 44–126, case file 44–1406, section 8 box 95, 5, RG 65

23 Meriwether County, Robert Gilbert statement FBI report 12 Sept. 1946, RD, file 44–116, case file 44–1406, section 8 box 96, 1, 15, RG 65 and FBI report 20 July 1946, file 44–116, section 1, box 95, 1

24 Grady County, FBI report 1 Aug. 1946, RD, file 44–129, case file 44–1406, section 3 box 95, 1, RG 65

25 Chatham County, Aaron Kravitch statement, FBI report 1 Aug. 1946, RD, file 44–41, case file 44–1406, section 3 box 95, 28, RG 65

26 Baker County, Phipps to Cowart 15 July 1946, FBI report 23 July 1946, RD, file 44–107, case file 44–1406, section 2 box 95, 2–4, RG 65

27 Fayette County, Mrs. J. W. Lunsford statement, FBI report 28 Aug. 1946, RD, file 44–165, case file 44–1406, section 6 box 96, 3, RG 65

28 Polk County, Thomas Davitte statements, FBI report 22 July 1946, RD, file 44–121, case file 44–1406, section 2 box 95, 3 RG 65 and FBI report 6 Sept. 1946, file 44–121, case file 44–1406, section 6 box 95, 2, RG 65

29 Monroe County, FBI report 25 July 1946, RD, file 44–123, case file 44–1406, section 2 box 95, 2, RG 65

30 Haralson County, Claude Driver statement, FBI report 29 Aug. 1946, RD, file 44–145, case file 44–1406, section 6 box 96, 5, RG 65

31 Clarke County, Henry West statement, FBI report 5 Sept. 1946, RD, file 44–185, case file 44–1406, section 6 box 96, 5, RG 65

32 Walton County, Emory Gordon statement, FBI report 24 July 1946, RD, file 44–127, case file 44–1406, section 2 box 95, 2–5, RG 95

33 *Atlanta Constitution* 6 July 1946

34 *Atlanta Constitution* 7 June 1946

35 *Atlanta Constitution* 10 July 1946

36 *Atlanta Constitution* 13 July 1946

37 *Atlanta Constitution* 5 July 1946

38 *Atlanta Constitution* 5 July 1946

39 *Atlanta Constitution* 5 June 1946

40 *Atlanta Constitution* 7 July 1946 and 13 July 1946

41 *Atlanta Constitution* 17 July 1946
42 Weeks report 5 Aug. 1946, 38, MF
43 JEH to Caudle 29 July 1946, MF
44 Redacted name statement 11 Nov. 1946, MF
45 Redacted name preacher statement 11 Nov. 1946, MF
46 Redacted name statement 11 Nov. 1946, MF
47 Redacted name statement 4–5 Sept. 1946, MF
48 Redacted name statement 29 Nov. 1946, MF
49 Lucius Briscoe statement 4 Aug. 1946, MF
50 Redacted name statement 24, MF Aug. 1946 and unidentified Barnett Hester brother 21 Oct. 1946, MF
51 Redacted name statement 21 Oct. 1946, MF
52 James Hanson statement 3 Oct. 1946, MF
53 Redacted name statement 24 Oct. 1946, MF
54 Redacted name statements 9 Oct. 1946 and 24 Oct. 1946, MF
55 Redacted name statement 18 Aug. 1946, MF
56 Redacted name statement 18 Sept. 1946, MF
57 Redacted name statements 19 Sept. 1946 and 1 Oct. 1946, MF
58 Perry Breedlove statement 26 Aug. 1946, MF and Redacted name statement 26 Sept. 1946, MF
59 James Verner statement 21 Sept. 1946, MF
60 *Walton Tribune* 19 July 1946 and *Atlanta Constitution* 19 July 1946
61 Redacted name statements, undated, in Weeks to Washington 25 Nov. 1946, MF

Chapter 4—Stabbing

1   Weeks memo 22 Aug. 1946, box 506, section 15, 6, PR
2   Weeks memo 22 Aug. 1946, box 506, section 15, 3, PR
3   Moena Williams statement 6 Aug. 1946, MF
4   Mattie Louise Campbell in *Atlanta Constitution* 31 May 1992
5   Buster Malcolm statement 17 Sept. 1946, MF
6   Dora Malcolm/Dora Mae Pryor statement 22 Aug. 1946, MF
7   Moena Williams statement 6 Aug. 1946, MF
8   Redacted name statement 28 Aug. 1946, MF
9   Redacted name statement 21 Aug. 1946, MF
10 Dora Malcolm/Dora Mae Pryor statement 22 Aug. 46, 1946, MF
11 Eugene "Doll" Johnson statement 12 Sept. 1946, MF
12 Buster Malcolm statement 22 Aug. 1946, MF
13 Redacted name statement 15 Aug. 1946, MF
14 Barnett Hester statement 21 Nov. 1946, MF
15 Redacted name statement 15 Aug. 1946, MF

16 Walton County Hospital Supt. statement 16 Aug. 1946, MF

17 Redacted name statement 15 Aug. 1946, MF

18 B. H. Hester statement 12 Aug. 1946, MF

19 Redacted name of mother of Roger Malcolm's baby and redacted names statement 17 Aug. 1946, MF

20 B. H. Hester statement 12 Aug. 1946, MF

21 Willie Lee Pitts statement 22 Aug. 1946 and redacted black name statement 21 Aug. 1946, MF

22 Claude Malcolm statement 7 Aug. 1946, MF

23 Redacted name statement 14 Nov. 1946, MF

24 Redacted name statement 28 Nov. 1946, MF

25 Moena Williams undated statement in Weeks reports 25 Nov. 1946 and 13 Dec. 1946, MF

26 Hillman Levy Adcock statement 8 Oct. 1946, MF

27 Weeks report 5 Aug. 1946, 38, MF

28 Ruther Reeves statement 15 Jan. 1947, MF

29 W. A. Stepp statement 9, 11 October 1946, MF

30 Willie Lee Pitts statement 22 Aug. 1946, MF

31 Redacted name statement 15 Aug. 1946, disk 5, 282

32 Grady Malcolm statement 5 Aug. 1946 in Weeks report 25 Nov. 1946, MF

33 Redacted name statement 8 Oct. 1946, MF

34 Wayman Malcolm statement 4 Aug. 1946, MF

35 Emory Gordon statement 14 Aug. 1946, 83, MF

36 Lewis Howard statement 14 Aug. 1946, MF

37 Weeks report 25 Nov. 1946, MF

38 FBI report 14 Aug. 1946, 39, MF

39 Redacted name statement 28 July 1946, MF

40 *Walton Tribune* 19 July 1946

41 Redacted name statements 31 July 1946, and 11 Aug. 1946, MF

Chapter 5—Jail

1 Major Jones statement 10 Oct. 1946, MF

2 Major Jones statement 10 Oct. 1946, MF

3 Redacted statement 15 Oct. 1946, MF

4 Major Jones statement 13 Nov. 1946, MF

5 Major Jones statement 4 Nov. 1946, MF

6 Redacted name statement 16 Aug. 1946, MF

7 Redacted name statement 29 Aug. 1946, MF

8 Lewis Howard and Sorrells statements 29 Aug. 1946 and Flanigan statement 6 Sept. 1946, MF

9 Redacted name statement 29 Aug. 1946, MF

10 Redacted name statement 14 Oct. 1946, MF

11 Redacted name statement 14 Aug. 1946, MF

12 *Atlanta Constitution* 31 May 1992

13 Redacted names statements 8 Aug. 1946 and 14 Aug. 1946, MF

14 Buster Malcolm undated statement 17 Sept. 1946, MF

15 Moena Williams statement 6 Aug. 1946, MF

16 Ruby Dorsey and Robert Lee Elder in Harrison interview with FBI 8 July–26 Sept. 1946, MF

17 Weeks report 25 Nov. 1946, MF

18 FBI remarks in Moena Williams statement 6 Aug. 1946, MF

19 Supt. Walton County hospital statement 16 Aug. 1946, MF

20 Redacted name statement 21 Aug. 1946, MF

21 FBI report 6 Aug. 1946, MF

22 Moena Williams statement 6 Aug. 1946, MF

23 Weeks report 5 Aug. 1946, MF

24 Weeks to Washington 25 Nov. 1946, and Lewis Howard statement 14 Aug. 1946, MF

25 Redacted name statement 19 Sept. 1946, MF

26 Weeks report 5 Aug. 1946, MF

27 Harrison statement 2 Aug. 1946 in Weeks report 5 Aug. 1946, MF

28 Redacted name statement 19 Nov. 1946, MF

29 Weeks report 5 Aug. 1946, MF

30 Weeks to JEH 11 Aug. 1946, MF

31 Harrison statement 26 Sept. 1946, MF

32 Will Perry statements 31 July 1946 and 7 Aug. 1946 and Harrison statement 2 Aug. 1946 in Weeks report 5 Aug. 1946, MF

33 Vivian Tillman statement 14 Aug. and 4 Sept.1946, MF

34 Redacted name statement 8 Aug. 1946, MF

35 Ridden Farmer statement 3 Aug. 1946, MF

36 Ernest Dillard statement 31 July 1946, MF

37 Lamar Hearn statement 30 July 1946, MF

38 Major Jones statement 8 Aug. 1946, MF

39 Redacted name statement 7 Aug. 1946, MF

40 Redacted name statement in Weeks report 24 Aug. 1946, MF

41 Redacted name statement in Weeks report 24 Aug. 1946, MF

42 Redacted name statement in Weeks report 24 Aug. 1946, MF

43 Redacted name statement 19 Sept. 1946, MF

44 Redacted name statement 29 Aug. 1946, MF

45 Lorena Howard statement 14 Aug. 1946, MF

46 Harrison statement 2 Aug. 1946, MF

Chapter 6—Ambushed

1 FBI report 2 Aug. 1946 in Weeks report 5 Aug. 1946, and Weeks report 25 Nov. 1946, MF

2 Redacted name statement 12 Sept. 1946, MF

3 Redacted name statement in Weeks pre-grand jury report 24 Aug. 1946, 55, MF

4 Redacted name statement in Weeks pre-grand jury report 24 Aug. 1946, 54, MF

5 Clinton Adams to *Atlanta Constitution* 31 May 1992

6 Weeks memo 13 Aug. 1946, MF

7 Harrison statement 2 Aug. 1946 in Weeks report 5 Aug. 1946, MF

8 Pearl Ramey statement 18–20 Sept. 1946, MF

9 Valley Mosley statement 11 Sept. 1946, MF

10 Nellie Foster statement 28 July 1946, MF

11 Bud Ramey statement 25 July 1946, MF

12 Ridden Farmer statement 11 Aug. 1946, MF

13 Emerson Farmer statement 11 Aug. 1946 and Reba Farmer statements 27 July 1946 and 29 July 1946, MF

14 Reba Farmer statement 27 July 1946, MF

15 Ridden Farmer statements 3 Aug. 1946 and 11 Aug. 1946, MF

16 Redacted name statement 3 Sept. 1946, MF

17 Ridden Farmer statement 11 Aug. 1946, MF

18 Harrison statement 2 Aug. 1946, MF

19 Harrison statement 26 Sept. 1946, Griffin Dooley statement 20 Aug. 1946, William Barnette statement 17 Aug. 1946, MF

20 Harrison to Associated Press, in *New York Herald Tribune* 27 July 1946, reprinted in 79C 2S p.10259

21 Harrison statement 2 Aug. 1946 in Weeks report 5 Aug. 1946, MF

22 Harrison statements 28 July 1946, 17, and 2 Aug. 1946 in Weeks report 5 Aug. 1946, MF

23 Redacted name statement 8 Sept. 1946, MF

24 Redacted name statement 8 Sept. 1946, MF

25 Harrison statement 28 July 1946, MF

26 Redacted name statement 30 July 1946, MF

27 Harrison to Associated Press, in *New York Herald Tribune* 27 July 1946, reprinted in 79C 2S p.10259

28 McElroy Griffie statement 21 Aug. 1946, MF

29 Harrison statement 2 Aug. 1946 in Weeks report 5 Aug. 1946, MF

30 Emerson Farmer statement 11 Aug. 1946, MF

31 Reba Farmer statement 29 July 1946, MF

32 Redacted name statement 13 Sept. 1946, MF

33 Nellie Foster statement 28 July 1946, MF

34 Redacted name statement 4 Aug. 1946, MF

35 Redacted name statement 5 Aug. 1946, MF

36 Redacted name undated statement, pre-grand jury 54, MF

37 Pearl Ramey statement 18–20 Sept 1946, MF

38 Redacted name statement 4 Sept. 1946, MF

39 FBI conclusion 6 Aug. 1946, MF

40 Mrs. Carl Aycock statement 6 Aug. 1946, MF

41 Unsigned transcript *Ten o'Clock Wire* 26 July 1946, section 17, PR

Chapter 7—The FBI Steps In

1 Robert Jackson and Hartley Shawcross, *Washington Post* 27 July 1946

2 Ladd to JEH 27 Dec. 1946, MF

3 *Washington Post* 27 July 1946 and Selective Service file seen by FBI 6 Aug. 1946, MF

4 Enlisted Record and Report of Separation, NAACP Group II box A413, LC

5 Moena Williams to Associated Press, in *New York Herald Tribune* 27 July 1946, reprinted in 79C 2S p.10259

6 Redacted name statement to JEH 30 July 1946, MF

7 Sneed to JEH 27 July 1946, PR

8 Crew to Tom Clark, box 506, PR

9 Cy Saltzman to Tom Clark 9 Sept. 1946, box 507, PR

10 Anonymous to JEH received Aug. 1946, PR

11 Washington State American Vets to JEH 30 July 1946, PR

12 American Vets Committee to JEH 13 Aug. 1946, PR

13 NAACP to Truman 26 July 1946, NAACP Part IX 221, LC

14 White, Walter. *A Man Called White.* New York: The Viking Press, 1948, 331

15 NAACP to attorney general 26 July 1946, NAACP Part IX 221, LC

16 Harold Wood to JEH 2 Aug. 1946, PR

17 Redacted name to JEH 29 July 1946, PR

18 Redacted name Z. A. Vane and Co. to JEH 29 July 1946, PR

19 Redacted name to JEH 27 July 1946, PR

20 Undecipherable Brink to HST 21 Aug. 1946, box 507, PR

21 Unidentified name to JEH 30 July 1946, PR

22 A Citizen to JEH 26 July 1946, PR

23 Redacted name to JEH 26 July 1946, PR

24 David Reid to JEH 29 July 1946, PR

25 Redacted name to JEH 29 July 1946, PR

26 Redacted name to JEH 30 July 1946, PR

27 Ohio Baptist state convention to JEH 3 Aug. 1946, PF

28 N. California Council of Churches to JEH 2 Aug. 1946, PF

29 Redacted name to JEH 27 July 1946, PR

30 Richard Russell, 79C 2S pp. 10259–10260

31 Public Papers of HST, 1946, 368, Govt. Printing Office, Washington, D.C. 1962

32 HST to Clark 20 Sept. 1946, in Niles papers, HST Library, Independence, MO.

33 Ellis Arnall to JEH 31 July 1946, MF

34 Arnall to White 31 July 1946, NAACP Group II box A412, LC

35 I. E. Nitschke report 10 Sept. 1938, TPF

36 Personnel status report JEH to SAC Aberdeen S. Dakota 9 Nov. 1938, TPF

37 H. H. Clegg to Clyde Tolson 13 May 1943, TPF

38 Tolson to JEH 26 May 1941, TPF

39 J. T. Madigan to JEH 21 July 1941, TPF

40 JEH to Trost 13 Nov. 1942, TPF

41 Ladd to Tolson 30 Dec. 1942, TPF

42 Inspector Crowl report 8 May 1944, TPF

43 J. C. Strickland to Ladd 26 July 1946, MF

44 R. C. Hendon to JEH 7 Aug. 1946, TPF

45 Theron Caudle to JEH 26 July 1946, TPF

46 R. C. Hendon to JEH 7 Aug. 1946, TPF

47 JEH to Clark 31 July 1946 and 2 Aug. 1946, PR

48 Tamm to JEH 30 July 1946, TPF

49 Strickland to Ladd 27 July 1946, MF

50 Tamm to JEH 30 July 1946, TPF

51 JEH to Trost 30 July 1946, TPF

52 R. C. Hendon to JEH 7 Aug. 1946, TPF

53 M. E. Gurnea to JEH 5 Aug. 1946, TPF

54 JEH to Trost 12 Aug. 1946, TPF

55 Trost to JEH 14 Aug. 1946 and Henry King to JEH 16 Aug. 1946, TPF

56 R. C. Hendon to JEH 7 Aug. 1946, TPF

57 *Black Dispatch,* Oklahoma City, OK. 31 Aug. 1946, TPF

Chapter 8—Hostility and Fear

1 Tamm to Ladd 30 July 1946 and Gurnea to Tamm 5 Aug. 1946, MF

2 J. S. Egan report 19 Jan. 1932, WPF

3 E. J. Connelley to JEH 10 Aug. 1946, WPF

4 Egan to JEH 26 Apr. 1932, WPF

5 F. N. Quinn report 21 June 1930 and H. C. Douglas to JEH 28 Jan. 1936, WPF

6 L. C. Schilder to JEH 6 Dec. 1932, WPF

7 JEH to Tolson 1 Aug. 1944, MF

8 JEH to Weeks 11 Aug. 1944, MF

9   Ladd to JEH 17 Sept. 1946, MF

10 Weeks to JEH 5 Sept. 1946, MF

11 JEH to Clark 19 Sept. 1946, MF

12 JEH to Clark 19 Sept. 1946, MF

13 Gurnea to JEH 5 Aug. 1946, MF

14 Weeks to JEH 8 Aug. 1946, MF

15 Trost to JEH 7 Aug. 1946, MF

16 Weeks to JEH 30 Aug. 1946, MF

17 JEH to Clark 19 Sept. 1946, MF

18 Ladd to JEH quoting Weeks 20 Dec. 1946, MF

19 Tamm to JEH 18 Sept. 1946, MF

20 Charles Towler statement 24 Oct. 1946 with comments by FBI and GBI, MF

21 Maj. Spence in *Atlanta Constitution* 28 July 1946

22 Conference report with NACW 2 Aug. 1946, box 507, PR

23 *Washington Post* 31 July 1946

24 *Washington Post* 30 July 1946

25 JEH to SAC Atlanta 6 Aug. 1946, MF

26 Acting SAC to JEH 30 Aug. 1946, MF

27 Joe Tom Malcolm statement 30 Sept. 1946, MF

28 Redacted name statement 10–11 Oct. 1946, MF

29 Lovett Clarence Malcolm statement 21 Sept. 1946, MF

30 Redacted name statement 11 Oct. 1946, MF

31 Dr. J. R. Trammell statement 4 Aug. 1946, MF

32 Weeks report 5 Aug. 1946, MF

33 Trost to JEH 28 July 1946, MF

34 Agent Charles Carroll in Clinton Adams to *Atlanta Constitution* 31 May 1992

35 Weeks report 5 Aug. 1946, MF

36 Weeks to JEH 23 Aug. 1946, MF

37 Weeks report 5 Aug. 1946, MF

38 Weeks to JEH 30 Aug. 1946, MF

39 Walton Tribune 9 Aug. 1946

40 Weeks to Washington 24 Sept. 1946, MF

41 Redacted name statement 24 Sept. 1946 MF and *Walton Tribune* 13 Sept. 1946

42 Gurnea to JEH 5 Aug. 1946, MF

43 *Walton Tribune* 9 Nov. 1945

44 Weeks to JEH 8 Aug. 1946, MF

45 Trost to JEH 29 July 1946, MF

46 Weeks to JEH 15 Aug. 1946, MF

47 Redacted name statement 11 Aug. 1946, MF

48 Weeks to JEH 8 Aug. 1946, MF

49 Redacted name statement 3 Oct. 1946, MF

50 Weeks to Washington in report 5 Aug. 1946, MF

51 O. B. Lindsey statement 16 Oct. 1946, MF

52 Redacted name statement 3 Oct. 1946, MF

53 Comer Parrish statement 14 Aug. 1946, MF

54 Redacted name statement 28 Sept. 1946, MF

55 James Verner statement 21 Aug. 1946 and James Ivey statement 13 Sept. 1946, MF

56 Clarence Malcolm statement 25 Sept 1946, MF

57 Clarence Malcolm statement 25 Sept. 1946, MF

58 C. D. Forsyth testimony 10 July 1871 vol. 6–7, 121, IS

59 Harry Jackson statement 19 Sept. 1946, MF

60 Redacted name statement 7 Sept. 1946, MF

61 Redacted name statement 9 Sept.–20 Oct. 1946, MF

62 Redacted name statement 11 Sept. 1946, MF

63 Redacted name statement 23 Sept. and 28 Sept. 1946, MF

64 Redacted name statement 17 Aug. 1946, MF

65 Louise Brown in Weeks to Washington 25 Nov. 1946, MF

66 Redacted names statements 20 Oct. 1946, MF

67 Redacted name statement 9 Oct. 1946, MF

68 Macon Thornton 8 Oct. 1946, MF

69 Ernest Harrison 7 Oct. 1946, MF

70 Lester Boyd Hester 3 Oct. 1946, MF

71 Melvin Hester statement 2 Oct. 1946, MF

72 Charles Thomas Hester Jr. statement 3 Oct. 1946, MF

73 Redacted name statement 11 Oct. 1946, MF

74 John Stewart statement 1 Sept. 1946, MF

75 Redacted name statement 9 Oct. 1946, MF

76 Leron Hester 4 Oct. 1946, MF

77 George Edmondson 19 Sept. 1946, MF

78 Redacted name statement 15 Aug. 1946, MF

79 Ernest Hawk statement 22–23 Oct. 1946, MF

80 Weeks to JEH 17 Sept. 1946 and Weeks memo 16 Sept. 1946, MF

81 James Felton and Annie Lou Malcolm 15 Sept. 1946, MF

82 Trost to JEH 1 Aug. 1946, MF

83 Weeks to JEH 8 Aug. 1946, MF

84 Weeks memo 3 Aug. 1946, MF

85 Redacted name statement 6, 7 Nov. 1946, MF

86 Redacted name statement 3 Oct. 1946, MF

87 Redacted name statement 6, 7 Nov. 1946, MF

88 Clarence Dillard statement 6 Oct. 1946, MF

89 Redacted name and date statement, MF

90 *Walton Tribune* 2 Aug. 1946

91 *Washington (State) Daily News* 14 Aug. 1946

92 Hoover quoted in *To Secure These Rights,* report of the President's Committee on Civil Rights, chapter III, p. 124, 29 Oct. 1947, Truman Library, Independence, MO.

93 Redacted name statement 20 Aug. 1946 in G. R. McSwain report 22 Aug. 1946, MF

94 Weeks to JEH 12 Aug. 1946, MF

95 Weeks to JEH 5 Sept. 1946, MF

96 Redacted name statement 12 Nov. 1946, MF

97 Redacted name statement 21 Aug. 1946, MF

98 Willie Lee Pitts statement 17 Sept. 1946, MF

99 Louise Brown statement in Weeks report 25 Nov. 1946, MF

100 Redacted name statement 9 Oct. 1946, MF

101 Strickland to Ladd 3 Sept. 1946, MF

102 Weeks memo 3 Aug. 1946, MF

103 Redacted name statement 17 Oct. 1946, MF

104 Eugene Johnson statement 12 Sept. 1946, MF

105 Redacted name statement 1 Sept. 1946, MF

106 Robert Lee Elder statement 9 Sept. 1946, MF

107 Loy Harrison statement 23 Aug. 1946, MF

108 FBI interviews with redacted names of three children 6 September 1946, MF

109 FBI comments on Johnnie Thrasher statement 13 Sept. 1946, MF

110 Weeks to JEH 8 Aug. 1946, MF

111 Redacted name statement 6 Oct. 1946, MF

112 Weeks memo 3 Aug. 1946, MF

113 Weeks to JEH 8 Aug. 1946 MF

114 White to NAACP Southern branches 21 Aug. 1946, NAACP Group II box A413, LC

115 Trost to JEH 2 Aug. 1946, MF

116 Weeks to JEH 8 Aug. 1946, MF

Chapter 9—Major Suspect

1 Unsigned transcript *Ten o' Clock Wire,* Pacific Northwest, 26 July 1946, case file 144–19M-14, section 17, box 507, PR

2 Anonymous to JEH 1 Aug. 1946, PR

3 Ralph Wright statement 20 Nov. 1946, MF

4 Willie Adams statement 12 Sept. 1946, Dept. of Justice, case 144–19M-14, section 17, Litigation case files 1936–1997, box 544

5 Weeks report 5 Aug. 1946, MF

6 Harrison criminal record 9–10 Sept. 1946, MF

7 Redacted name statement 19 Sept. 1946, MF

8 Redacted name statements 1 Oct. 1946 and 19 Sept. 1946, MF

9 Harrison statement 2 Aug. 1946 in Weeks report 5 Aug. 1946, MF

10 Harrison statement 23 Aug. 1946, MF

11 Marshall Pollock statement 26 Aug. 1946 and Harrison statement 10 Nov. 1946, MF

12 Redacted name statement 21 Sept. 1946, MF

13 Robert Lee Elder statement 23 Oct. 1946, MF

14 Grace Thurmond statement 30 Aug. 1946, MF

15 Tax collector records Watkinsville, GA for 1945, MF

16 Weeks to JEH in Weeks report 5 Aug. 1946, MF

17 Harrison statement 10 Nov. 1946, MF

18 Weeks to JEH 23 Aug. 1946, MF

19 Weeks report 25 Nov. 1946 and Grace Thurmond statement 30 Aug. 1946, MF

20 Willie Adams statement 28 Aug. 1946, MF

21 Anderson Elder statement 15 Oct. 1946, redacted name statement 24 Sept. 1946, Eugene Johnson statement 12 Sept. 1946, redacted names statements 22 Aug. 1946, 6 Sept. 1946 and Willie Adams statement 28 Aug. 1946, MF

22 Harrison statement 26 Sept. 1946, MF

23 Grace Thurmond statement 3 Sept. 1946, MF

24 Willie Adams statements 12 Sept. 1946 and 28 Aug. 1946, box 506, PR

25 Willie Adams statement 12 Sept. 1946, box 506, PR

26 Grace Thurmond statement 30 Aug. 1946, MF

27 Grace Thurmond statements 3 Sept. 1936 and 6 Sept. 1946, MF

28 Harrison statement 26 Sept. 1946, MF

29 Redacted name statement 22 Aug. 1946, MF

30 Redacted name statement 25 Aug. 1946, MF

31 Weeks report 25 Nov.1946, MF

32 Redacted names statement 30 Aug. 1946 and 25 Aug. 1946, MF

33 Harrison statement 26 Sept. 1946, MF

34 Redacted name statement 16 Aug. 1946, MF

35 Redacted name statement 6 Sept. 1946, MF

36 Redacted name statement 24 August 1946, MF

37 William Jackson statement 22 Aug. 1946, MF

38 Redacted name statement 6 Sept. 1946, MF

39 Redacted name statement 21 Aug. 1946, MF

40 Charlie Boy Dorsey statement 8 Sept. 1946, MF

41 Weeks memo 16 Sept. 1946, MF

42 Weeks to JEH 11 Aug. 1946, MF

43 Harrison statement 26 Sept. 1946, MF

Chapter 10—Prime Suspects

1   Redacted names statements 12 Aug. 1946, MF
2   Redacted names statements 13 Aug. 1946, MF
3   Redacted name statement 10 Aug. 1946, MF
4   Weldon Hester statement 13 Aug. 1946, MF
5   Sheriff Gordon statement 14 Aug. 1946, MF
6   Grady Malcolm statement 5 Aug. 1946, MF
7   Weldon Hester statement 13 Aug. 1946, MF
8   Grady Malcolm statement 5 Aug. 1946, MF
9   Preston Peters statement 27 Nov. 1946, MF
10 Redacted name statement 14 Aug. 1946, MF
11 Redacted name statement 19 Aug. 1946, MF
12 Weldon Hester statement 13 Aug. 1946, MF
13 Redacted name statement 10 Oct. 1946, MF
14 Dora Malcolm and Dora Mae Pryor joint statement 22 Aug. 1946, box 506, PR
15 Dora Malcolm and Dora Mae Pryor joint statement 22 Aug. 1946, box 506, PR
16 Weldon Hester statement 13 Aug. 1946, MF
17 Redacted name comment 13 Aug. 1946, MF
18 Weldon Hester statement 13 Aug. 1946, MF
19 Weldon Hester statement 13 Aug. 1946, MF
20 Mrs. Weldon Hester statement 13 Aug. 1946, MF
21 Redacted name statement 20 Aug. 1946, MF
22 Weldon Hester statement 13 Aug. 1946, MF
23 Redacted name statement 20 Nov. 1946, MF
24 Louis Malcolm statement 23 Aug. 1946, MF
25 Lamar Howard statement 2 Jan. 1947 in Joseph Sylvester report 9 Jan. 1947, box 507, PR
26 Redacted name undated statement in Joseph Sylvester report 9 Jan. 1946, box 507, PR
27 Weeks report 25 Nov. 1946, MF
28 Harrison statement 26 Sept. 1946, MF
29 FBI comment in agent Joseph Sylvester Jr. report to Washington 9 Jan. 1947, 61, box 507, PR
30 James Verner statement 30 July 1946, MF
31 James Verner statement 21 Aug. 1946, MF
32 Vivian Tillman statement 4 Sept. 1946, MF
33 James Verner statement 6 Sept. 1946 and Evelyn Patterson statement 24 Aug. 1946, MF
34 James Verner statement 21 Aug. 1946, MF
35 Weeks report 25 Nov. 1946, 218, MF
36 James Verner statement 30 July 1946, MF

37 James Verner statement 30 July 1946, MF

38 James Verner statement 21 Aug. 1946, MF

39 Evelyn Patterson statements 24 Aug 1946 and 26 Aug. 1946, MF

40 Sam Bradley statement 25 Aug. 1946, MF

41 Evelyn Patterson statement 24 Aug. 1946, MF

42 James Verner statement 21 Aug. 1946, MF

43 James Verner statement 30 July 1946, MF

44 James Verner statement 21 Aug. 1946, MF

45 James Verner statement 21 Sept. 1946, MF

46 James Verner statement 21 Aug. 1946, MF

47 Weeks report 25 Nov. 1946, MF

48 Redacted name statement 27 Aug. 1946, MF

49 FBI comment in Bob Hester statement 15 Aug. 1946, MF

50 FBI comment in 12 and 15 Aug. 1946, MF

51 Redacted name statement and FBI comment 9 Sept. 1946, MF

52 Redacted name statement 9 Sept. 1946, MF

53 Lewis Howard statements 14 and 29 Aug. 1946, MF

54 Weeks report 25 Nov, 1946, MF

55 Sorrells and Howard statements 14 Aug. 1946, MF, and FBI pre-Grand Jury report p.81, MF

56 Lewis Howard statement 14 Aug. 1946, MF

57 FBI Pre-Grand Jury report p. 81, MF

58 Ida Hester statement 12 Aug. 1946, MF

59 Bob Hester statement 15 Aug. 1946, MF

60 George Hester statement 28 July 1946, MF

61 George Hester statements, 28 July and 15 Aug. 1946, MF

62 FBI comment in George Hester summary 8 Aug. 1946, MF

63 George Hester statement 8 Aug. 1946, MF

64 FBI comment in Bob Hester statement 15 Aug. 1946, MF

65 George Hester statements 28 July & and 15 Aug. 1946, MF

66 Grady Malcolm statements 31 July 1946 and 3 Aug. 1946, MF

67 FBI comment in redacted name statements 9 and 11 Aug. 1946, MF, and Redacted name statement 3 Oct. 1946, MF

68 Grady Malcolm statement 5 Aug. 1946, MF

69 Grady Malcolm statement 5 Aug. 1946, MF

70 Wayman Malcolm statement 5 Aug. 1946, MF

71 Wayman Malcolm statement 4 and 5 Aug. 1946, MF

72 Grady Malcolm statement 5 Aug. 1946, MF

73 Alvin Adcock statement 1 Aug. 1946, MF

74 Alvin Adcock statement 9 Aug. 1946, MF

75 Redacted name statement 9 Aug. 1946, MF

76 Alvin Adcock statement 9 Aug. 1946, MF
77 Alvin Adcock statements 1 Aug. 1946, 4 Aug. 1946 and 9 Aug. 1946, MF
78 Redacted name statement 27 July 1946, MF
79 Leonius Adcock statement 9 Aug. 1946, MF
80 Leonius Adcock statements 1 Aug. 1946 and 9 Aug. 1946, MF
81 Leonius Adcock statement 1 Aug. 1946, MF
82 Leonius Adcock statements 1 Aug. 1946 and 9 Aug. 1946 MF
83 FBI remarks 9 Aug. 1946, MF
84 Redacted name statement 21 Aug. 1946, MF
85 Willie Pitts statement 22 Aug. 1946, MF
86 Powell Adcock statement 1 Aug. 1946, MF
87 Redacted name statement 16 Aug. 1946, MF
88 Redacted name statement 8 Aug. 1946, MF
89 FBI comment in redacted name statement 11 Aug. 1946, MF
90 Powell Adcock statement 1 Aug. 1946, MF
91 Willie Pitts statement 17 Sept. 1946, MF
92 Willie Pitts statement 22 Aug. 1946, MF
93 FBI comment in redacted name statement 11 Aug. 1946, MF
94 FBI comment in Powell Adcock statement 1 Aug. 1946, MF
95 FBI comment in Melvin Hester statement 30 July 1946, MF
96 Melvin Hester and Redacted name statements 30 July 1946, MF
97 Clarence and Melvin Hester statements 1 Aug. 1946 and 30 July 1946, MF
98 Redacted name statement 13 Aug. 1946, MF
99 Redacted name statement synopsis in Weeks summary to Washington, 30 Oct. 1946, MF
100 Melvin Hester statement 2 Oct. 1946, MF
101 FBI remarks 3 Oct. 1946, MF
102 FBI description 2 Oct. 1946, MF
103 Melvin Hester statement 2 Oct. 1946, MF
104 Melvin Hester statement 2 Oct. 1946, MF
105 Clarence Hester statement 1 Aug. 1946, MF
106 Clarence Hester statement 2 Oct. 1946, MF
107 FBI comment in Melvin Hester statement 2 Oct. 1946, MF
108 Clarence Hester statement 2 Oct. 1946, MF
109 Clarence Hester description 1 Aug. 1946, MF
110 Redacted name statement 13 Aug. 1946, MF
111 Clarence Hester statement 2 Oct. 1946, MF
112 Redacted name statement in Clarence Hester statement 1 Aug. 1946, MF
113 Clarence Hester statements 1 Aug. 1946 and 2 Oct. 1946 MF
114 Weeks to Washington 24 Sept. 1946, MF
115 Redacted name statement 26 Aug. 1946, MF

116 Redacted name statement 5 Nov. 1946, MF

117 Redacted name statement 11 Nov. 1946, MF

Chapter 11—Sexual Relations

1   Ridden Farmer statement 12 Aug. 1946, MF
2   Redacted names statements 3, 9 Oct. 1946, MF
3   Ridden Farmer statement 12 Aug. 1946, MF
4   Hillman Levy Adcock statement 10 Aug. 1946, MF
5   Ridden Farmer statement 12 Aug. 1946, MF
6   Redacted name statement 13 Sept. 1946, MF
7   Redacted name statement 14 Sept. 1946, MF
8   Henry Thomas statement 19 Sept. 1946, box 507, PR
9   Ben Dickinson statement 10 Sept. 1946, MF
10 Charlie Boy Dorsey statement 17 Sept. 1946, MF
11 Redacted name statement 14 Aug. 1946, MF
12 Charlie Boy Dorsey statement 17 Sept. 1946, MF
13 FBI comment in Charlie Boy Dorsey statement 17 Sept. 1946, MF
14 Redacted name statement 14 Aug. 1946, MF
15 Ridden Farmer statement 12 Aug. 1946, MF
16 Redacted name statement 3 Sept. 1946, MF
17 Redacted name statement 14 Aug. 1946, MF
18 Redacted name statement 13 Sept. 1946, MF
19 Martie Adams statement 14 Aug. 1946, MF
20 Ridden Farmer statement 12 Aug. 1946, MF
21 Martie Adams statement 13 Aug. 1946, MF

Chapter 12—Hoover Offensive

1   Lincoln to Joseph Hooker 26 Jan. 1863
2   JEH to Clark 29 July 1946, MF
3   JEH to Clark 30 July 1946, MF
4   JEH to House Committee on Un-American Activities, reprinted in CR, 80C 1S 2692
5   McKellar to JEH 23 Oct. 1947, McPF
6   Hearings before subcommittee of Senate Committee on Appropriations 74C 2S 199
7   Weeks to JEH 31 July 1953 McPF
8   Ladd to JEH 10 Sept. 1946, MF
9   JEH to SAC Washington 10 Sept. 1946, MF
10 Ladd to JEH 4 Oct. 1946 and SAC Washington report 20 Sept. 1946, MF
11 Caudle to JEH 26 July 1946, JEH to Clark 3 Oct. 1946, Weeks to JEH 21 Oct. 1946, JEH margin note in Weeks to JEH 19 Nov. 1946, JEH to Clark 17 Dec. 1946, MF

12 JEH margin notes on Ladd to JEH 16 Sept. 1946, MF
13 Clark to Robeson 18 Sept. 1946, MF
14 JEH to Tolson, Tamm, Ladd and Nichols 4 Sept. 1946, MF
15 Ned Brooks, *Scripps-Howard* 7 Oct. 1946, MF
16 JEH margin note on Ned Brooks, *Scripps-Howard* 7 Oct, 1946, MF
17 *Washington Post* 28 July 1946
18 Weeks to JEH 23 Aug. 1946, MF
19 Strickland to Ladd 3 Sept. 1946, MF
20 Ladd to JEH 6 Sept. 1946, MF
21 Ladd to JEH 16 Aug. 1946, MF
22 Ladd to JEH 3 Sept. 1946 disk
23 Weeks to JEH 6 Aug. 1946, MF
24 Weeks to JEH 8 Aug. 1946, MF
25 Weeks to JEH 14 Aug. 1946, MF
26 Weeks to JEH 11 Aug. 1946, MF
27 Weeks to JEH 29 Aug. 1946, MF
28 JEH to Weeks 22 Aug. 1946, MF
29 Weeks to JEH 31 Aug. 1946, MF
30 Weeks to JEH 22 Sept. 1946, MF
31 Tamm to JEH 18 Sept. 1946, MF
32 Weeks memo 16 Sept. 1946, MF
33 Weeks to JEH 30 Aug. 1946, MF
34 Tamm to JEH 18 Sept. 1946, MF
35 Weeks to JEH 30 Aug. 1946 and Weeks to Washington 25 Nov. 1946, MF
36 JEH to Clark 19 Sept. 1946, MF

Chapter 13—Pre-Grand Jury

1   Clark to JEH 3 Oct. 1946, MF
2   Weeks to JEH 21 Oct. 1946, MF
3   Weeks memo, 16 Sept. 1946, MF
4   JEH comment on Weeks to JEH 19 Nov. 1946, MF
5   JEH to Clark 3 Oct. 1946, box 507, PR
6   Clark to JEH 7 Oct. 1946, MF
7   JEH to Weeks 10 Oct. 1946, MF
8   Weeks to JEH 21 Oct. 1946, MF
9   Weeks to JEH 4 Nov. 1946, MF
10 Weeks to JEH 21 Oct. 1946, MF
11 Weeks to JEH 19 Nov. 1946, MF
12 Weeks to Hoover 29 Nov. 1946, MF
13 Weeks to JEH 19 Nov. 1946, MF
14 JEH to Clark 3 Oct. 1946, MF

15 Weeks to JEH 21 Oct. 1946, MF

16 JEH to Clark 3 Oct. 1946, MF

17 Weeks to JEH 23 Sept. 1946, MF

18 Weeks to JEH 23 Sept. 1946, MF

19 Weeks to JEH 23 Sept. 1946 and JEH to Clark 3 Oct. 1946, MF

20 JEH to Clark 3 Oct. 1946, box 507, PR

21 Weeks to JEH 21 Oct. 1946, MF

22 Walton Tribune 15 Nov. 1946, MF

23 JEH to Caudle 13 Nov. 1946, MF

24 Ladd to JEH quoting Weeks 20 Dec. 1946, MF

25 J. S. Egan report 19 Jan. 1932, WPF

26 Lewis Howard and Sorrells statements 29 Aug. 1946, Sorrells statement 14 Aug. 1946, and Flanigan statement 6 Sept. 1946, MF

27 Weeks to JEH 19 Nov. 1946, MF

28 Ladd to Tamm 12 Nov. 1946, MF

29 JEH to Caudle 29 Oct. 1946, MF

30 Ladd to Tamm 12 Nov. 1946, MF

31 Weeks to JEH 4 Nov. 1946, MF

32 Weeks to JEH 21 Oct. 1946 and 4 Nov. 1946, MF

33 Weeks to JEH 4 Nov. 1946, MF

34 Weeks to JEH 3 Dec. 1946, MF

35 Weeks to JEH 4 Nov. 1946 MF

36 *New York Herald Tribune* 3 Dec. 1946

37 Weeks to JEH 19 Nov. 1946, MF

38 *Daily Worker* 3 Dec. 1946

39 *New York Times* 3 Dec. 1946

Chapter 14—Grand Jury

1   Tamm to JEH 9 Dec. 1946, MF

2   JEH to Tolson 12 Dec. 1946, MF

3   Tamm to JEH 9 Dec. 1946, MF

4   JEH to Tolson 12 Dec. 1946, MF

5   JEH appendage to Caudle to JEH 7 Nov. 1946, MF

6   Weeks to JEH 27 Nov. 1946, MF

7   Tamm to JEH 9 Dec. 1946, MF

8   *Walton Tribune* 6 Dec. 1946

9   George Hester statement 8 Aug. 1946, MF and *Walton Tribune* 6 Dec. 1946

10 *Atlanta Constitution* 4 Dec. 1946

11 *Walton Tribune* 6 Dec. 1946

12 *Atlanta Constitution* 4 Dec. 1946

13 *Atlanta Constitution* 5 Dec. 1946

14 *Atlanta Constitution* 4 Dec. 1946

15 *Atlanta Constitution* 5 Dec. 1946

16 Tamm to JEH 9 Dec. 1946 MF

17 Tamm to JEH 9 Dec. 1946, MF

18 Tamm to Ladd 18 Dec. 1946, MF

19 JEH to Clark 17 Dec. 1946, MF

20 Weeks to JEH 20 Dec. 1946, MF

21 Weeks to JEH 20 Dec. 1946, MF

22 Weeks to JEH 20 Dec. 1946, MF

23 Weeks to JEH 20 Dec. 1946, MF

24 Major Jones statement 10 Dec. 1946 in Weeks to Washington Bureau 21 Dec. 1946, MF

25 Major Jones statement 10 Dec. 1946 in Weeks to Washington Bureau 21 Dec. 1946, MF

26 Weeks to Washington Bureau 25 Nov. 1946, MF

27 Weeks to Washington Bureau 21 Dec. 1946, MF

28 Weeks to JEH 20 Dec. 1946, MF

29 JEH to Clark 17 Dec. 1946, MF

30 Weeks to JEH 20 Dec. 1946, MF and *Atlanta Constitution* 3 Dec. 1946

31 Jury decision, 19 Dec. 1946 and Weeks to Washington Bureau 21 Dec. 1946, MF

32 Ladd to Tamm 20 Dec. 1946, MF

33 Weeks to JEH 20 Dec. 1946, MF

34 A. Devitt Vanech to JEH 23 Dec. 1946, MF

35 Stroupe, Henry S. in *Dictionary of North Carolina Biography*. Chapel Hill: University of North Carolina Press, 1979

36 *Walton Tribune* 3 Jan. 1947

37 *Walton Tribune* 20 Dec. 1946

38 Alvin Adcock description E. J. Foltz to Washington Bureau 13 Jan. 1947, MF

39 E. J. Fritz to Washington Bureau 13 Jan. 1947, MF

40 Alvin Adcock confession 12 Dec. 1946 in E. J. Fritz to Washington Bureau 13 Jan. 1946, MF

41 Leonius Adcock statement 12 Dec. 1946, MF

42 Weeks to JEH 16 Dec. 1946, MF

43 SAC Atlanta to JEH 16 June 1948 and John Balls 16 Mar. 1949, MF

44 Weeks to JEH 20 Dec. 1946, MF

45 Weeks to JEH 19 Dec. 1946, MF

46 Weeks to JEH 20 Dec. 1946

47 Ladd to Tamm 20 Dec. 1946, MF

48 Devitt Vanech to JEH 23 Dec. 1946, MF

49 Nichols to Tolson 31 Dec. 1946, MF

50 Weeks to JEH 20 Dec. 1946, MF

51 JEH margin notes in Weeks to JEH 20 Dec. 1946, MF

52 Walter White to NAACP staff 12 July 1946 part 2, B99 folder 7, Thurgood Marshall, general, 1946, records of NAACP, LC

53 Marshall to White 1 Oct. 1946, part 2, B99 folder 7, Thurgood Marshall, general, 1946, records of NAACP, LC

54 Marshall to Clark 27 Dec. 1946, group 2, box A410, general office file, folder 7, LC

55 Clark to Marshall 13 Jan. 1947, group 2, box A410, general office file, folder 7, LC

56 JEH to Walter White 13 Jan. 1947, group 2, box A410, general office file, folder 7, LC

57 White to Marshall 20 Jan. 1947, group 2, box A410, general office file, folder 7, LC

58 Marshall to White 23 Jan. 1947, group 2, box A410, general office file, folder 7, LC

Chapter 15—Vengeance

1 JEH to Caudle 3 Jan. 1947, box 507, PR

2 Lamar Howard undated statement, box 507, PR

3 Lamar Howard undated statement, box 507, PR

4 Lamar Howard statement 2 Jan. 1947, box 507, PR

5 Cowart to Clark 4 June 1947, box 507, PR

6 Lamar Howard statement 1 Aug. 1946, MF

7 Lamar Howard undated re-interview, box 507, PR

8 Lamar Howard statement 9 Jan. 1947, box 507, PR

9 Francis Peek statement 5 Jan. 1947, box 507, PR

10 FBI description of Tom Verner, box 507, PR

11 Willie Howard statement 6 Jan. 1947, box 507, PR

12 Associated Press quoted in *Washington Star* 3 Jan. 1947 and William Fowlker statement 6 Jan. 1947, box 507, PR

13 Will Perry statement 3 Jan. 1947 and William Fowlker statement 6 Jan. 1947, box 507, PR

14 Lamar Howard undated statement, box 507, PR

15 Mercine Simmons statement 5 Jan. 1947 and William Borders statement 6 Jan. 1947, box 507, PR

16 Associated Press quoted in *Washington Star* 3 Jan. 1947 and Reverend William Holmes Borders statement 6 Jan. 1947, box 507, PR

17 Associated Press quoted in *Washington Star* 3 Jan. 1947

18 Jack Simmons, statement 6 Jan. 1947, James Howard statement 6 Jan. 1947, Lillie Simmons statement 6 Jan. 1947, box 507, PR

19 Lamar Howard undated statement, box 507, PR

20 Lamar Howard statement 2 Jan. 1947, box 507, PR
21 Paul Brice statement 6 Jan. 1947, box 507, PR
22 Paul Brice statement 6 Jan. 1947, box 507, PR
23 Lillie Simmons statement 6 Jan. 1947, box 507, PR
24 Dr. Homer Head 5 Jan. 1947, box 507, PR
25 C. J. "Doc" Sorrells statement 5 Jan. 1947, box 507, PR
26 Lamar Howard statement 2 Jan. 1947 and Lewis Howard statement 5 Jan. 1947, box 507, PR
27 Martin to White 24 Aug. 1946, NAACP Group II box A412, LC
28 Richard Hackney statement 6 Jan. 1947, box 507, PR
29 Associated Press quoted in *Washington Star* 3 Jan. 1947
30 William Fowlker statements 3 Jan. 1947 and 6 Jan. 1947, box 507, PR
31 *Walton Tribune* 10 Jan. 1947 and Ben Dickinson statement 4 Jan. 1947, box 507, PR
32 *Walton Tribune* 10 Jan. 1947 and charge sheet US vs James and Tom Verner, 11 Feb. 1947, box 507, PR
33 FBI report 31 Jan. 1947, box 507, PR
34 FBI description in Howard Peters statement 11 Aug. 1946, MF
35 FBI report in statement by Howard Leonius Peters 11 Aug. 1946, MF, *Walton Tribune* 10 Jan. 1947 and FBI addenda, box 507, PR
36 Agent Thomas Davis undated statement box 507, PR
37 Gerdine Banks statement 7 Jan. 1947, box 507, PR
38 JEH to Caudle 14 Jan. 1947, box 507, PR
39 Bowdry Crutchfield statement 16 Jan. 1947, box 507, PR
40 Daniel Young statement 16 Jan. 1947, box 507, PR
41 Daniel Young statement 16 Jan. 1947, box 507, PR
42 JEH to Caudle 20 Jan. 1947 and Caudle to JEH 28 Jan. 1947, box 507, PR
43 Mahlon Bloodsaw statement 16 Jan. 1947, box 507, PR
44 JEH to Clark 3 Jan. 1947, box 507, PR
45 Will Perry statement 3 Jan. 1947, Box 507, PR

Chapter 16—Defective Juries

1 FBI undated notation, box 507, PR
2 Cowart to Clark 6 Mar. 1947, box 507, PR and *Atlanta Daily World* 25 Feb. 1947
3 Agent E. DeWitt Wingo statement 4 Jan. 1947, box 507, PR
4 *Atlanta Daily World* 25 Feb. 1947
5 *Atlanta Daily World* 25 Feb. 1947
6 *Atlanta Daily World* 26 Feb. 1947
7 Cowart to Clark 6 Mar. 1947, box 507, PR
8 Cowart to Clark 6 Mar. 1947, box 507, PR
9 *Atlanta Constitution* 4 June 1947

10 Cowart to Clark 4 June 1947, box 507, PR
11 Cowart to Clark 4 June 1947, box 507, PR
12 Agent E. DeWitt Wingo statement 4 Jan. 1947 and FBI report 9 Jan. 1947, box 507, PR
13 Agent E. DeWitt Wingo statement 4 Jan. 1947, FBI report 9 Jan. 1947, box 507, PR and *Atlanta Constitution* 4 June 1947
14 Cowart to Clark 4 June 1947, box 507, PR
15 Cowart to Clark 4 June 1947, FBI report 10 June 1947 US vs James and Tom Verner, box 507, PR, and *Atlanta Constitution* 4 June 1947
16 Cowart to Clark 4 June 1947, box 507, PR
17 Cowart to Clark 4 June 1947, box 507, PR
18 Cowart opinion 30 June 1949, box 507, PR
19 Maceo Hubbard opinion 29 Apr. 1949, box 507, PR and Cowart to Clark 31 Oct. 1947, MF
20 Cowart to Clark 6 May 1949, box 507, PR
21 Cowart to Clark 15 Jan. 1948, box 507, PR
22 SAC Atlanta to JEH 7 Jan. 1953, MF

Chapter 17—Eyewitnesses

1 *Atlanta Constitution* 31 May 1992
2 *Atlanta Constitution* 31 May 1992
3 Jim Procopio to FBI Director 18 July 1991, FBI Airtel, file # 63–21063-3
4 SAC Atlanta to FBI Director 1 May 1991, 62D-AT-66422
5 *Atlanta Constitution* 31 May 1992
6 Procopio to FBI Director 18 July 1991, FBI Airtel, file # 63–21063-3
7 Clinton Adams in *Athens Banner-Herald* 19 May 2013
8 Clinton Adams, quoted in OnlineAthens, *Athens Banner-Herald* 9 June 1999 from *The Secret Inside* by Adams's wife, Marjorie, and Ann Varnum, self-published
9 Clinton Adams to *Atlanta Constitution* 31 May 1992
10 Emerson Farmer statements 28 July and 11 Aug. 1946, MF, and Reba Farmer statement 27 July 1946, MF
11 Emerson Farmer statement 28 July 1946, MF
12 Procopio to FBI Director 18 July 1991, FBI Airtel, file # 63–21063-3
13 *Atlanta Constitution* 31 May 1992
14 SAC Atlanta to FBI Director 1 May 1991, 62D-AT-66422
15 *Atlanta Constitution* 31 May 1992
16 *Athens Banner-Herald* 13 July 2008
17 Watson in video recording Apr. 2013
18 Wayne Watson in video recording Apr. 2013, *The Guardian* 16 Feb. 2015, *Washington Post* 18 Feb. 2015

19 *Atlanta Journal-Constitution* 20 Feb. 2015
20 *Walton Tribune* 6 June 1999

Chapter 18—Court Action

1 Joseph Bell to Michael Moore, US District Attorney for Middle District of Georgia 20 Aug. 2013
2 Joseph Bell re Petition of Anthony S. Pitch, US District Court for Middle District of Georgia, 29 Jan. 2014.
3 Michael Moore to US District Court for Middle District of Georgia 5 March 2014
4 Weeks to JEH 20 Dec. 1946, MF
5 SAC Atlanta to FBI Director 1 May 1991, 62D-AT-66422
6 Weeks to JEH 20 Dec. 1946, MF
7 John Fox to the author 21 May 2015
8 Judge Treadwell Order, US District Court for Middle District of Georgia, 19 Aug. 2014
9 Bell to Lynch 27 June 2015, copy in the author's possession
10 Attorney General's 4th annual report to Congress pp. 3–4, 2012

Chapter 19—Afterword

1 Richard Rusk, Secretary MFMC, in *Reflections Along the Truth and Reconciliation Trail,* for Emory University conference 3–6 Oct. 2002
2 Rusk in *Walton Tribune* 6 Aug. 1997
3 Rusk to *Athens Banner Herald* 22 Mar. 1998
4 Andrew Lee in *The Red & Black,* University of Georgia student newspaper 6 Nov. 1997
5 Editorial in *Athens Banner-Herald* 22 Mar. 1998
6 *Athens Banner-Herald* 26 July 2005
7 Rusk in *Athens Banner-Herald* 7 Aug. 2008
8 Benford Stellman in *Athens Banner-Herald* 26 July 2005
9 *Athens Banner-Herald* 26 July 2005
10 *Walton Tribune* 31 July 2013
11 *Walton Tribune* 31 July 2013
12 *Athens Banner-Herald* 26 July 2005
13 Rusk in *Athens Banner-Herald* 7 Aug. 2008
14 *Athens Banner-Herald* 21 July 2010
15 Rusk in *Athens Banner-Herald* 7 Aug. 2008
16 Editorial, *Athens Banner-Herald* 21 July 2010
17 Jason Winders in *Athens Banner-Herald* 3 Aug. 2008
18 Interview with the author 25 July 2011

19 Records of NAACP group 2 boxes A407 and A412, lynching miscellaneous reports 1940–46, LC

20 NACW meeting with Peyton Ford 2 Aug. 1946, box 507, PR

21 Ladd to JEH quoting Weeks 20 Dec. 1946, MF

22 Statement by [redacted name] African American woman to FBI 19 Aug. 1946, MF

23 FBI report on interview with [redacted name] 21 Sept. 1946, MF

24 *http://www.wsbtv.com/news/news/local/georgia-state-rep-tyrone-brooks-resigns/ nkqZj/*

25 http://www.11alive.com/story/news/politics/2015/04/09/state-rep-tyrone-brooks-set-to-enter-plea-on-fraud-tax-charges/25512529/

26 *http://www.wsbtv.com/news/news/local/georgia-state-rep-tyrone-brooks-resigns/ nkqZj/*

27 Tyrone Brooks telephone conversation with the author 3 June 2015

28 Martin to White 24 Aug. 1946, NAACP Group II box A412, LC

29 Rusk in *Athens Banner-Herald* 7 Aug. 2008

30 Rusk in *Stuck at the Moore's Ford Bridge,* undated 2005

31 *Athens Banner-Herald* 26 July 2005

Acknowledgments

W hen I began researching this book with a trip down to the site of the lynchings near Monroe, Georgia, I met two men who had a profound effect on me for their courage and tenacity. They refused to abandon the case, and did all they could to commemorate the lives of the four African American victims. Bobby Howard and Rich Rusk were in the forefront of these twin missions. They risked their lives in these endeavors. Bobby, an African American civil rights advocate of the highest stature, survived a firebombing and jail in his quest for justice and remembrance. Rich, secretary of the Moore's Ford Memorial Committee, and son of former Secretary of State Dean Rusk, whom I had interviewed more than a quarter century earlier, kept the issue alive through newspaper articles and in scholarship and other programs to better race relations in Georgia. At different times, both showed me homes and sites connected with the lynchings and reeled off their extensive knowledge of the crime. Admiration for them is inadequate to express my awe for their bravery.

Gratitude is insufficient to thank attorney Joseph J. Bell, of Bell, Shivas & Fasolo P.C., Rockaway, New Jersey. I had met him years ago when he invited me to lead a group on a tour of sites connected with Abraham Lincoln's assassination in Washington, DC, based on my book, *"They Have Killed Papa Dead!"—The Road to Ford's Theatre, Abraham Lincoln's Murder, and the Rage for Vengeance*. We became friendly when he repeated the tour many times with aspiring lawyers, friends, and staff. He volunteered to represent me pro bono in my quest to unseal the secret grand jury testimony in this case, heard in Athens, Georgia, on December 3–19, of 1946. In the many years he devoted to this crucial aspect of the book, he even went through the tedious and expensive process of being admitted to the Georgia bar to plead my case, should it become necessary. It was a lengthy process, involving countless hours of research, a US attorney, a Georgia District Court judge, help from the FBI historian, inquiries at archival repositories, and requests through the Freedom of Information Act. And all the while he dedicated his time and legal skills to helping me. It was a mark of his devotion to the law and the blessings he bestowed on me. Thanks are also due to his staff, most notably Cheryl Capo, Patricia Melia, and Michael Edwards, who gave so much of their time and expertise to the issues.

My appreciation is also due to Dr. John Fox Jr., FBI historian, based in Washington, DC. At all times he was approachable and exceedingly helpful, especially in advising me on how to search for the personnel files of John Trost and his successor, Charles Weeks, who led the FBI investigation at different times in Monroe, Georgia. He also gave much of his precious time in trying hard to try and track down the elusive grand jury testimony and specific requested letters.

I made many requests under the Freedom of Information Act for details about this tragedy. Sometimes I drew a blank, as with the grand jury testimony. But I received bulky material on the search for the murderers and back-channel correspondence between Washington and Georgia, then on the massive personnel files of US Senator Kenneth McKellar, and FBI Special Agents in Charge, John Trost and Charles Weeks. For their prompt help I want to thank David Hardy, FOIA Section Chief, and David Sobonya, Public Information Officer, of the FBI Records Management Division, Winchester, Virginia.

Richard Peuser, Chief, Textual Reference Operations at the National Archives, College Park, Maryland, has always brought his acute knowledge of the extensive records collection to my attention, and he was again indispensable and forthcoming when approached. Both he and his colleague, Dr. Christina Violeta Jones, were generous with their knowledge and busy schedules, particularly in their hunt for evidence given to the grand jury. Acting on information I gave them, Rick Peuser authorized, and James Mathis declassified, a huge FBI file on civil rights violations, particularly the massive disenfranchisement of African Americans from voter rolls in Georgia for the first all-race primary in 1946. This was enormously useful in detailing an orchestrated campaign to suppress the black vote in that election. I acknowledge the professional and profuse assistance I received from so many other experts at Archives II. Without them I would be lost in the labyrinth of finding aids. Special thanks are due to Tab Lewis, Archivist RDT2, to Amy Reytar, Civilian Archivist, and David Castillo and Haley Maynard, Archives Technicians, who were indispensable.

Without the enviable help from experts at the Library of Congress, particularly in the Madison building, I would have fumbled or strayed helplessly on many topics. I am so grateful to the following for their expertise, which they shared with much enthusiasm, whether it was in locating the right manuscripts and documents, photographic images, or copyright needs: Adrienne Cannon, Manuscript Specialist; Jeffrey Flannery, head of the reference and reader services section in the Manuscripts Division, and his assistants, Jennifer Brathovde, Joe Jackson, Patrick Kerwin, Bruce Kirby, and Lewis Wyman. Jonathan Eaker, Reference Technician and Jan Grenci, Reference Specialist, in Prints and Photographs; Rosemary Kelly, Head of Records Research and Certification, and Patricia Rigsbee, Senior Copyright Research Specialist, both at the Copyright Office.

Many institutions scoured their collections for the grand jury testimony and I would like to thank them publically for their diligent efforts, although they were unable to trace it. It may be that any written testimony was among masses of files reportedly destroyed by a confidant of FBI Director J. Edgar Hoover after his death in 1972. Those who searched for the missing record include individuals already noted above, and the office of the US attorney in Macon, Ga., Guy Hall, Archivist at the National Archives and Records Administration at Atlanta, in Morrow, Georgia; Kayla Barrett of the Georgia State Archives; Linda Wilkins, Public Affairs Specialist at FBI headquarters in Washington, DC; Jen Erdman, Records Manager at the Georgia Department of Community Affairs, Atlanta; Mazie Bowen, Public Service Coordinator, University of Georgia, Special Collections Library, Athens, who got the same reply from the Richard B. Russell Library for Political Research and Studies, also at Athens; Melinda Castels, Chief Deputy Clerk, and Tasha Parker, Deputy Clerk, Walton County Superior Court, Monroe, Georgia.

Karen Needles, who is digitizing online all federal records created during the administration of Abraham Lincoln, and housed at the National Archives, saved me many hours of precious time when arranging for files to be pulled well in advance of my arrival at Archives II.

Requests for the official coroner's reports on all four victims were handled by Melinda Castels, Chief Deputy Clerk, Walton Superior Court, Monroe, Georgia, and forwarded by Kathy Trost, Clerk.

Stephen Emmett, FBI Special Agent in the Atlanta bureau, took several questions relating to the 2008 search by the FBI for evidence in the unsolved lynchings.

Time and again I drew on the *Congressional Record* in the US Senate Library for excerpts of debates. Assistance from three reference librarians, Brian McLaughlin, Nancy Kervin, and Meghan Dunn, was extraordinarily fulfilling. Not only did they locate, prepare, and explain the contents, but Nancy Kervin even sent me a link to C-Span's TV coverage of the Senate apology for not having passed anti-lynch laws in the past.

Special mention is due to Hilary Shelton, Director, NAACP Washington Bureau and Senior Vice-President for Policy and Advocacy, and Adam Lee, the Office Operations Manager, for their invaluable assistance in providing me with the full interview between then NAACP National President Benjamin Jealous and Wayne Watson, which was handed over to Thomas Perez, then head of the Justice Department's Civil Rights Division, before his appointment as secretary of labor.

Teresa Sharkey and Mary Kay Schmidt, of Archives II, found crucial file numbers that enabled me to request thousands of documents maintained by the FBI. Wes Swietek, formerly managing editor of the *Walton Tribune* and now editor of the *Daily News,* Bowling Green, Kentucky, shared confidences of his intimate knowledge of the crime. His deep and beautifully written feature on the case is mentioned in the bibliography. Randy Sowell, Archivist at the Harry S. Truman Library at Independence, Missouri, kindly supplied information on President Truman's reaction to the bestiality and alarm at nationwide racial feelings;

J. Edgar Hoover's comments on obstruction by local residents; and his own view on whether the attorney general kept a diary. Arlene Royer, of the National Archives—Southeast Region, at Morrow, sent a copy of the jury's decision in the Moore's Ford killings. Barbara Hawley, of the Monroe-Walton County Library, supplied dates and past copies of articles on the murders.

Lindsay Sheldon, Reference Assistant at the Georgia Historical Society, provided valuable information on the Georgia election of 1946. Ariel Young Sullivan, former President and Funeral Director of the Young Funeral Home in Monroe, spoke willingly and briefly, without an appointment, of her late father, Dan, who conducted autopsies on the two lynched African American couples. Joanne Tetreault Eldridge, Deputy Clerk of Court, US Army Court of Criminal Appeals, Arlington, Virginia, checked court martial records to see if either of the Verner brothers were included. Andy Malcom, of Malcom & Malcom, Realty Professionals in Monroe, supplied me with an article so that I could walk to the pinpointed location of the since-destroyed Monroe Hotel. Erica Bruchko, Librarian for US History and African American Studies at Emory University's Robert W. Woodruff Library, Atlanta, sent me a specific article from the *Atlanta Daily World.* Kiara Boone, paralegal with the Equal Justice Initiative in Montgomery, Alabama, provided me with their latest annual report and publication on *Lynching in America: Confronting the Legacy of Racial Terror.* Mark Potok, editor of the Southern Poverty Law Center's *Intelligence Report,* was able to confirm no breaks in the case even though the Justice Department said it had partnered with them for assistance. My wife, Marion, transcribed the recorded video interview by then NAACP President Benjamin Jealous with Wayne Watson in Monroe.

Olga Hill, assistant to the CEO of Real Times Media, ended a long search for *Atlanta Daily World* archival photographs by telling me where I might find them, since the paper was sold. M. Alexis Scott, former publisher of the *Atlanta Daily World,* searched for missing photographs and forwarded one to me that she found in her father's trunk. Matthew Lutts, of Associated Press Images in New York, transferred most of the selected photographs after I had been advised by Ellen Johnston, of

Special Collections, Georgia State University Library. Rebecca Petersen, Public Services Archivist, Special Collections and Archives, Wake Forest University, was exceedingly quick in sending material on an assistant to the attorney general. Sitesh Patel, Account Manager, Books, for the Press Association in England, assisted with copyright questions on other photographs.

I am also very grateful to my Skyhorse editors. My thanks to the extraordinarily talented Rain Saukas for an awesome cover. Finally, I am deeply indebted to my son, Michael, for his expertise with computers. The technological revolution swept me by without my comprehending much. My son came to the rescue on so many occasions that this book would never have seen the light of day without his steady hand and understanding of my iMac. My daughter, Nomi, gave me the encouragement so necessary to continue with this endeavor.

Bibliography

Bartoletti, Susan Campbell. *They Called Themselves The K.K.K.: The Birth of an American Terrorist Group*. Boston: Houghton Mifflin Harcourt, 2014.

Bernd, Joseph L. "White Supremacy and the Disenfranchisement of Blacks in Georgia." The Georgia Historical Society: *Georgia Historical Quarterly*, vol. 66, No.4 (winter 1982) pp. 492–513.

Holden-Smith, Barbara. "Lynching, Federalism, and the Intersection of Race and Gender in the Progressive Era." Yale Journal of Law and Feminism.1966.

Odum-Hinmon, Maria E. *The Cautious Crusader: How the Atlanta Daily World Covered the Struggle for African American Rights from 1945 to 1985*. College Park, Maryland: University of Maryland Press, 2005.

Swietek, Wes. "Moore's Ford—Lifting the Veil of Silence," Prelude, Parts 2 and 3, 2015. Access via www.mooresford.wordpress.com.

Primary Sources

Congressional Record 74C 2S 199

Congressional Record 75C IS 3563

Congressional Record 75 2S 11

Congressional Record 75C 2S 41

Congressional Record 75C 2S 122–23

Congressional Record 75C 2S 208–89

Congressional Record 75C 3S 139

Congressional Record 75C 3S 145–46

Congressional Record 75C 3S 305

Congressional Record 75C 3S 313

Congressional Record 75C 3S 370

Congressional Record 75C 3S 374

Congressional Record 75C 3S 1101–2

Congressional Record 75C 3S 1105

Congressional Record 75C 3S 1115

Congressional Record 75C 3S 1537

Congressional Record 75C 3S 1943

Congressional Record 75C 3S 2007

Congressional Record 79C 2S 10259–10260

Congressional Record 80C 1S 2692

Congressional Record 109C 1S S6364-S6388

C-SPAN TV coverage Senate apology for lynching 13 June 2005

C-SPAN TV coverage Senate press conference 13 June 2005

FBI Case File No. HQ44–1421, Unknown Subjects: Roger Malcolm and wife, Dorothy, and George Dorsey and wife, Mae, Civil Rights and Domestic Violence.

FBI personnel file John Frank Trost

FBI personnel file Charles Everett Weeks

FBI personnel file US Senator Kenneth Douglas McKellar

General Records, Department of Justice, Civil Rights Division, RG 60

Hearings before the Sub-Committee of the Committee on Appropriations US Senate 74C 2S

Lynching in America: Confronting the Legacy of Racial Terror. Equal Justice Initiative, Montgomery, Alabama, 2015

Records of DOJ, CRD, classified subjects file 1930–87, case file 144–19M-14–25, boxes 506, 507, RG 60, NA

Records of DOJ, CRD, case file 144–19M-14, sections 15–16, boxes 543–544, Class 144, RG 60, NA

Report of the President's Committee on Civil Rights, titled *To Secure These Rights,* presented to President Truman 29 Oct.1947, Govt. Printing Office, Washington, DC, 1947

Report of the Joint Select Committee to Inquire into the Conditions of Affairs in the Late Insurrectionary States, made to the two Houses of Congress, 19 Feb. 1872, Govt. Printing Office, Washington, D.C., 1872

Report of Marianna, Florida, lynching to the National Association for the Advancement of Colored People, New York, 20 Nov. 1934, Department of Justice, straight numerical file #158260, box 1279, RG 60, National Archives

Unknown subjects: Racial Discrimination in Registration of Negro Voters, FBI reports, 1946, files #44–62, Case file # 44–1406, RG 65).

US Senate Election, Expulsion and Censure Cases 1793–1990. Government Printing Office, Washington, DC, 1995.

Newspapers and Wire Services:

Associated Press
Athens Banner-Herald
Atlanta Constitution
Atlanta Daily World
Black Dispatch, Oklahoma
Daily Worker
New York Herald Tribune
New York Times
Pittsburgh Courier
Scripps-Howard
The Guardian
The Red & Black
United Press
Walton Tribune
Washington Star
Washington (State) Daily News
Washington Post

Index